Complete PET

Teacher's Book

Emma Heyderman and Peter May
with Rawdon Wyatt

CAMBRIDGE
UNIVERSITY PRESS

CAMBRIDGE UNIVERSITY PRESS
Cambridge, New York, Melbourne, Madrid, Cape Town, Singapore,
São Paulo, Delhi, Dubai, Tokyo

Cambridge University Press
The Edinburgh Building, Cambridge CB2 8RU, UK

www.cambridge.org
Information on this title: www.cambridge.org/9780521741378

First published 2010
Reprinted 2010

Printed in the United Kingdom at the University Press, Cambridge

A catalogue record for this publication is available from the British Library

ISBN 978-0-521-74137-8 Teacher's Book
ISBN 978-0-521-74648-9 Student's Book with CD-ROM
ISBN 978-0-521-74136-1 Student's Book with answers and CD-ROM
ISBN 978-0-521-74138-5 Class Audio CDs (2)
ISBN 978-0-521-74141-5 Student's Book Pack
ISBN 978-0-521-74139-2 Workbook with Audio CD
ISBN 978-0-521-74140-8 Workbook with answers and Audio CD

Contents

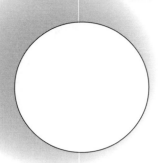

Introduction

Who *Complete PET* is for

Complete Pet is an enjoyable and motivating topic-based course designed to give thorough preparation for the Preliminary English Test (PET), Common European Framework (CEF) level B1. It is particularly suitable for teenagers but can also be used with young adults. It offers:

- stimulating reading and listening tasks providing strategies and training in the techniques needed to deal with exam tasks

- a systematic approach to exam speaking tasks providing models for students to follow and clear outcomes for improved exam performance

- many opportunities for personalisation with further speaking activities

- a step-by-step approach to writing tasks with models to work from and sample answers

- comprehensive coverage of all major grammar areas tested in the PET exam. These are supported by work on correcting common grammar mistakes made by PET candidates in the exam as revealed by the Cambridge Learner Corpus (see below)

- vocabulary input, particularly focusing on and correcting common vocabulary mistakes and confusions made by PET candidates in the exam, as revealed by the Cambridge Learner Corpus.

What the Student's Book contains

- 12 topic-based units of 8 pages each covering topic areas frequently encountered in the PET Exam.

- Each unit covers a selection of tasks from each of the three papers which comprise the exam, so all units contain work on Reading, Listening, Speaking and Writing. They also contain systematic coverage of grammar and vocabulary.

- Each exam-style task is integrated into a range of classroom work designed to give students the strategies and techniques to deal with exam questions.

- The tasks are accompanied by information about what the task involves and advice about how best to approach it.

- Six two-page review sections (one after every two units), covering the grammar and vocabulary encountered in each unit.

- A Grammar reference section giving clear and detailed explanations of the grammar covered in each unit.

- Writing and Speaking reference sections containing detailed advice to students on how to approach writing and speaking tasks in the exam, and writing and speaking models as examples.

- A complete, authentic PET Exam past paper supplied by Cambridge ESOL.

- A free CD-ROM intended for self-study with further practice of reading, writing, listening, pronunciation, grammar and vocabulary.

The Cambridge Learner Corpus (CLC)

The Cambridge Learner Corpus (CLC) is a large collection of exam scripts written by students taking Cambridge ESOL English exams around the world. It currently contains over 85,000 scripts and is growing all the time. It forms part of the Cambridge International Corpus (CIC) and it has been built up by Cambridge University Press and Cambridge ESOL. The CLC currently contains scripts from over:

- 85,000 students
- 100 different first languages
- 180 different countries

Exercises in the Student's Book which are based on the CLC are indicated by this icon: **◉**.

What the Teacher's Book contains

- Unit notes for the 12 units of the Student's Book which:
  - state the objectives of each unit
  - give step-by-step advice on how to treat each part of each Student's Book unit
  - offer a wide range of ideas for extension activities to follow up Student's Book activities
  - include a selection of 'alternative treatment' ideas so activities can be adapted to suit different types of learners
  - contain comprehensive answer keys for each activity and exercise
  - contain complete recording scripts. The sections of text which provide the answers to listening tasks are underlined. There are also six pages of photocopiable recording scripts.

- 12 photocopiable activities, one for each unit, designed to provide enjoyable recycling of work done in the Student's Book unit, but without a specific exam-style focus. All photocopiable activities are accompanied by detailed teacher's notes outlining:
  - the objectives of the activity
  - a suggested procedure for handling the activity in the classroom.

- 4 photocopiable progress tests, one every three units, to test grammar and vocabulary taught in the units

- 12 photocopiable word lists covering vocabulary encountered in the Student's Book. The vocabulary items are accompanied by definitions supplied by corpus-informed Cambridge dictionaries. These lists can be given to students for private study, reference or revision after they have completed the unit, or for reference while they are working on the unit if you prefer. The lists are intended as an extra tool for extending students' vocabulary.

See below for suggestions on how to use the word lists.

Other components of Complete PET

- 2 audio CDs containing a wide range of exam-style listening materials, recordings for the authentic PET past Exam supplied by Cambridge ESOL and recordings of different parts of the Speaking test to serve as models for students. The listening material is indicated by a different coloured icon in the Student's Book for each of the CDs.

- A Student's Workbook to accompany the Student's Book, with:
  - four pages of exercises for each unit. These exercises practise the reading, writing and listening skills needed for the PET exam. They also give further practice in grammar and vocabulary.
  - a twelve-page 'Vocabulary Extra' section (one for each unit), containing a variety of exercises to revise, extend and consolidate the vocabulary in the Student's Book.
  - **an audio CD** containing the listening material.

The word lists

In general you should give students the word lists when they have finished, or are near to finishing a unit as reinforcement of vocabulary encountered during the unit.

With a weak or insecure class, you can give them the word lists in advance, but it is always useful to train students to guess the meanings of unfamiliar vocabulary from the context before resorting to a dictionary explanation. They can then use the word lists to check whether their deduction has been correct.

If you wish, you can give out the word lists before students do the final writing task in the unit and ask them to check through the list beforehand to see if they can use any of the vocabulary in the task.

Unit 1　Homes and habits

Unit objectives

- **Topics:** house and home, daily life
- **Listening Part 4:** identifying parallel expressions
- **Reading Part 5:** reading for gist and main points
- **Speaking Part 1:** questions and answers
- **Writing Part 1:** identifying target structures, writing an email
- **Grammar:** prepositions of time, frequency adverbs, question forms, present simple / present continuous, state verbs, prepositions of place, quantifiers: *a few, a little, many, much, a lot of, lots of*
- **Vocabulary:** house and home, daily life, countable and uncountable nouns

Starting off

❶ This introduces the topics and some basic vocabulary. Encourage speculation on which might be her room, possibly with prompts such as 'How old do you think Julia might be?', and focus on objects shown in the pictures such as books, magazines, phone, computer and guitar, plus the verbs *play, put on, log on*, etc.

❷ 🎧 After they have heard the recording once or twice, elicit the correct room (B) and forms using the present simple, e.g. spends much of her time there, has her things there, uses the PC for emailing, etc., loves texting, does homework there, reads a lot, listens to music, plays the guitar.

Answer
B

Recording script   CD1 Track 2

Julia:　　　Hi. My name's Julia Davies and this is my room. I spend most of my evenings there and part of the weekend, though I'm out quite a lot then. It's not a particularly big room, but I've got all my favourite things there. There's my <u>computer</u>, which I use mainly for emailing, online chat and looking around on the Internet, and my <u>mobile</u> – I love texting people!

I do my homework there too, as you can see from the <u>pile of textbooks</u>. They should really be on the <u>bookshelf</u>, but there just isn't any space there. I read a lot, actually – that's why there are so many <u>books</u> and <u>magazines</u>. Also I play the <u>guitar</u> a bit, and though I'm not very good yet my mum says I'm starting to get better! Then there's the <u>DVD player</u>. I don't often use that, but when I have someone round, we sometimes watch a film or two.

❸ This provides practice in identifying parallel expressions (paraphrase). This is a useful language sub-skill in itself, which will be helpful when tackling exam task types including Listening Part 4, and Writing Part 1 (at the end of this unit).

Answers
2 e　3 a　4 f　5 d　6 b

Extension idea Get groups to study an intermediate-level text and think of parallel expressions for as many words and phrases in it as possible.

Listening Part 4

❶ Allow time for the class to read the instructions and Exam advice, and answer any questions they may have.

❷ Explain that the answer they hear is unlikely to be in the same words as those they are reading, so they need to practise listening for expressions with meanings that are similar (correct answers), or opposite (incorrect answers). Suggest they begin by thinking of similar expressions to key words (plus their opposites), and then listening out for them. Explain that the noun *routine* means the things you do regularly, and how and when you do them.

Suggested answers
1 doesn't shut late, lots of places stay open late
2 cost a lot of money, charge low prices
3 sometimes doesn't feel safe, is always very safe
4 get out of bed before, stay in bed longer
5 a sensible thing to do, not very clever

❸ 🎧 Play the recording twice. Remind them always to give an answer to every question, even if they are not sure.

> **Answers**
> **1** No **2** Yes **3** Yes **4** No **5** Yes

Extension idea Photocopy the recording script on page 139 for students, who then match the underlined expressions with the exact words in the text.

Recording script CD1 Track 3

Lucas: When you're travelling abroad, Zoe, do you find that people do things at different times of the day?

Zoe: Well, I guess the first thing you notice is how early people have dinner here in the UK, maybe at 6 o'clock. And often in the USA and Canada, too. But in Spain or South America, for instance, they don't usually have their main meal until late in the evening, and they often go out after that. By then, in a town like this, everything's closing, isn't it?

Lucas: Well, I don't think that's *always* true. <u>Some places stay open very late</u> these days, particularly in the town centre.

Zoe: But how do you get home here? The buses and trains all stop running around eleven-thirty.

Lucas: There are usually taxis around after that. There always seem to be people getting into them, or waiting for them.

Zoe: Well, even if you can get one, they <u>cost far too much</u>, in my opinion anyway.

Lucas: <u>You're right about that</u>. That's why I never take them. But I suppose you could walk home.

Zoe: All the way from the town centre? You must be joking! And that's another thing. At night in places like Italy or Greece or the Middle East, there are always lots of people around. Families, I mean. So you don't worry about anything bad happening there, but when I'm <u>here in your town there are times when I feel, well, not as safe</u>. I know it seems silly, but it's true.

Lucas: You may be right that older people go to bed early most nights. But doesn't that make it more fun when you're out? Everyone you see is young!

Zoe: That's true!

Lucas: So do people in the south of Europe get up later the next morning?

Zoe: Well, school starts just as early as in the north of Europe so <u>I don't think they stay in bed any later</u>. And the school day is normally about the same as here.

Lucas: And when there's no school?

Zoe: They have lunch later, perhaps at two or three. A proper meal, that is – not just a sandwich. After that people sometimes have a quick sleep.

Lucas: <u>I think that's sensible, if it's just for a few minutes</u>. I'd like to do that, every day.

Zoe: It's certainly a good idea when it's hot. Maybe the different routines in different parts of the world are because of the weather there?

Lucas: That's possible, yes.

Prepositions of time

❹ ⊙ Explain that 1–5 are actual mistakes made by students taking the PET exam, and are particularly common ones.

> **Answers** **2** in **3** on **4** at **5** in

❺ Elicit more, such as 'on my birthday', but point out that other prepositions may be possible, e.g. 'during' (the holidays, 2009, the winter, etc.), or 'around' (two o'clock, etc.). Note also 'on the weekend' in US English, now sometimes used in the UK, too.

> **Answers**
> AT half past two, bedtime; IN the morning, summer, 2010, the holidays; ON April 24, Saturdays

❻ Ask whether there are any regional differences within their own country, and if so why.

Grammar
Frequency adverbs; question forms

❶ Explain that 'main verb' excludes modals and auxiliaries, such as *don't* in the second sentence. Elicit as many frequency adverbs and expressions as possible, perhaps writing them on the board prior to the next activity. Adverbs: *always, frequently, hardly ever, never, normally, often, occasionally, rarely, regularly, seldom, sometimes, usually*; adverbial expressions: *every day, from time to time, now and then, once a week, twice a month, most weekends*, etc.

> **Answers**
> **1** before **2** they go after it **3** at the end

❷ Before they begin, point out that *hardly ever* (7) means *almost never*.

> **Suggested answers**
> **2** I check my email every two hours.
> **3** I'm never late for school.
> **4** I sometimes write letters to friends.
> **5** I don't always have lunch at home.
> **6** I'm sleepy in the morning almost every day.
> **7** I hardly ever go out on Monday nights.
> **8** I stay in bed late most weekends.

❸ Students work individually. Point out that in most cases they can use longer expressions like *once a day* instead of words such as *often*, or vice versa, but if they do so they will have to change the word order.

Extension idea Each student rewrites 1–8 so that it is true, in their opinion, for their partner. Then they compare sentences to see whether they were right about each other.

❹ If necessary, refer the class back to 'prepositions of time' in Listening Part 4.

❺ Point out the negative answers: 'No, I never chat online / send text messages.'

❻ You may want them to work with different partners for this.

Reading Part 5

❶ The third picture shows the windmill described in the text on the next page, but the class should not be told this yet.

Background information The first recorded uses of windmills were in the Middle East and China, and they are still in use in many parts of the world, most famously in Holland, central Spain and the Cyclades islands of Greece. The basic design is a number of rotating 'sails' powered by the wind. The energy these generate is traditionally used to grind grain or pump water. Their present-day successors, called *wind turbines*, generate electricity.

❷ Suggest that in Reading Part 5 they begin by quickly reading through the text for gist, ignoring the gaps. Make sure that everyone understands 1–8, and set a time limit of 2 or 3 minutes for the reading. Point out that this windmill is in the village of Wraysbury, pronounced /ˈreɪzbri/.

> **Answers**
> Article. A windmill built to be a home. C. On one side, near the top of the windmill (sails); around the lower part of the windmill (balcony). Points in text: 1, 3, 4, 6, 7

❸ Explain that Part 5 mainly focuses on vocabulary, but may also test prepositions, determiners, phrasal verbs, linking words, frequently confused words, pronouns, etc.

Background information Students may be interested to know that since this text was written, the Wraysbury Windmill has become a hotel, complete with four-poster bed. Further information from: http://www.riverthames.co.uk/accommodation/2718.htm.

> **Answers**
> **2** ground **3** third **4** like **5** few **6** corners
> **7** as **8** in **9** job **10** electricity

❹ *Background information* Cappadocia is an inland region of western Turkey, famous for the strangely shaped pillars and caves formed by the erosion of the soft volcanic deposits there. For many centuries, the local inhabitants have built underground houses, churches and monasteries to avoid the extremes of temperatures there – and also as hiding places.

> **Answers**
> News report; modern cave homes.
> *Suggested points*: As the climate becomes hotter, cave homes are becoming more popular; it's never very hot or cold in caves; modern cave homes are pleasant places to live.

❺ Revise prepositions of time if weaknesses are apparent, but leave *a few / a little / a lot*, etc. until the next section.

> **Answers**
> **1** D **2** A **3** B **4** A **5** C **6** B **7** B **8** D

Extension idea Focus on any points that cause particular difficulty, such as *rise/raise, all/every, since/although* and reflexive pronouns.

❻

> **Suggested answers**
> Reasons: the lack of natural light, the possibility of damp, claustrophobia, etc.
> Other places: tree houses, converted lighthouses, aeroplanes, boats, etc.

Grammar
Present simple and present continuous; state verbs

❶ Point out that English regularly uses two different verb tenses for the present – this may not be the case in the students' first language. Elicit the form of the present continuous (correct form of *be* + *-ing* form of main verb), the negative and interrogative, and the contracted forms of both tenses, including negatives. The use of the present continuous for future arrangements could be introduced now, or left until Unit 7.

> **Answers**
> 1 b   2 d   3 a   4 c

Extension idea Put some more examples on the board and ask the class which they illustrate; for example:
1 I usually <u>sleep</u> about eight hours, except at weekends.
2 Paul <u>is watching</u> the match on the TV in his room.
3 This week <u>I'm staying</u> at my grandparents' house.
4 Our apartment <u>has</u> three bedrooms and two bathrooms.

❷ Begin with some gist-reading practice, e.g. *Where is she? What does she want to do? How does she feel?* Go through each answer, asking why the continuous/simple is needed.

> **Answers**
> 2 am/'m sitting   3 is   4 am/'m looking   5 love
> 6 stay   7 go   8 is getting/'s getting   9 leave   10 is blowing
> 11 am/'m having   12 don't think

❸ Explain that many of these verbs describe thoughts, possession and existence. Go through the answers, possibly eliciting more, e.g. *appear, imagine, recognise, suspect, wish.*

> **Answers**
> All state verbs except: *change, dream, fill, improve, paint, relax*

Extension idea 1 With a strong class, point out that certain verbs – particularly of senses and feelings, e.g. *think, see* – are sometimes considered to be state verbs but can be used in the continuous when they relate to actions: 'What are you thinking?', 'I'm seeing the doctor', etc. Elicit examples of both uses with more verbs such as *feel, taste, smell, be, weigh.*

Extension idea 2 For the next lesson, students go back through their recent written work, and note down the verbs they most often use incorrectly in the present simple or continuous. They report back to groups, who draw up a list of the 'top ten' common errors involving these forms. Draw up a class 'hit list' of frequently misused present-tense verbs that can be pinned up, or photocopied and handed out.

❹ This is a useful ice-breaking activity. Encourage use of state verbs, and explain they will need the answers for the next part, when their answers will be given to others.

❺ Pairs compare completed sentences.

> **Answers**
> **2** Do you prefer to get up early or late?
> **3** Is anybody at your house watching TV at the moment?   **4** What colour clothes are you wearing today?   **5** Which things in your house belong to you?   **6** What do you sometimes forget to do in the morning?
>
> ***Suggested answers***
> **2** I prefer to get up late.   **3** No, nobody at my house is watching TV at the moment.   **4** I'm wearing blue and black clothes today.   **5** The small bed, the computer and the desk belong to me.
> **6** I sometimes forget to brush my teeth in the morning.

❻ Encourage the use of both tenses, and if necessary refer students back to the verbs they have practised in earlier activities.

Alternative treatment Each writes six sentences about themselves based on the prompts in Exercise 5, but two contain false information. Their partner has to guess which two are false. Examples: I prefer to get up late – *true*; My dad is watching TV at the moment – *false*.

Vocabulary
House and home; countable and uncountable nouns

❶ Elicit other rooms or parts of homes, e.g. *patio, study, basement, cloakroom, cellar, conservatory, attic, spare room, storeroom, shed, lift.*

❷ Explain that some of these, e.g. *cupboards*, could be found in a number of rooms. Elicit more common items: *freezer, wardrobe, bedside table, dining table, desk*, etc.

> **Suggested answers**
> Living room – sofa, cushions, armchair;
> Bathroom – bath, cupboards, mirror, taps, toilet, towels, washbasin; Kitchen – cooker, cupboards, dishwasher, microwave, sink, taps, washing machine, fridge; Bedroom – blankets, cupboards, mirror, chest of drawers, pillow; Hall – bell.

❸ ⊙ Remind the class that countable nouns usually have singular and plural forms, and are preceded by *a/an* or *the* in the singular. Uncountable nouns tend to be things like qualities, topics and substances that only have one form and are not normally used with *a/an* or *the*. Get the class to circle the correct answer (*furniture*), and then check with the dictionary entry.

❹ [U] tells you the noun is uncountable; [C] is the symbol for a countable noun. Tell them to look for the [C] or [U] symbol whenever they want to check whether a word is countable or uncountable.

Grammar

A few, a little, many, much, a lot of and *lots of*; prepositions of place

❶ Pairs study the examples in the text. Point out that we can use *much/many* in affirmative sentences, but usually only in more formal situations, e.g. *There is much work to be done.*

> **Answers**
> **1** a few, a few   **2** a little, a little
> **3** many, many, many   **4** much, much, much
> **5** a lot of / lots of, a lot of / lots of, a lot, a lot

❷ Remind the class to decide whether the noun (if there is one) that follows the gap is countable or uncountable. This is also good practice for exam tasks such as Reading Part 5.

> **Answers**
> **2** much / a lot of / lots of, a few   **3** a few / lots of / a lot of, a lot of / lots of   **4** much / a lot of / lots of, a lot of / lots of   **5** much / a lot of / lots of, a few, a lot   **6** much / a lot of / lots of, many / a lot of / lots of

❸ ◉ Point out that the wrong alternatives to 1–6 are among the most common errors made by candidates writing about homes.

> **Answers**
> **2** in   **3** in   **4** on   **5** on   **6** on

❹ Encourage the use of all language in this section. Point out that these need only be very rough sketches, showing the main items of furniture, etc.

> **Alternative treatment** Show the class photos or a diagram of your own house or flat, describing the layout, each room and its contents. Then get pairs or groups to draw plans of their own homes (or bring in photos), and describe them in the same way.

> **Extension idea** Pairs imagine their ideal house or flat, and describe the building, the interior, the fittings, furniture, colours, materials, etc.

Speaking Part 1

❶ This activity provides practice using actual questions used in PET Speaking Part 1. Learners will need to use these forms accurately to role play examiner/candidate. The answers extend the uses of prepositions of place from the Vocabulary section.

> **Answers**
> **2** How do you spell it? d
> **3** Where do you live?   a
> **4** What do you do?   e
> **5** Do you enjoy studying English?   c

❷ Elicit more expressions with each, e.g. **at** the station, **in** a village, **on** a mountain.

> **Answers**
> at (school, etc.), in (a town, etc.), on (the coast, etc.)

❸ Pairs role play examiner/candidate. Stress the importance of keeping to the exact wording of the questions, though the 'candidates' may answer as they choose.

❹ Maria clearly has a good level of spoken English and makes no mistakes here. Draw attention to the fact that she gives full answers to questions, not just one or two words.

> **Answers**
> **2** in   **3** do you work   **4** are you   **5** at   **6** in
> **7** do you study   **8** 're studying   **9** do you enjoy
> **10** like   **11** at   **12** in   **13** go out   **14** in   **15** at

❺ ∩ Go through the answers with the class.

> **Recording script**   CD1 Track 4
>
> John: Maria, where do you come from?
>
> Maria: I'm from Vari. It's a small town <u>in</u> Greece, near Athens.
>
> John: And <u>do you work</u> or <u>are you</u> a student?
>
> Maria: I'm a student, <u>at</u> a secondary school <u>in</u> the town.
>
> John: What subjects <u>do you study</u>?
>
> Maria: All the usual ones like maths and history, but this month <u>we're studying</u> modern music, too. It's really interesting.
>
> John: Ah! What <u>do you enjoy</u> doing in your free time?
>
> Maria: Well, I <u>like</u> listening to music <u>at</u> home, <u>in</u> my room. And I sometimes <u>go out</u> with friends <u>in</u> the evenings, or <u>at</u> weekends.

❻ Encourage students to work with others that they don't know: this can be a good ice-breaking activity.

Writing Part 1

❶ If any difficulties are apparent, elicit the reasons why each answer is correct, e.g. 1 'on' with specific date, 2 'sunlight' is uncountable.

> **Answers**
> **2** a little **3** 'm waiting **4** at **5** often

❷ If necessary, remind the class what each point consists of, e.g. 'frequency adverbs': *usually, every week.*

> **Answers**
> **b** 3 **c** 1 **d** 2 **e** 4

❸ They match the items with the five grammar points in 2. Do 1 as an example: the answer required is a quantifier, in this case *a few.*

> **Answers**
> **2** e) prepositions of place **3** b) present tenses
> **4** a) frequency adverbs **5** d) quantifiers
> **6** e) prepositions of place

❹ Stress the importance of correct spelling.

> **Answers**
> **2** aren't / are not at **3** is having / 's having
> **4** ever **5** a little **6** at the

Extension idea The class identify and make a note of the pairs of structures that change in the two sentences of each item, e.g. *aren't many / only a few.* Explain that the same grammar points tend to recur in exam tasks of this kind.

❺ For a model text, refer the class back to the email in Grammar on page 12. The format used here is similar to Writing Part 2, although study of the actual task type should be left until Unit 2.

Unit 1 photocopiable activity: The right words   Time: 20 mins +

This activity provides material for the first lesson, perhaps before students have bought their books.

Objectives
- To review target language (frequency adverbs/ quantifiers/prepositions of time and place) from Unit 1
- To encourage student participation and cooperation
- To allow free practice of target language (in extension activity)

Before class

Make one copy of the activity for each group of four students in your class. Cut the bottom of the activity sheet into six 'sentence' cards. You will also need dice and counters (one die and two counters for each group of four students). Ideally, each student group should also have two pens of different colours.

In class

❶ Divide your class into groups of four, and ask each group to divide into two teams of two players. Tell them that they will find it useful during the activity if each team uses a pen with different-coloured ink.

❷ Give each group a copy of the activity grid, the cards, a set of instructions, a die and two counters. Ask them to look at the sentences on the cards (they should not write anything yet) and explain that these sentences can all be completed using words on the grid.
Each space needs just one word.

❸ Ask them to look at the instructions, answer any questions they have, and then play the game.
They should either play until their cards have been completed, or you can set a time limit of 15 minutes.

❹ Review their answers. For each correct word they chose, they award themselves one point. The winning team is the team in each group with the most points.

> **Suggested answers**
> **A** I **never/rarely** go out **in** the evening because I **always/normally/usually** have a **lot** of homework to do.
>
> **B** There aren't **many** students **in** my English class, and **on** Monday morning **sometimes/normally/ usually** it's just me and the teacher!
>
> **C** My family **usually/normally/always** eats our evening meal **in** the kitchen, but there are a **few** occasions (especially **at** the weekend) when we eat in the dining room.
>
> **D** Our school canteen is **on** the first floor, but I hardly **ever** go there **at** lunchtime because there's too **much** noise.
>
> **E** My birthday is **on** 1st April and I **usually/ normally/always/sometimes** have a party at a club, but this year I'm staying **at** home and celebrating with a **few** close friends.
>
> **F** Our train leaves at half seven, but it's **never/rarely** on time. I've got a **little** money, so why don't we have a coffee **at** that café over there while we wait?

Unit 1 photocopiable activity
The right words

ever	at				many
		at	on	much	
	sometimes		at		
		never			
	on		few	usually	
	in				
		at	at	in	
			rarely		
		lot		little	
	in		normally		
always				on	few

Team 1 Start → here   **Team 2 Start ← here**

✂ Cut along the dotted lines to divide these into cards.

A I .... go out .... the evening because I .... have a .... of homework to do.	**B** There aren't .... students .... my English class, and .... Monday morning .... it's just me and the teacher!
C My family .... eats our evening meal .... the kitchen, but there are a .... occasions (especially .... the weekend) when we eat in the dining room.	**D** Our school canteen is .... the first floor, but I hardly .... go there .... lunchtime because there's too .... noise.
E My birthday is .... 1st April and I .... have a party at a club, but this year I'm staying .... home and celebrating with a .... close friends.	**F** Our train leaves .... half seven, but it's .... on time. I've got a .... money, so why don't we have a coffee .... that café over there while we wait?

Word list

Unit 1

Note: the numbers show which page the word or phrase first appears on in the unit.

armchair *n* (13) a comfortable chair with sides that support your arms

balcony *n* (10) a small area joined to the wall outside a room on a high level where you can stand or sit

bell *n* (13) an electrical object that makes a ringing sound when you press a switch

belong *v* (12) to feel happy and comfortable in a place or with a group of people

blanket *n* (13) a thick, warm cover that you sleep under

bulb *n* (14) a glass object containing a wire which produces light from electricity

cave *n* (11) a large hole in the side of a cliff (= straight, high rock next to the sea), mountain, or under the ground

chest of drawers *n* (13) a piece of furniture with drawers for keeping clothes in

consist (of) *v* (12) to be formed or made from two or more things

contain *v* (11) If one thing contains another, it has it inside it.

cooker *n* (13) a piece of equipment used to cook food

corridor *n* (13) a passage in a building or train with rooms on one or both sides

cosy *adj* (11) comfortable and warm

cottage *n* (11) a small house, usually in the countryside

cushion *n* (13) a cloth bag filled with something soft which you sit on or lean against to make you comfortable

design *n* (11) the way in which something is planned and made

exist *v* (12) to be real or present

fridge *n* (13) a large container that uses electricity to keep food cold

guess *v* (12) to give an answer or opinion about something without having all the facts

improve *v* (12) to get better or to make something better

include *v* (12) to have something or someone as part of something larger or more general, such as a group, price, or process

matter *v* (12) to be important, or to affect what happens

microwave *n* (13) an electric oven that uses waves of energy to cook or heat food

mirror *n* (13) a piece of glass with a shiny metallic material on one side which produces an image of anything that is in front of it

own *v* (12) to have something that legally belongs to you

pillow *n* (13) a soft object which you rest your head on in bed

relax *v* (12) to become happy and comfortable because nothing is worrying you

remain *v* (11) to continue to be in the same state; to continue to exist when everything or everyone else has gone

right *adv* (12) exactly in a place or time

sink *n* (13) a bowl that is fixed to the wall in a kitchen or bathroom that you wash dishes or your hands, etc. in

suppose *v* (12) to think that something is likely to be true

tap *n* (13) the part at the end of a pipe which controls the flow of water

tidy *v* (10) to make a place tidy

upstairs *adv* (11) on or to a higher level of a building

washbasin *n* (13) a bowl in a bathroom that water can flow into, used for washing your face or hands

windmill *n* (10) a building with long parts at the top that turn in the wind, used for producing power or crushing grain

Unit 2 Student days

Unit objectives

- **Topics:** education, work
- **Listening Part 1:** taking notes
- **Reading Part 3:** understanding important information
- **Reading Part 1:** recognising what each message says
- **Speaking Part 4:** turn-taking and active listening
- **Writing Part 2:** thanking, explaining, apologising, inviting and suggesting, opening and closing a message
- **Grammar:** past simple, past continuous and *used to*
- **Vocabulary:** (ir)regular past tense forms, verb + noun combinations

Starting off

❶

Answers
A alarm clock rings **B** set off for school
C catch the school bus **D** teacher takes register
E have lunch in the school canteen

❷

Answers
2 E **3** D **4** C **5** B

Recording script CD1 Track 5

One.
[alarm clock ringing]
Two.
[Sound of school canteen]
Three.
Teacher: [taking register] Kelly Ashby.
Kelly: Yes, Ms Truman.
Teacher: Max Atkinson.
Max: Yes, Ms Truman.
Teacher: Gemma Brown.
Gemma: Yes, Ms Truman.
Four.
[school bus]

Five.
Boy: Bye, Mum! [front door closing]
Mother: Bye!

❸ Students should extend their answers using follow-up questions: *When?/Why?*, etc.

Reading Part 3

❶

Suggested answer
The text is probably about the typical school day of Wayne, a 16-year-old secondary school student in Beijing, China.

❷

Possible answers
Wayne sets off for school after breakfast; he catches the school bus near his house; when he gets to school, the teacher takes the register; he has lunch in the school canteen at 12.10.

❸ Set a time limit to discourage students from trying to understand every word.

❹

Suggested answers
2 by car **3** punished, later than 7.20
4 some sports facilities **5** midday, none, home, lunch
6 leaves, at 17.20 **7** homework until, dinner
8 never sleeps, more than six hours

❺ Tell the students to write the question number next to the words they have underlined in the text (Sentence 1 has been done as an example).

Suggested answers
1 fry myself an egg for breakfast. My sister buys something from the market stalls

2 I sometimes go to school by bus. However, I normally go to school by bicycle

3 in school at least 20 minutes before lessons begin. It's a school rule. If you don't arrive on time, you can expect punishment (the clock in the next paragraph shows that lessons begin at 7.40).

4 didn't use to have a football pitch, basketball courts or a running track but now it does

5 All of us eat in the school canteen

6 We finish school but we can't go home; we have an exam after class

7 It takes me 30 minutes to eat and then I have to do my homework

8 I always wake up less than six hours later

Answers
2 B   3 A   4 A   5 A   6 B   7 B   8 A

❻ *Alternative treatment* Students could begin this exercise by making the statements in Exercise 4 true for them, e.g. *My mum makes my breakfast*, etc.

Vocabulary

Take, sit, pass, fail, lose, miss, learn, teach and *study*

❶❷ ⊙

Answers
2 sitting   3 taking   4 missing   5 study   6 learn
7 teach

❸❹

Suggested questions
1 How many marks do you need to pass exams at your school?   2 What happens if you fail an exam?   3 How often do you miss school?
4 Do you study every weekend?   5 Would you like to learn something new? What?

Grammar

Past simple

As a warmer Ask students if they or anybody they know has been an exchange student. Invite a brief discussion about what you could learn by being an exchange student.

❶ Students should consider daily life, language, family and free-time activities.

❷ 🎧 Before listening, students should predict the missing information.

Answers
2 shopping centre   3 (large) cinema(s) (with choice of films)   4 Spanish   5 (being with) new family and friends

Recording script   CD1 Track 6

Interviewer: Today we have Nadine with us to talk about the six months she spent in Chile. Hello, Nadine.

Nadine: Hi!

Interviewer: You're a normal 16-year-old school student. Where did you go last year?

Nadine: Last year I lived in Chile for six months as an exchange student. I lived with a Chilean family. I went to school every day and I had to wear a uniform. In Canada I don't have to wear a uniform. It's so uncool!

Interviewer: Where did you stay?

Nadine: I stayed in San Pedro de Atacama – high in the Atacama desert. Unlike Toronto, there's no disco, no shopping centre, no large cinemas with choice of films.

Interviewer: How did you feel when you first arrived?

Nadine: To tell you the truth, I was scared. San Pedro is so different from my home town.

Interviewer: Did you speak Spanish before you went?

Nadine: Yes, I did. I studied Spanish at school in Canada and I thought I was good at it. But when I got to Chile I couldn't say anything. It was awful.

Interviewer: What about school? What subjects did you study?

Nadine: I did maths, chemistry, biology, physics, history, Spanish and art.

Interviewer: Was it a good experience?

Nadine: Yes, it was. I'm really glad I went there. My Spanish improved and I even began to dream in Spanish. I also stopped missing expensive activities like going to the cinema or the disco and began to realise that fun in San Pedro was being with my new family and friends.

Interviewer: Thank you, Nadine … and if *you'd* like to know more about being an exchange student, contact our hotline number on 0800 444 …

❸ Do not correct the questions; students listen again in Exercise 4.

Answers
2 Where did you stay?   3 How did you feel when you first arrived?   4 Did you speak Spanish before you went?   5 What subjects did you study?
6 Was it a good experience?

❹ 🎧 If necessary, play the recording twice; the first time to check the questions and then to listen for Nadine's answers.

Answers
b stayed   **c** was   **d** studied   **e** did   **f** was … went

❺

Answers
Regular: **a** lived   **b** stayed   **d** studied
Irregular: **c** was   **e** did   **f** was, went

6

> **Answers**
> **2** ~~plaied~~ – played (vowel before *y*) **3** ~~planed~~ –
> planned (consonant + vowel + consonant)
> **4** ~~traveled~~ – travelled (British English always
> doubles the *l*, although this answer would be
> correct in US English) **5** ~~openned~~ – opened (final
> syllable is **not** stressed) **6** ~~happend~~ – happened
> (add *-ed* to infinitive without *to*) **7** ~~studyed~~ –
> studied (consonant before *y*, the *y* changes to *i*)

7

> **Answers**
> **2** ~~buyed~~ – bought **3** ~~choosed~~ – chose
> **4** ~~felt~~ – fell **5** ~~weared~~ – wore **6** ~~writed~~ – wrote

Extension idea Encourage the students to keep a list
of their common mistakes.

Past simple and past continuous

1

> **Suggested answer**
> The sun was shining and Nadine was walking to
> school. Suddenly she saw a group of dogs. She was
> very frightened.

2

> ### Recording script   CD1 Track 7
> Nadine: It was in my second week. <u>The sun was shining
> and I was feeling good. I was walking to school
> when I saw a group of dogs. I was frightened</u> but
> I didn't know what to do.

3 ***Extension idea*** Students produce a comic strip to
illustrate this journey.

> ### Recording script   CD1 Track 8
> Nadine: Suddenly a woman appeared from nowhere and
> she started screaming at the dogs. The dogs ran
> off. I said 'Gracias!' and went to school.

4

> **Answers**
> **1** Underline: appeared, started, ran off
> No, the actions happened one after the other.
> The dogs ran off last.
> **2** Circle: was shining, was feeling
> We don't know when the sun started shining or
> if it stopped shining.
> **3** Circle: was walking; underline: saw
> No, Nadine began walking to school and in the
> middle of this activity, she saw the dogs.

5

> **Answers**
> **2** past continuous **3** past simple **4** past
> continuous **5** past continuous **6** past simple

6 Pre-teach *slippers*.

> **Answers**
> **2** looked **3** was raining **4** had **5** got
> **6** drove **7** changed **8** was putting
> **9** started **10** were

7

> ### Recording script   CD1 Track 9
> Tommy: This morning I <u>woke up</u> early to visit Ryukoku
> High School. I <u>looked</u> out of the window. It <u>was
> raining</u>. I <u>had</u> a quick breakfast and we <u>got</u> ready
> to go. We <u>drove</u> to school. At the school we
> <u>changed</u> our shoes for slippers. As I <u>was putting</u>
> on my slippers, my Japanese friend <u>started</u>
> looking at my feet. The slippers <u>were</u> too small!

8 Elicit questions to talk about these things first, e.g.
*Have you ever had an unusual journey to school? What
happened?* If necessary, model a full answer first.

Listening   Part 1

1 Point out that in the PET Listening Part 1 exam, there
are seven questions.

> **Suggested answers**
> **2** do today, 11 am **3** What, buy
> **4** weather, tomorrow

2

> **Suggested answers**
> **1 A** one fifty or ten to two **B** one forty-five or
> (a) quarter to two **C** two fifteen or (a) quarter
> past two **2 A** a sports class **B** a (school) play/
> performance **C** a maths class **3 A** table tennis
> balls **B** table tennis bats **C** trainers
> **4 A** sunny weather **B** cloudy and rainy weather
> **C** cloudy weather

3 Remind students that they **can** write on the exam
paper in the PET exam.

> **Suggested answers**
> **2 A** 11 tomorrow **B** after break, finish 11.15
> **C** 11.15 **3 A** cheap **B** lend brother's **C** got
> some **4 A** too much sun **B** today **C** Internet,
> dry but cloudy

Recording script   CD1 Track 10

One. What time does John have to leave school today?

Mrs Drew: Woodland High School. Mrs Drew speaking.

Mother: Yes. This is John Fuller's mother. He's got <u>another doctor's appointment</u> today at <u>a quarter past two</u>. Last week I <u>picked him up at ten to two</u> but we got there late. <u>Can I get him five minutes earlier today – at a quarter to two?</u>

Two. What are the students going to do today at 11 am?

Teacher: There'll be some changes to your timetable today. <u>After break</u> we're going to see <u>a play performed</u> by some Year-10 students. That should <u>finish by 11.15</u>. We'll do <u>maths then</u>. I know we <u>normally do sport at 11</u> but we'll have to <u>do that tomorrow instead</u>.

Three. What does Nathan have to buy?

Nathan: I've just joined the table-tennis team but I'm not sure I've got enough money to buy the equipment.

Jacob: Don't worry! <u>The balls are really cheap</u> and <u>I can lend you my brother's bat</u>. He never uses it. You'll have to <u>get some good trainers, though</u>.

Nathan: <u>I've already got some</u>.

Four. What will the weather be like tomorrow?

Father: Are you ready for your school trip tomorrow, Beth? You're going to those new outdoor swimming pools, aren't you? Lucky you didn't go <u>today</u>. <u>It hasn't stopped raining</u>.

Beth: That's what I'm worried about. Our teacher looked it up on the Internet and <u>it says it'll be dry, but cloudy</u>. Let's hope it's right.

Father: Yeah, that's <u>better than too much sun</u>, I think.

4 🎧 Encourage the students to say why the other two pictures are incorrect. Point out that in the PET exam, students will listen to each individual recording twice rather than listening to the whole recording twice.

> **Answers**
> 1 B   2 B   3 A   4 C

Grammar
Used to

As a warmer With books closed, encourage a brief open class discussion on the differences between going to primary and to secondary school.

1

> **Answer**
> *used to*

2

> **Suggested answers**
> **1** No (we can say *I/you/he*, etc. *used to* go)
> **2** There is no *d* at the end of *use* (we didn't <u>use</u> to take exams)
> **3** The infinitive without *to*

3 ***Extension idea*** Encourage stronger students to include new information, e.g. about school uniform, subjects, punishment, etc.

4

> **Suggested questions**
> **1** Did you use to get a lot of homework?
> **2** Did you use to play in a team?
> **3** How often did you use to meet your friends?
> **4** Did you use to choose your own clothes?
> **5** What did you use to do in your free time?

5 ***Extension idea*** Students write an article for *Teen* magazine about these changes.

Reading   Part 1

1

> **Answers**
> 1 B   2 C   3 C   4 B   5 A

Vocabulary
Earn, have, make, spend and *take*

1 ⊙ Highlight the difference between *spend time doing* and *take time **to** do*.

> **Answers**
> **2** make   **3** take   **4** spend   **5** earn

2 Tell the students that there is no one correct answer.

Speaking   Part 4

1 ***Alternative treatment*** With a weaker class, start with Exercise 2 first.

②

> **Suggested answers**
>
> Linh, Vietnam:
> 1 No. Very few work. Parents don't allow them. They have to study hard.
> 2 No.
> 3 No, but could be a good thing for some teenagers (learn about money and society). Studying is the most important thing.
>
> Marcelo, Colombia:
> 1 Yes. To earn extra spending money.
> 2 Yes, in father's office.
> 3 Yes, but with more rules / limit on number of hours worked. Working can be good experience / can work more in school holidays

Recording script   CD1 Track 11

Linh: Do teenagers work in Colombia?

Marcelo: Yes, they do. Teenagers in my country work to earn extra spending money. What about in Vietnam?

Linh: Well, I don't work and actually very few teenagers in Vietnam work. In my country, most parents don't allow their children to have a part-time job. We have to go to school and study hard. In my opinion, it's not a good idea for teenagers to work and study at the same time. What do you think?

Marcelo: I'm not so sure. I agree that teenagers need enough time to study and do their homework. If they work too many hours, their marks will go down. However, working part-time can be a good experience … don't you think so?

Linh: Maybe. For some teenagers, working could be a way to learn about money and society. However, we have to think about the future. I think that studying is the most important thing. Do you agree?

Marcelo: Yes and no. As I said before, I think having a part-time job can be a good experience. However, we need more rules. For example, teens shouldn't work more than 15 hours a week and only two or three days a week, like at the weekend. I think they can work more hours during the school holidays.

Linh: Have you got a part-time job?

Marcelo: Yeah. I sometimes work in my father's office. I have to deliver letters and documents around the building. I earn a little bit of extra money.

Linh: Really? That sounds interesting. What do your teachers say?

Marcelo: Teachers complain that students who work don't do their homework well and they often do badly in tests. I think that students can work to earn some pocket money if they are good students.

Linh: Good point! I haven't got a job. I'm going to concentrate on my studies and look for a job when I'm older.

③ 🎧

> **Answers**
> 1 think   2 so   3 agree   4 no   5 part-time job
> 6 Really   7 say   8 point

Extension idea Photocopy the recording script on page 140 for the students to highlight useful expressions.

④ ***Extension idea*** Students change pairs two or three times and do the same task.

Writing Part 2

①

> **Suggested answers**
> can't, sports practice, note, coach, apologise, explain, suggest another time

②

> **Answers**
> **Question 1**: 1 email   2 English-speaking friend, Isabel   3/4 thank, tell, invite
> **Question 2**: 1 note   2 coach, we don't know name   3/4 apologise, explain, suggest

③

> **Answers a** 1   **b** 2

④

> **Answers**
> *invite*: would you like to come; *suggest*: why don't I train …; *explain*: (I won't be able …) because (I …); *apologise*: I'm sorry that …

⑤

> **Answers**
> 1 an email   2 Jason   3 to tell him you can't meet him   4 apologise, explain, suggest

⑥

> **Model answer**
> Hi Jason
>
> I'm sorry that I can't meet you tomorrow. It's because I have exams next week and I have to study hard. I'll finish my exams on Friday. Why don't we meet then? We could go to the cinema.
> Yours

Vocabulary and grammar review Unit 1

Answers

Grammar

❶ 2 in   3 on   4 in   5 in   6 at   7 In   8 at   9 in   10 at
11 at   12 in   13 on

❷ 2 a little   3 a lot   4 a little   5 time   6 much
7 a little   8 a few

❸ 2 ~~I call~~ I'm calling   3 ~~do you stand~~ are you
standing   4 ~~Do you sleep ever~~ Do you ever sleep
5 ~~I'm never believing~~ I never believe   6 I make my
own bed every day.   7 How often do you have a bath?
8 ~~I get normally home~~ I normally get home

Vocabulary

❹ **Across:** 1 fridge   4 own   6 upstairs   7 cosy   8 sink
9 blanket   10 cave   11 garage   12 hall
Down: 1 floor   2 remain   3 tap   5 tidy
7 cooker   8 sofa   9 bell

Vocabulary and grammar review Unit 2

Answers

Vocabulary

❶ 2 study   3 had   4 made   5 take   6 missed   7 sitting
8 learn

Grammar

❷ 2 ~~planing~~ → planning   3 ~~payed~~ → paid
4 ~~founded~~ → found   5 ~~baught~~ → bought
6 ~~felt~~ → fell   7 ~~bringed~~ → brought
8 ~~studing~~ → studying   9 ~~teached~~ → taught
10 ~~puted~~ → put

❸ 2 was shining, were singing   3 was having, rang
4 chose, was   5 saw, was buying   6 escaped, was
cleaning   7 thought, was   8 read, wrote
9 enjoyed   10 laughed, appeared

❹ **Suggested answers**
2 used to go home for lunch
3 didn't use to live near our school
4 didn't use to be a good student
5 used to give us a lot
6 used to be very late for school

Unit 2 photocopiable activity: It's all in the past   Time: 20–30 mins

> **Objectives**
> - To review the past simple, the past continuous and *used to / didn't use to*
> - To practise question forms with *what* to ask about the past
> - To involve the whole class in an information-exchange activity that practises speaking, listening and writing skills

Before class

Make one copy of the activity for each pair of students in your class. Cut into two sections, Part 1 and Part 2.

In class

❶ Divide your class into pairs, and give each pair Part 1 of the activity.

❷ Explain that they are going to interview each other about past experiences. They will need to find out what their partner did at the weekend, what they were doing at eight o'clock last night, what they used to do when they were younger that they don't do now, and what they didn't use to do when they were younger but do now. They should write their partner's answers as complete sentences on a separate sheet of paper, following the example they are given. Allow them about five to eight minutes for this.

❸ Each student then reads out their sentences to the rest of the class. The other students should listen and try to remember as much information as possible (they should not take notes, but you might find it useful to take notes yourself, which you can refer to in Step 5 below).

❹ Give each pair Part 2 of the activity. Explain that they need to work together to fill in the tables with numbers (in the second column of each table) and activities (in the fourth column of each table) that are true about the other students in the class. They *cannot* include information about themselves. Allow them about five to eight minutes for this. It doesn't matter if they cannot fill in all of the spaces in that time.

❺ Review their answers and award each pair two points for each correctly completed box. The number in the second column must be correct (for one point), and the information in the fourth column must be factually *and* grammatically correct (for one point). The winning pair is the pair with the most points.

Unit 2 photocopiable activity

It's all in the past

Part 1

Ask your partner:

- What he/she did at the weekend.
- What he/she was doing at 8 o'clock last night.
- What he/she *used to do* when he/she was younger but *doesn't do* now.
- What he/she *didn't use to do* when he/she was younger but *does do* now.

Write his/her answers on a separate sheet of paper using complete sentences (for example: *At the weekend, Ahmed played football. At eight o'clock last night, he was playing computer games. When he was younger, he used to fight with his sister. When he was younger, he didn't use to eat fish.*)

✂ -

Part 2

Complete these tables with information that is true about the other students in your class. You <u>cannot</u> include your or your partner's information in this part.

Example:

	Number		Rest of sentence with past *simple* verb
At the weekend,	3	student(s) in our class	went to the cinema

	Number		Rest of sentence with past *simple* verb
At the weekend,		student(s) in our class	

❷

	Number		Rest of sentence with past *continuous* verb
At eight o'clock last night,		student(s) in our class	

❸

	Number		Rest of sentence with *used to*
When they were younger,		student(s) in our class	

❹

	Number		Rest of sentence with *didn't use to*
When they were younger,		student(s) in our class	

Complete PET by Emma Heyderman and Peter May with Rawdon Wyatt © Cambridge University Press 2010 PHOTOCOPIABLE

Word list

Unit 2

Note: the numbers show which page the word or phrase first appears on in the unit.

apologise *v* (23) to tell someone that you are sorry about something you have done

canteen *n* (16) a restaurant in an office, factory, or school

earn a wage *v* (22) to get money for doing work

explain *v* (23) to make something clear or easy to understand by giving reasons for it or details about it

fail an exam *v* (18) to not pass a test or an exam

have fun *v* (22) to enjoy yourself

invite *v* (23) to ask someone to come to a social event

learn *v* (17) to get knowledge or skill in a new subject or activity

lose *v* (18) to not be able to find someone or something

make friends *v* (22) to begin to know and like someone

miss the bus *v* (18) to arrive too late to get on a bus, train or aircraft

pass an exam *v* (18) to succeed at a test or an exam

ring *v* (16) If something rings, it makes the sound of a bell, and if you ring a bell, you cause it to make a sound.

set off *v* (16) to start a journey

sit an exam *v* (18) to take an exam

spend time doing something *v* (22) to use time doing something or being somewhere

study *v* (17) to learn about a subject, usually at school or university

suggest *v* (23) to express an idea or plan for someone to consider

take an exam *v* (18) to do an official test

take time to do something *v* (22) to do something without hurrying

teach *v* (18) to give lessons in a particular subject at a school, university, etc.

thank *v* (23) to tell someone that you are grateful for something they have done or given you

Unit 3) Fun time

Unit objectives

- **Topics:** hobbies and leisure, free time
- **Listening Part 2:** identifying type of information needed
- **Reading Part 4:** focusing on multiple-choice stems, identifying the writer's purpose
- **Speaking Part 2:** making suggestions and replying politely to them, word stress for new information
- **Writing Part 1:** identifying words to change, error correction, describing free-time activities
- **Grammar:** verbs followed by *to* or *-ing*
- **Vocabulary:** hobbies and leisure, free time, negative prefixes, phrasal verbs

Starting off

❶ Focus on any new language prompted by the pictures. The collocations can be done quickly, but check that the differences between *diving, surfing* (this meaning may be new) and *sailing* are clear. This activity previews the focus on *-ing* forms in the Grammar section. Get them to match the photos with six of the activities, but leave any discussion of these until Exercise 2. (The unusual collection is of rubbers.)

> **Answers**
> **b** seeing   **c** going   **d** flying   **e** collecting
> **f** playing   **g** surfing   **h** sending   **i** keeping
> **j** diving **Pictures: 2** i   **3** f   **4** e   **5** c   **6** j

❷ A count could be taken to establish the overall favourite free-time activity of the six.

Listening Part 2

❶ Tell the class what they will hear in 2: a radio talk by one person, on a number of leisure activities. Then explain that this part of the test consists of a longer text, usually factual, and that the questions normally focus on specific information and possibly opinion/attitude. Stress that the four types of information in a–d are examples only: there are many other kinds (places, people, emotions, etc.), and in some cases it may only be possible to say 'detail'. Remind them to do this each time they tackle Listening Part 2.

> **Answers**
> **a** 2   **b** 1   **c** 4   **d** 3

Extension idea Get the class to study some old PET Listening Part 2 questions. Ask what kind of information is needed in each item, and what clues tell them, e.g. 'Why' in the question indicates a reason is required.

❷ 🎧 Draw attention to the Exam advice and explain that the order of the questions follows the order of the information in the recording. They will also hear 'cues' that correspond to the language of the questions, e.g. the speaker mentions *safety advice* before giving the answer to Question 2. Play the recording twice, and check answers.

> **Answers**
> 1 B   2 A   3 C   4 B

Extension idea Go through the part of the recording script that relates to each item, eliciting both the 'cue' and the words that mean the same as the correct answer. You can photocopy the script on page 141.

Recording script   CD1 Track 12

Spencer: Hi, I'm Spencer Watson and I'm here to tell you about four unusual ways to have a great day out. First, how about going back in time with a steam-train journey through the beautiful Scottish countryside? This is on the railway line made famous by the *Harry Potter* films. Starting at Fort William, near Britain's highest mountain, the train departs each morning at twenty past ten, getting into the lovely fishing village of Mallaig at 12.25. The return journey to Fort William starts at 14.10 and takes an hour and fifty minutes. The fares are good value for money and it's a great experience for steam-train fans of any age. It's very popular in summer, so it's best to book ahead.

For a really exciting day out, *Go Wild* adventure courses offer hours of fun in 17 different locations. For a fairly small admission fee, you can climb tall trees, go from tree-top to tree-top on a high wire, cross waterfalls far below, go through tunnels – and lots more. Before you start, though, they give you full safety advice. To prevent accidents they put a belt round your waist and the tops of your legs, and attach it to wires. And then you're off – completely on your own! To take part you have to be fit, over nine years old and at least 1 metre 40 tall. Opening hours are usually 9.30 to 3.30.

If the adventure course isn't really your thing, but you like seeing really big wildlife, you can't do much better than dolphin and whale watching in Wales. *Voyages of Discovery* organises regular trips out to sea, passing small islands with their enormous seabird populations and then on to even deeper waters. And there, very occasionally, you will see whales, while <u>on almost all the trips dolphins will appear</u>. You may also see huge sharks, although they are quite rare these days. The voyage isn't cheap, but most people who've done it agree that it's well worth the money.

If instead you'd like to be up in the sky, try a balloon flight, from any of the hundreds of sites across the country. It usually begins early in the morning when you meet the pilot, crew and other passengers, and the huge balloon slowly fills with hot air. It rises gently, and then you go whichever way the wind is blowing. The actual flying time is about an hour, and although <u>I think it could last a bit longer</u>, it's certainly a wonderful experience. It's also possible to book a flight just for two, for any time of the year.

❸ After the class have listened twice, they should be able to recall the collocations and fixed expressions. Check understanding – *return journey* and *book ahead*, for example, may need explaining.

Answers
2 hours   **3** fee   **4** value   **5** journey   **6** advice
7 ahead

❹ For the first part, allow time for them to give their reasons, possibly using expressions from Exercise 3. Prompt, if necessary, for the second part with suggestions such as a theme park or fairground they've been to, and make sure they ask and answer using the complete questions from Exercise 3.

Extension idea Pairs tell the class which of the four activities they chose. Find out which is the most popular overall, and why. Then do the same with their own suggestions for a day out.

Vocabulary
Negative prefixes

❶ Point out that none of these forms hyphenated words. You may want to practise distinguishing the pronunciation between *un/in/im*.

Answers
un- fit/fair/healthy, in- correct/dependent/active, im- possible/polite/probable

❷ Perhaps check first that all the words given, e.g. *patient*, are understood. Also elicit/explain the meaning of *theme park*: similar to a large fairground, but based on one subject, e.g. *a Western theme park*.

Answers
3 informal   **4** unkind   **5** untrue   **6** impatient

❸ Give more examples, such as 'go everywhere by car'.

Suggested answers
2 stay in all the time.   **3** get up early to go somewhere.   **4** fly in balloon number 13.   **5** charge such high admission fees.   **6** I sometimes have to run for the bus.

Reading Part 4

❶ Elicit vocabulary such as *boat*, *sailing*, *voyage*, *sea*, *land*, *ocean*, *waves*, *wind*, *storm*, *dangerous*, *sink* and *rescue*. Explain that Michael Perham was just 14 then. At the end of Reading Part 4, you may want to add that in 2009 he became the youngest person to sail solo around the world.

❷ Before they start, give examples such as 'to describe a real event', 'to tell an imaginary story', 'to tell readers how to do something', 'to give safety advice', 'to talk about different kinds of boats', 'to encourage people to visit the Caribbean', etc. Allow three minutes, then elicit answers. Do not give the correct answer yet.

Suggested answers
'tell the story of how a young person sailed alone across the Atlantic.'

❸ When they have finished, give the answer.

Answer   B

❹ These three questions are the stems of the multiple-choice items to follow, but the class do not need to be told this yet. The aim is to train them to look for their own answers in the text first, and only then to compare their understanding with the four options provided. Point out that they only need to think of approximate answers.

Answers
1 'It feels fantastic … out of a can!'(second half of Paragraph 2)   **2** '… he too would like to break the record' (Paragraph 3)   **3** '… he hadn't felt afraid … never felt like giving up' (Paragraph 4)

Alternative treatment With a strong class, ask them to write down their own answer to each question. This can be difficult if the question is quite broad in scope, e.g. 'What does X say about …', but in those cases they could note down two or three different answers.

❺ Refer the class to the options, which are in the same order as the questions in Exercise 4. You may want to explain that 'distractors', i.e. the three incorrect options, are intended to do just that: distract readers from a correct understanding of the text, which is why it is so important for them to find the true meaning for themselves.

> **Answers**
> 1 C   2 C   3 B

❻

> **Answer**
> Yes, and they always are in Reading Part 4 questions on detail. Exam question 5, however, usually requires understanding of different parts, or all, of the text, as does Exam question 1, which normally focuses on the author's purpose in writing the text.

❼ Tell the class they can discuss any kind of record, sporting or not. When they have finished, find out from the class which are the most popular choices, and consider this as a possible future classroom topic.

Grammar
Verbs followed by *to* or *-ing*

❶ Allow time for them to look back at the context in the Reading Part 4 text and check their answers. Then they complete the table with the verbs below. Check these, possibly eliciting more verbs of each type. With a strong class, explain that *like/love/hate/prefer* + *-ing* tends to mean 'in general', whereas the infinitive is used more for particular situations, e.g. *I like singing / I like to sing in the shower.*

> **Answers**
>
> | Verb + *-ing* | Verb + infinitive |
> | --- | --- |
> | feel like, practise, admit, avoid, fancy, finish, mind, miss, suggest | seem, afford, decide, expect, hope, learn, manage, promise, want, would like |
> | deny, dislike, can't help, imagine, mention, put off, can't stand | appear, attempt, intend, offer, pretend, refuse |

❷ ⊙ Remind the class that these are all very common errors.

> **Answers**
> 2 ~~decided catch~~ decided to catch   3 ~~enjoy to be~~ enjoy being   4 ~~forget to visit~~ forget visiting
> 5 correct   6 ~~fancy to come~~ fancy coming
> 7 correct   8 ~~finished to eat~~ finished eating
> 9 ~~forgot asking~~ forgot to ask   10 correct

❸ *Forget* and *remember* can be followed by both, with a change in meaning.

◖ page 121 *Grammar reference: Verbs followed by* to *or* -ing

Extension idea With a strong class, elicit or present verbs that change meaning depending on whether they are followed by *-ing* or the infinitive, e.g. *stop, try, regret* (*to do / doing* something), and ask for example sentences, such as 'While I was walking to school, I stopped to talk to a friend.'

❹ Remind them that where the infinitive is needed, it must be the full *to* infinitive. Students should both ask and answer all the questions about themselves.

> **Answers**
> 2 listening to   3 to do   4 going   5 to bring
> 6 to do

❺

> **Suggested answers**
> 2 I'm learning to speak a third language.
> 3 I decided to stop spending too much last week.
> 4 I'm planning to go shopping on Saturday.
> 5 I want to start learning to ride a motorbike.
> 6 I must remember to phone my best friend tomorrow.   7 I'll finish doing this exercise soon.
> 8 I shouldn't forget to watch that film on TV next weekend.   9 I always hate waiting for the bus.
> 10 I really love dancing to good music.

Extension idea They draw up a three-column table headed 'verbs followed by *-ing*', 'verbs followed by infinitive' and 'verbs followed by either *-ing* or infinitive', in their notebooks. They add more verbs during lessons, and while reading/listening at home.

Vocabulary
Phrasal verbs

❶ Focus on the entry from the *Cambridge Learner's Dictionary* (CLD), explaining that some phrasal verbs can have both an adverb and a preposition. Pairs fill in the gaps with *look after*, *work out* and *make up for* (which is a verb + adverb + preposition).
Point out that the three sentences are also from the *Cambridge Learner's Dictionary*: they're the examples in the entries for these three phrasal verbs. Explain that *inconvenience* means 'something that causes difficulty'.

> **Answers**
> **1** work out   **2** make up for   **3** look after

❷ Let pairs study the Reading Part 4 text, then elicit the answers. For the follow-up questions, explain that certain phrasal verbs can be separated, for example by an object or time expression, but do not go into the issue of separability in any detail at this level.

> **Answers**
> **2** looking forward to   **3** turn (his dream) into
> **4** set out on   **5** giving up   **6** go on   **7** deal with
> **8** get on with. **Three words**: 2, 4, 8. **Separated**:
> 3 (*his dream*)

❸ Point out that there are other verbs in some of the sentences but they have to identify the phrasal verbs.

> **Answers**
> **2** took up – c   **3** put (my name) down – b
> **4** joined in – a   **5** go off (it) – f   **6** set off – d

❹ Explain that not all the phrasal verbs in the preceding activities are needed, though students will have to be careful with tenses.

> **Answers**
> **2** went off   **3** take up   **4** put down   **5** gave up
> **6** go on   **7** catch up with   **8** looking forward to

❺ 🎧 Play the recording through twice, if necessary.

> **Recording script** CD1 Track 13
>
> Chris: Hi, Ava. Are you and Megan going away on holiday soon?
>
> Ava: Yes, on Saturday. We want to <u>set off</u> very early in the morning.
>
> Chris: Are you going to the coast?
>
> Ava: No, we <u>went off</u> beach holidays last summer. There were too many people. We've decided to <u>take up</u> skiing instead. We're off to the Alps.
>
> Chris: Do you know how to ski?

> Ava: Er, not really! That's why I'm going to <u>put</u> my name <u>down</u> for lessons.
>
> Chris: I tried it once but I found it really difficult. After three days I <u>gave up</u> and went home!
>
> Ava: Well, the lessons <u>go on</u> until late in the evening, every day, so I should improve quickly. Megan's a good skier and I've got a lot to learn, but I'm sure I can <u>catch up with</u> her. I'm really <u>looking forward to</u> trying, anyway!
>
> Chris: Yes, I'm sure you'll have a great time.

❻ If necessary, give more prompts and point out that in some cases, the suffix *-er/-or* is added for the person. *Cook* is an obvious exception that can create difficulties: 'my mother is wonderful cooker', etc.

> **Answers**
>
> | hobby | person | equipment |
> |---|---|---|
> | chess | *player* | *board, pieces* |
> | camping | camper | tent, backpack |
> | collecting | collector | collection |
> | cooking | cook | cooker, oven |
> | cycling | cyclist | bike, helmet, |
> | music | musician | instrument |
> | painting | painter | brush, paint |
> | photography | photographer | camera |

❼ These can be any relevant words or phrases, e.g. *playing the guitar: guitarist, electric guitar, practise, band, concert, rock star.*

> **Suggested answers**
> **camping**: sleeping bag, put up, fire, campsite
> **collecting**: album, coins, stamps, objects, art, valuable
> **cooking**: recipe, saucepans, frying pan, boil, roast, bake
> **cycling**: wheels, seat, pedals, chain, lock, ride
> **music**: practise, performance, solo, notes, keys, melody
> **painting**: portrait, landscape, frame, picture, oils
> **photography**: flash, focus, digital, zoom, close-up

❽ Suggest the speakers begin their descriptions with more general points, e.g. where it takes place, what you have to do, before giving more direct clues and mentioning words closely linked to the hobby.
The listeners should not interrupt until they are fairly sure they know the answer.

Speaking Part 2

❶ 🎧 Make sure everyone knows what these activities are, possibly eliciting the advantages and disadvantages of each. Play the recording once without pausing: this is essentially a gist-listening activity and students won't be expected to produce language at this level in the speaking exam.

> **Answers**
> **1** fishing   **2** rock-climbing, canoeing, water-skiing, mountain-biking   **3** mountain-biking

Recording script   CD1 Track 14

Olivia: There's never anything to do in this town, is there? Let's choose a hobby, an outdoor one, for the weekends and holidays.

Daniel: OK then, <u>how about</u> going <u>fishing</u>? We could go to the river in the valley over there, or even down to the lakes.

Olivia: Well, I think I'd <u>prefer</u> to do something a bit more exciting. And anyway I'd feel sorry for the poor fish! Perhaps we <u>could</u> try a water sport? Something like <u>canoeing</u>, or <u>water-skiing</u>, maybe.

Daniel: Yes, but we can't afford to hire a boat. I think we <u>should</u> do something cheaper. Or better still, free!

Olivia: All right, <u>why</u> don't we go <u>rock-climbing</u>? That's free, and it can be exciting, too.

Daniel: Hmm. I think it'd be <u>better</u> to do something less dangerous.

Olivia: OK, let me see … I know – what about <u>mountain-biking</u>? It's outdoor, quite safe, fairly cheap …

Daniel: … <u>Yes, we could hire a couple of bikes and see if we like it</u>. So <u>shall</u> we do that, then?

Olivia: <u>I think it would be great</u>. We could ride through the hills and into the forest. So, yes, <u>let's</u> go for that one.

❷ 🎧 Give them time to study 1–8. Play the recording, pausing if and where necessary. Check answers for accuracy, as many of these are expressions they will need to use.

> **Answers**
> **2** prefer   **3** could   **4** should   **5** why   **6** better
> **7** shall   **8** let's

❸ 🎧 Play the sentences, possibly more than once. Check everyone agrees which are the stressed words, then elicit the kind of information they convey. Pairs practise stressing 'new information' words in questions by asking about other activities, e.g. 'How about going **dancing**?', 'How about going **swimming**'?

> **Answers**
> The strongest stress is on: **1** fishing   **3** water sport
> **5** rock-climbing   **8** that (they give new information)

Recording script   CD1 Track 15

Daniel: OK then, how about going <u>fishing</u>?

Olivia: Perhaps we could try a <u>water sport</u>?

Olivia: All right, why don't we go <u>rock-climbing</u>?

Olivia: Yes, let's go for <u>that</u> one.

❹ 🎧 Point out the importance of using a polite tone when rejecting a suggestion (and an enthusiastic one when accepting). Play the recorded sentences and focus on this tone. To put the extracts from Exercises 3 and 4 into their broader context, you may want to play the recording from Exercise 1 again.

Recording script   CD1 Track 16

Olivia: Well, I think I'd prefer to do something a bit more exciting.

Daniel: I think we should do something cheaper.

Daniel: I think it'd be better to do something less dangerous.

❺ The aim here is to practise making suggestions and responding to these suggestions, as preparation for the exam task in Exercise 6. Encourage the use of verbs + -ing/infinitive such as *enjoy doing* and *don't want to do*. If necessary, prompt with more hobbies, which could also be indoor activities.

❻ Monitor pairs, making sure they are taking turns and reacting sensitively to each other's suggestions. Discourage them from coming to a decision too quickly, advising them to consider each idea carefully and give reasons why they are in favour of or against it. Give feedback to pairs or to the class as a whole.

Writing Part 1

❶ Tell the class not to try to write the answer yet, just to concentrate on the two sentences. The aim of the activity is to isolate the words that candidates need to change, and then avoid wrong answers. Elicit the answer to Question 2.

> **Answers**
> **1** *have enough money for*   **2/3** *afford* is followed by the *to* infinitive, so it must be *afford to buy*

❷ Students could do these in pairs. Check answers, the reasons why those given are wrong, and the words they have underlined. Point out that *can't wait* is another verb form followed by the infinitive.

❸ This is a technique that students can apply whenever they do transformation sentences. Make it clear that they don't need to fill in the second sentences at this stage, and check their answers.

❹ Elicit the structures tested in each item: **1** verb + *ing* **2** verb + inf **3** expression for making suggestion + *ing* **4** phrasal verb **5** verb + inf **6** phrasal verb (and *too/enough*)

❺ Encourage the use of linking expressions, e.g. *also*, *although*, *because*, etc. to form the paragraph, rather than a series of disjointed sentences.

❻ Allow plenty of time for them to discuss each other's writing. Ask groups about the accuracy of use of verbs followed by *-ing*/infinitive, adjectives with negative prefixes and phrasal verbs. Provide further practice if any weaknesses are still apparent.

Unit 3 photocopiable activity: What's my hobby? Time: 15–20 mins

Objectives
- To review hobbies and verbs from Unit 3
- To practise asking *yes/no* questions

Before class

Make one copy of the activity for each student. Also make one copy only of the hobby cards at the bottom of the sheet.

In class

Write these 18 words on the board. (One of the words is deliberately written twice.)
*biking   canoeing   chess   climbing   dancing   fishing
fit   guitar   horse   keeping   mountain   painting
playing   playing   riding   rock   sailing   the*

❶ Explain that the words make 11 hobbies. Some of these hobbies use just one word from the board, but some need two, or even three, words. Allow them a minute or two to try to identify these hobbies.

❷ Ask one student to come to the front of the class and give them the hobby card marked *Student 1*. Tell that student to imagine that the hobby on the card is their favourite hobby, but they should not tell the others in the class what it is.

❸ Tell the other students that they must try to find out what the hobby on the card is. They can do this by asking the student with the card questions, but that student can only answer with *Yes* or *No*. The class can ask a maximum of ten questions.

❹ The students ask their ten questions. Make sure that a handful of students do not dominate this activity (for example, you could tell them that they can only ask a maximum of one or two questions each).

❺ When the ten questions have been asked, the student at the front of the class returns the card to you and sits down. The other students then decide what the hobby was, and write their answer on a separate sheet of paper. They mark their answer *Student 1*.

❻ Repeat Steps 2–5 with the other cards. Again, try to ensure that the activity is not dominated by the same students.

❼ Give each student a copy of the crossword grid. Tell them that unlike other crosswords, there are **no black spaces**. They must complete the grid with the hobbies they identified. The *numbers* represent the students who answered the questions, and the *arrows* indicate the direction on the grid that they must write their answers. They should not leave blank spaces between words.

❽ The first to complete the grid correctly 'wins'.

What's my hobby?

Crossword grid

									1↓				
		2↓			3↓								4↓
5→										6↓			
7→													
					8↓			9↓					
10→													
11→													

Hobby cards

✂ Cut along the dotted lines to divide these into cards.

Student 1 You enjoy canoeing in your free time.	**Student 2** You enjoy playing the guitar in your free time.	**Student 3** You enjoy dancing in your free time.
Student 4 You enjoy rock climbing in your free time.	**Student 5** You enjoy playing chess in your free time.	**Student 6** You enjoy sailing in your free time.
Student 7 You enjoy painting in your free time.	**Student 8** You enjoy keeping fit in your free time.	**Student 9** You enjoy fishing in your free time.
Student 10 You enjoy mountain biking in your free time.	**Student 11** You enjoy horse riding in your free time.	

Word list

Unit 3

Note: the numbers show which page the word or phrase first appears on in the unit.

admission fee *n* (27) the amount of money that you pay to enter a place

(can) afford *v* (30) to have enough money to buy something

art gallery *n* (27) a room or building that is used for showing paintings and other art to the public

backpack *n* (32) a bag that you carry on your back

book ahead *v* (27) to arrange to use or do something at a particular time in the future

catch up with *v* (31) to reach someone or something in front of you, by going faster, working harder, etc. than them

chess *n* (32) a game that two people play by moving differently shaped pieces around a board of black and white squares

cyclist *n* (32) someone who rides a bicycle

deal with *v* (29) to take action in order to achieve something or to solve a problem

diving *n* (26) the activity or sport of jumping into water with your arms and head going in first

feel like *v* (29) to want something, or want to do something

formal *adj* (28) used about clothes, language, and behaviour that are serious and not friendly or relaxed

get on with *v* (29) to continue doing something, especially work

give up *v* (29) to stop doing something before you have completed it, usually because it is too difficult

go off *v* (31) to stop liking someone or something

go on *v* (29) to last for a particular period of time

healthy *adj* (27) physically strong and well, or good for your health

helmet *n* (32) a hard hat that protects your head

instrument *n* (32) an object that is used for playing music, for example a piano or drum

join in *v* (31) to become involved in an activity with other people

look forward to *v* (28) to feel happy and excited about something that is going to happen

make up for *v* (30) to reduce the bad effect of something

mountain-biking *n* (32) riding a bicycle with thick tyres, originally made for people to ride on hills and rough ground

opening hours *n* (27) the times of the day when a place is open to the public

oven *n* (32) a piece of kitchen equipment with a door which is used for cooking food

patient *adj* (28) having patience

put someone's name down *v* (31) to write someone's name on a list or document

set out *v* (28) to start a journey

sightseeing *n* (27) the activity of visiting places which are interesting because they are historical, famous, etc.

surfing *n* (26) the sport of riding on a wave on a special board

take up *v* (31) to start doing a particular job or activity

tent *n* (32) a structure made of metal poles and cloth which is fixed to the ground with ropes and used as a cover or to sleep under

turn into *v* (28) to change and become someone or something different, or to make someone or something do this

value *n* (27) how useful or important something is

water-skiing *n* (32) a sport in which someone is pulled behind a boat while standing on skis

work out *v* (30) to calculate an amount

PROGRESS TEST Units 1–3

❶ Look at this email, and put the verbs in *italics* into their correct form (present simple, present continuous, past simple or past continuous).

0 Last night I (*watch*) …*watched*………… an interesting programme about South Africa.

Hi John

Thank you for your text message. I (1) (*get*) …………………… it earlier this morning while
I (2) (*go*) …………………… to work. How is Spain? I'm really glad you
(3) (*have*) …………………… a nice holiday there and that the sun (4) (*shine*)
…………………… . Unfortunately, right now I (5) (*sit*) …………………… at my computer
trying to do some work! I'm bored and tired and I (6) (*want*) …………………… to go home!
I (7) (*not have*) …………………… much news at the moment. I (8) (*see*) ……………………
Amy last weekend when I (9) (*do*) …………………… my shopping in the supermarket.
We (10) (*go*) …………………… for a coffee in that new café on the High Street.
Anyway, call me when you get back home.

Harriet

❷ Read the text below and choose the correct word.

0 I always …B… fun with my friends at the weekend.

    A do   **B** have **C** take   **D** make

My name's Charles. I'm 15 years old, and I live (1) …….. home with my mother, my father
and my younger sister. I like the area where I live because there are so (2) …….. cafés,
restaurants, shops and cinemas. During the week I go to school. I'm working very hard at the
moment because we have exams soon and I want to (3) …….. them. However, on Saturday
morning I have a part-time job. I wash cars for my neighbours. I don't (4) …….. much money
for this, but I usually have enough to spend on the things I like doing. Last year I took
(5) …….. photography, so I spend most of my money on cameras and computer software.

1	**A** in	**B** at	**C** on	**D** by
2	**A** many	**B** few	**C** much	**D** lots
3	**A** sit	**B** take	**C** fail	**D** pass
4	**A** take	**B** spend	**C** have	**D** earn
5	**A** over	**B** on	**C** up	**D** out

❸ **Here are some sentences about someone's free time. For each question, complete the second sentence so that it means the same as the first, *using no more than three words*. (Contractions, e.g. *he'll*, count as two words: *he will*.)**

0   How do you spend your free time?
     What ..*do you do*............ in your free time?

1   I played football when I was younger, but I don't now.
     When I was younger I .... football.

2   I really enjoyed football, but I stopped liking it.
     I really enjoyed football, but .... off it.

3   These days, I don't play it very often and prefer to watch DVDs instead.
     These days, I .... it and prefer to watch DVDs instead.

4   There are 200 DVDs in my collection.
     I .... 200 DVDs in my collection.

5   I can't afford any more because they are very expensive.
     I can't afford any more because they .... money.

❹ **Read this interview and put the words in *italics* in their correct order to make questions. Don't forget to begin each sentence with a capital letter.**

you old how are?

0   ......*How old are you?*..

Mr Jones:	Hello, Tony. I'd like to ask you a few questions.
Tony:	Fine.
Mr Jones:	Good. *surname is what your?*
	(1) ....?
Tony:	Buxton.
Mr Jones:	Thank you. *spell you do that how?*
	(2) ....?
Tony:	B-U-X-T-O-N.
Mr Jones:	Right, next question. *school to you where go do?*
	(3) ....?
Tony:	In Cassington, a town near my home.
Mr Jones:	*do school you to subjects like at study what?*
	(4) ....?
Tony:	Lots of things, but history, maths and English are my favourite.
Mr Jones:	Great. Just one more question. *enjoy your you what with friends doing do?*
	(5) ....?
Tony:	Going to the cinema, playing football and watching DVDs.

㉛

❺ Add prefixes to the words in *italics* to make them negative.

0 It's very .. *un* .. healthy to sit in front of the television all day.

1 My brother never takes any exercise, so he's .... *fit* and .... *healthy*.

2 My bedroom is so .... *tidy* it's .... *possible* to find anything.

3 My sister is sometimes very .... *polite*, which makes her .... *popular* with other people.

4 My teacher gets so .... *patient* with me whenever I give an answer that is .... *correct*.

5 Jenny was very .... *kind* to me, which I thought was very .... *fair* of her.

❻ Rearrange the letters in *italics* to make words. The first letter of each word is in its correct place.

0 I'm *lnnegiar* .. *learning* ... Japanese, but it's really difficult.

At home I prefer to keep my bicycle in the (1) *gregaa* .... , but my father prefers me to leave it outside in the (2) *gndear* ....

Our kitchen is very small, with a fridge, a cooker, a (3) *movwicaer* .... and a (4) *dhweishsra* ....

I have two hobbies: (5) *cgleciolnt* .... unusual objects and (6) *sinugfr* .... the Internet.

My favourite subjects at school are (7) *pssycih* .... and (8) *cetirmyhs* ....

I'm (9) *lnnegiar* .... French at school and my brother's (10) *sunyidgt* .... mathematics at Singapore university.

❼ Decide if the verbs in *italics* should take an infinitive or -ing form.

0 I always enjoy *see* ...... *seeing* ...... my friends at the weekend.

1 Tonight, I'd like *try* .... the new Italian restaurant on Alamy Street.

2 We decided *meet* .... our friend outside the cinema at 7 o'clock.

3 Laurence suggested *go* .... to the beach for a picnic.

4 The computer course was difficult and at first I felt like *give up* ....

5 I couldn't afford *fly* .... to Paris, so I took the train.

6 When you finish *tidy* .... your room, I want you to wash the car.

7 Ian admitted *break* .... my new camera.

8 The bus was late, but we managed *get* .... to school on time.

9 I must remember *phone* .... my mother tonight.

10 Do you remember *meet* .... that strange girl at the party last week?

Unit 4 Our world

Unit objectives

- **Topics:** travel and holidays, buildings and places
- **Listening Part 3:** reading the question notes, focusing on the gaps
- **Reading Part 3:** highlighting key words, reading statements carefully
- **Speaking Part 3:** listening to a model answer, using language from model to describe pictures
- **Writing Part 3:** (*letter*) answering the question, use of language
- **Grammar:** comparative and superlative adjectives, (*not*) *as … as …*, gradable and non-gradable adjectives, modifiers
- **Vocabulary:** holiday activities, *travel, journey, trip,* buildings and places, adjectives used to describe places

Starting off

❶ Students should think about what each photo represents before looking at the vocabulary in the box.

> **Answers**
> **2** go snowboarding   **3** sunbathe   **4** take photos
> **5** go trekking   **6** go sightseeing   **7** go snorkelling

❷ 🎧

> **Answer**
> **1** snorkelling   **2** snowboarding

Extension idea Students listen to the recording again and write down the expressions Abi uses to talk about things she likes doing / would like to do (**in bold in the recording script**).

Recording script   CD1 Track 17

Toby: Where did you go on holiday, Abi?

Abi: Well, last year we went to Zanzibar. It's an island but it belongs to Tanzania, in East Africa.

Toby: You always do exciting things, don't you? Which activities did you do in Zanzibar?

Abi: Um, we stayed in Stone Town for a few days and went sightseeing.

Toby: Ah! What did you see there?

Abi: There were palaces and markets and we visited the museums.

Toby: Do you like visiting museums?

Abi: Um … **it's OK, but I prefer** go**ing** shopping.

Toby: Did you buy anything?

Abi: Oh yes! You know **I love** buy**ing** souvenirs. I bought some clothes and jewellery.

Toby: Which activity <u>did you enjoy doing most</u>?

Abi: Um … in the second week we stayed on the north coast and <u>I went snorkelling</u> for the first time. **It was fantastic**.

Toby: Are there any activities you'd still like to try?

Abi: Um … well, <u>I've never been snowboarding</u>. **I'd love to try** that. All my friends say it's the most exciting winter sport. Have you tried it?

❸ Encourage the students to use some of Abi's expressions in their answers.

Reading Part 3

❶ Use the photos to pre-teach *orang-utan, rainforest, jungle, island, wildlife, sick, injured.*

> **Suggested answers**
> trekking, snorkelling, sightseeing, buying souvenirs

❷ Encourage the students to read the sentences very carefully by asking general questions, e.g. *Does Sentence 1 say Borneo is the smallest island in the world?*

❸

> **Suggested answers**
> **3** first part, sleep, city centre   **4** water sports, South China Sea   **5** airport, Sukau   **6** animals, Sepilok, all sick or injured   **7** impossible, get near, orang-utan   **8** Orang-utans, only, meat   **9** includes, free trip, Mount Kinabalu   **10** buy gifts, after, sightseeing tour

❹ Remind the students that the statements follow the order of the text and they should write the question number in the text margin.

> **Answers and suggested answers**
> **1** B *Not* quite *as big as* its neighbour, the island of New Guinea

2 A Temperatures are generally *between 24° C and 30° C all year round*

3 A your comfortable *accommodation* in the *heart of this city*

4 A on the shores of the *South China Sea* where you can go *swimming or snorkelling* in its clear blue water

5 B *the only way to continue our journey* to Sukau … is *by bus*

6 B young orang-utans whose *parents have died. Some* of these animals arrive in *very bad condition*

7 B this extraordinary opportunity *to get close to* these creatures

8 B collect *the plants* that are part of *their diet*

9 B *For a small fee,* book our day trip to Mount Kinabalu

10 A And *when the tour is over,* it's a short ride to the modern shopping centres, local stores or markets *for some last-minute souvenirs*

5 Encourage the students to explain why each sentence is correct or incorrect.

6 **Extension activity** Appoint a spokesperson for each group to report back. Feed in some useful expressions, e.g. *Our group talked about …, We also decided …,* etc.

Vocabulary

Travel, journey and *trip*

1 Encourage the students to find examples of *travel, journey* and *trip* noun in the text about Borneo. Point out that *travel* is used as both a noun and a verb.

2

> **Answers**
> **2** trip   **3** travelled   **4** trip   **5** journey

Extension idea In groups, students choose a holiday destination and write a short description for a brochure, using *trip, travel* and *journey*.

Grammar

Comparative and superlative adjectives;
(not) as … as …

As a warmer With books closed, students brainstorm what they can remember about Borneo from the reading text.

1 Students should explain why a sentence is false.

> **Answers**
> **1** False (New Guinea is bigger)   **2** False (Kota Kinabalu is the most important city)   **3** True
> **4** True

2

> **Answers**
> 2 4   4 3

3 ☉

> **Answers**
> **1** (the) noisiest   **2** (the) biggest   **3** (the) most beautiful   **4** (the) best   **5** (the) worst   **6** (the) farthest or furthest   **7** add *-r* or *-st* to adjectives that finish in *-e*   **8** double the final consonant if the adjective finishes in vowel–consonant   **9** use *more* or *most* with adjectives with two or more syllables

4 ☉

> **Answers**
> **2** ~~more quiet~~ – quieter   **3** ~~worse~~ – worst   **4** ~~nearst~~ – nearest   **5** ~~more better~~ – better   **6** ~~hotest~~ – hottest

5 Other answers may be possible.

> **Suggested answers**
> **3** the most dangerous   **4** more intelligent
> **5** lighter   **6** the noisiest   **7** the slowest
> **8** the tallest   **9** the biggest   **10** the deepest
> **11** colder   **12** larger

6 ∩ Check that students have spelt the comparative or superlative adjective correctly.

Alternative treatment Treat as a team game. Groups score one point for every correctly written answer (focus on language), one point for correct information (focus on content) and extra points if they hear any more information on the recording.

> **Recording script**   CD1 Track 18
>
> **Fergus:** And here are the answers to this week's general-knowledge quiz. Did you know that <u>Asia is bigger than Africa</u>?
>
> **Alyssa:** Yes, and more people live in Asia than any other continent. Well, <u>Russia is the largest country in the world</u>.
>
> **Fergus:** And now for the animal facts. <u>The most dangerous animal on the planet is</u> not the lion or the shark but <u>the tiny mosquito</u> because it carries diseases. In the list of the top ten most intelligent animals <u>there are</u> dolphins, <u>orang-utans</u>, some types of elephant and whales – <u>but definitely no dogs</u>. The African elephant is the largest and heaviest land animal, but <u>the blue whale is the heaviest living creature</u>. On average, it can weigh around 150 tonnes – that's 150,000 kilos. I wouldn't like to share my home with a <u>howler</u>

monkey. They are the noisiest animals in the world. The slowest-moving fish is the sea horse. It would take this fish about an hour to move 15 metres. The tallest dog in the world is the Great Dane and the smallest is the chihuahua. You've got some answers about places, haven't you, Alyssa?

Alyssa: Yes, I have. Did you know that Nagoya train station in Japan is the biggest in the world and Shinjuku station in the same country is the busiest? If you like diving, then you should go to Belgium. Nemo 33 is the deepest pool in the world.

Fergus: And the last two answers. Antarctica is the coldest, driest and windiest continent. And while we're talking about large places, the Amazon rainforest is larger than any other forest in the world.

❼

Answers
2 Mount Everest is a bit / a little higher than K2.

3 Arica is much / far / a lot drier (or dryer) than Death Valley.

4 Atlanta International Airport is much / far / a lot busier than Heathrow Airport.

5 The sperm whale's brain is much / far / a lot heavier than a human adult's brain.

❽

Answers
1 True **2** True **3** False (the male is normally twice the size of the female)

❾

Answers
1 *as* + adjective + *as* **2** not **3** no

❿ Remind the students **not** to use more than three words.

Answers
2 large as **3** as straight as **4** as dangerous as / more dangerous than **5** as intelligent as

Extension idea Each group chooses a topic of interest, e.g. music, sport, etc., researches information about record breakers and produces a poster display. As a follow-up, produce (or ask the students to produce) a list of (in)correct statements (as in the PET Reading Part 3) about all the information on display.

Vocabulary
Buildings and places

As a warmer Ask students to close their eyes and imagine they are taking a group of visitors around their town. They should try to visualise all the places they see.

❶ Make sure the students can pronounce these words correctly.

Answers
2 department store **3** youth club **4** market
5 port **6** fountain **7** bridge **8** town hall

❷ Revise frequency adverbs from Unit 1 before students do this exercise.

❸ Change the pairs after a few minutes to encourage peer teaching. If necessary, write the opposites on the board in a different order.

Answers
2 wide **3** low **4** old (also ancient or old-fashioned) **5** clean **6** ugly **7** dull/calm
8 boring **9** dangerous **10** cheap **11** quiet
12 shallow **13** near **14** flat

Grammar
Big and *enormous* (gradable and non-gradable adjectives)

❶

Answers
1, 2 and **3** (in any order): quite, very, really **4** and **5** (in any order): absolutely, really **6** and **7** (in any order): quite, very

❷

Suggested answers
2 small **3** hot **4** cold **5** bad **6** dirty
7 interesting **8** good

Extension idea Elicit more non-gradable adjectives for *good* (*great, wonderful, delicious,* etc.), *bad* (*awful, horrible, disgusting,* etc.) *big* (*huge*), etc.

❸

Answers
2 really **3** absolutely **4** quite **5** very

❹❺

Alternative treatment Dictogloss. Students first listen to the recording all the way through (without stopping) to understand the general idea. Then play the recording again, stopping after each line, and encourage the students to write down the key words, e.g. *come, Sweden, town*. Do NOT give the students enough time to write down every word. Students then have to reconstruct the text using these key words.

Recording script   CD1 Track 19

Selma: Um … I come from Sweden. I live in a town about an hour away from the capital, Stockholm. There are only about 4,000 people – it's really tiny. It's a very nice place to live in because it never gets too crowded. There are several interesting sights, including a castle. Because it's a small town, it's extremely safe. Sometimes, I find living here quite boring. I'd like to live somewhere with a more lively nightlife. There are no youth clubs or night-clubs and we often have to spend the evening outdoors, even when it's absolutely freezing.

Listening Part 3

❶ Pre-teach 'Northern Pole of Cold'. Encourage the students to use the pictures to help answer the questions.

Suggested answers

1 Oymyakon is a village in East Russia (Siberia).
2 lowest temperature (−71.2° C); oldest man (109)
3 Ewan McGregor visited Oymyakon in 2004 on his motorbike.   4 Life for young people there is probably quiet.

❷

Suggested answers

1 date   2 number   3 noun   4 adjective   5 noun
6 noun

❸❹❺ 🎧 The students should try to write something for each gap as they listen. If necessary, play the recording for a third time, stopping after each answer is given.

Answers

1 1926   2 9/nine   3 television   4 oldest
5 mobile(s) (phone)(s)   6 motorbike

Recording script   CD1 Track 20

Presenter: Oymyakon, in East Russia, is extremely cold and people live there! The lowest temperature, of minus 71.2 degrees, was recorded in 1926, beating all records. Dave Gunhill reports.

Dave: Extremely low temperatures are frequent in Oymyakon, with temperatures going below minus 45 degrees Celsius regularly. Winters are long and cold and often last at least nine months. The summers are much warmer than the winters. Temperatures can rise to 35 degrees Celsius but then there is the problem of mosquitoes … About 2,300 people live in Oymyakon. Life is very much the same as 100 years ago – apart from television. For example, there are no indoor bathrooms and people use ice instead of water from the tap. The valley used to be famous because some of the oldest people in the country lived there. Fiodor Arnosow, Oymyakon's oldest-ever inhabitant, died in 1967. He was 109. There are about 300 children in the local school. Up until recently, there didn't use to be any heating in the school. The children did their classes in their coats. These young people dream of having mobile phones, an Internet café and a disco with a CD player that works. A local businessman, Alexander Krylov, wants to bring tourists to the area. He has also built the town's first hotel to attract these tourists. Each of the ten rooms has hot and cold water. The most famous visitor until now is the Hollywood actor Ewan McGregor, who visited this place - in summer of course- on the back of a motorbike.

❻ Encourage students to use some of the words and expressions from this unit.

Speaking Part 3

❶ Focus on the example and encourage students to use full sentences in their answers.

Answers

2 Marrakech, Morocco
3 Machu Picchu, Peru   4 The Great Wall, China
5 Hikkaduwa Beach, Sri Lanka

❷ First revise the holiday activities from Starting off.

Suggested answers

1 buy souvenirs, visit museums   2 buy souvenirs, go sightseeing   3 go trekking, go camping   4 go trekking, take photos   5 sunbathe, go snorkelling

❸ Encourage students to predict what they think Laura will describe. She describes *all* eight things.

Recording script CD1 Track 21

Laura: In this photo <u>I can see a lot of boats on water</u>. It <u>looks like</u> a traffic jam. The water <u>looks</u> really dirty. I <u>think</u> it's a market <u>in the morning</u> – <u>it could be somewhere in Asia</u>. There <u>seems to be a lot of fruit and vegetables</u> on the boats. There <u>are some green vegetables</u> but I don't know what they are. On each boat, I <u>can see</u> a person … no … I can see men and women. Some people <u>are wearing hats</u>. I think <u>they're selling things</u> but there aren't any people buying … er … on one of the boats, there <u>appears to be</u> somebody wearing <u>a colourful shirt</u>. Next to this boat, there's another man but I can't see him very well. I think <u>it's the morning</u>. <u>The weather is hot and sunny</u>. I <u>don't think</u> it will rain. Er …

❹

Answers
2 looks like **3** looks **4** think, could be **5** seems to be **6** can see **7** appears to be **8** don't think
We use *look like* (it *looks like a traffic jam*) with a noun and *look* (without *like*) with an adjective (*the water looks really dirty*).

❺ *Alternative treatment* The listener draws what their partner describes.

Writing Part 3

❶ Point out that in PET Writing Part 3 students can choose to write a letter or a story.

Answers
1 a letter **2** about 100 words **3** the name of a city in your country and more information about this city

❷ Refer students back to the list of adjectives in the Vocabulary section.

❸ Clear up any problems with vocabulary in Kirsty's model.

❹

Answer
Yes (this is a model answer and would get full marks in the PET exam)

❺ Brainstorm some alternatives to Kirsty's words and expressions, e.g. *Durban is one of the largest cities in South Africa* = *this city is (one of) the busiest / noisiest / most beautiful*, etc. *city (cities) in my country*.

Suggested answers
As you know, I've lived in … so why don't you write about …? It's one of the … cities in … In fact, over … live there … is famous for … People say that … is on the east coast of … which are … they are … for (verb + *-ing*). There are absolutely … and … too. The weather is … because … I hope this is enough information

❻ Make sure the students are using Kirsty's model and help them with vocabulary.

❼ If classes are not used to peer correction, some students may be **over**critical. Peer correction will need to be introduced gradually by first focusing on very good work. For example, ask the students to use the writing checklist to evaluate two of the very best answers and say why they got such high marks.

❽ Check the students' work before you ask them to write a final copy.

Vocabulary and grammar review Unit 3

Answers

Vocabulary

❶ **2** unfit **3** unfair **4** unpopular **5** unhealthy **6** informal **7** impatient **8** unsafe **9** unnecessary **10** inactive

❷ **2** e **3** a **4** h **5** b **6** g **7** d **8** f

Grammar

❸ **2** to do **3** to get **4** going **5** to buy **6** to have **7** to look for **8** to see **9** spending **10** to buy **11** to do **12** being

❹ **2** a **3** c **4** a **5** c **6** b **7** b

Vocabulary and grammar review
Unit 4

Answers

Vocabulary

❶ Suggested answers

2 fantastic/wonderful/great   3 coldest   4 freezing
5 lively/busy   6 enormous/huge   7 boring/dull
8 empty

❷ 2 than   3 very   4 far   5 travel   6 shopping centres

Grammar

❸ 2 ~~more better~~ → better   3 ~~more safe~~ → safer
4 ~~that~~ → than   5 ~~as~~ → than   6 ~~then~~ → than

❹ 2 farther/further   3 most popular   4 better than
5 the hottest

Unit 4 photocopiable activity:
Absolutely wonderful! Time: 15-20mins

Objectives
• To review and practise non-gradable (*strong*) adjectives
• To practise asking someone to repeat something
• To identify a new non-gradable adjective not featured in Unit 4

Before class

Make one copy of the activity for each group of three students in your class. Cut into two sections.

In class

❶ On the board, write the following adjectives:

*boiling   enormous   fantastic   fascinating   filthy
freezing   terrible   tiny   wonderful*

Review the meanings of these adjectives with your students, asking them to explain what each word means, using synonyms (for example, *boiling = very hot*). Ask them to verbally give examples of these words in sentences of their own (or, alternatively, ask students to come to the board and write an example for each one). When you have done this, erase the words from the board.

❷ Divide your class into groups of three. Give one student a copy of the sentences. They should not show these to the other students in their group. Give the other two students a copy of the grid.

❸ Explain that the student with the sentences is going to read these to the others in their group. They must listen carefully, and then replace the *last two words* in each sentence with one *strong* adjective. These adjectives will be those that were written on the board. They can ask the student to repeat the sentences, but they should only do this using appropriate expressions (for example, *Could you repeat that, please?* or *I'm sorry, could you say that again?*). Pre-teach these expressions if necessary.

❹ They should write the words in the spaces (one letter for each space: in most cases, they will be left with some empty spaces). Number 1 has been done for them.
If they do this correctly, they will reveal a new word by adding together the letters in the shaded spaces. This word can be used to complete the sentence at the bottom of their sheet.

❺ The winning group is the first group to identify this word.

Answers
1 wonderful   2 terrible   3 fascinating   4 fantastic
5 enormous   6 boiling   7 filthy   8 tiny
9 freezing

The sentence can be completed with the word *deafening.*

Unit 4 photocopiable activity
Absolutely wonderful!

Sentences

1 Rosanne's just had a baby girl. That's *very good*.
2 I didn't like the film. In fact, I thought it was *very bad*.
3 I'm interested in modern art. I think it's *very interesting*.
4 We had great fun at the party. It was *very good*.
5 The cake my mother made for my birthday was *very big*.
6 Can you open a window? The room's *very hot*.
7 Don't swim in the river. It's *very dirty*.
8 The food in this restaurant is nice, but the portions are *very small*.
9 Close the window. The room's *very cold*.

- -

Grid

Listen to the sentences you will hear, and change the last two words in each one to a single *strong* adjective. The first one has been done for you. You will not always need to write a letter in every space (in number 1, for example, you are left with two empty spaces).

| 1 | w | o | n | d | e | r | f | u | l | | |

| 2 | | | | | | | | | | | |

| 3 | | | | | | | | | | | |

| 4 | | | | | | | | | | | |

| 5 | | | | | | | | | | | |

| 6 | | | | | | | | | | | |

| 7 | | | | | | | | | | | |

| 8 | | | | | | | | | | | |

| 9 | | | | | | | | | | | |

Use the letters in the shaded spaces to change the two words in **bold** in Sentence 1 below to a single, *strong* adjective in Sentence 2. You do not need to change the order of the letters.

Sentence 1: 'The sound of the crowd cheering at the football match was **very noisy**.'
Sentence 2: 'The sound of the crowd cheering at the football match was d _ _ _ _ _ _ _ _.'

Word list

Unit 4

Note: the numbers show which page the word or phrase first appears on in the unit.

boiling *adj* (38) very hot

calm *adj* (38) peaceful and quiet

crowded *adj* (38) very full of people

deep *adj* (36) having a long distance from the top to the bottom

department store *n* (38) a large shop divided into several different parts which sell different types of things

dull *adj* (38) not interesting

empty *adj* (38) If something is empty, it does not contain any things or people.

enormous *adj* (38) extremely large

extremely *adv* (38) very, or much more than usual

filthy *adj* (38) extremely dirty

flat *adj* (38) smooth and level, with no curved, high, or hollow parts

fountain *n* (38) a structure that forces water up into the air as a decoration

freezing *adj* (38) very cold

hilly *adj* (38) having a lot of hills

journey *n* (36) when you travel from one place to another

lively *adj* (38) full of energy and interest

market *n* (35) a place where people go to buy or sell things, often outside

narrow *adj* (38) Narrow things measure a small distance from one side to the other.

noisy *adj* (36) Noisy people or things make a lot of noise.

port *n* (38) a town or an area of a town next to water where ships arrive and leave from

shallow *adj* (38) not deep

shopping centre *n* (35) a place where a lot of shops have been built close together

snorkel *n* (34) a tube that you use to help you breathe if you are swimming with your face under water

snowboard *n* (34) a large board that you stand on to move over snow

souvenir *n* (34) something which you buy or keep to remember a special event or holiday

sunbathe *v* (34) to sit or lie in the sun so that your skin becomes brown

take photos *v* (34) to produce pictures using a camera

tiny *adj* (38) extremely small

tourist office *n* (38) a building where someone who visits a place for pleasure can get information

town hall *n* (38) a large building where local government is based

travel *n* (36) the activity of travelling

travel *v* (36) to make a journey

trek *n* (34) a long, difficult journey that you make by walking

trip *n* (34) a journey in which you visit a place for a short time and come back again

youth club *n* (38) an organisation for young people who want to take part in a sport or social activity together, or the building they use for this

Unit 5 Feelings

Unit objectives

- **Topics:** personal feelings, opinions, experiences, relations with others
- **Listening Part 4:** identifying the language of opinions
- **Reading Part 5:** identifying focus of individual items, using the context to guess missing words
- **Speaking Parts 3 and 4:** describing photos, describing personal experiences
- **Writing Part 3:** (*letter*) cause and effect links, formal/informal expressions
- **Grammar:** modal verbs: ability and possibility; advice, obligation and prohibition
- **Vocabulary:** adjectives with *-ed* and *-ing*, adjectives and prepositions, adjectives of emotion and their opposites

Starting off

❶ Check that the meanings of 1–5, especially *jealousy*, are clear. Point out that *envy* (adjective: *envious*) has a similar meaning of 'wanting something that another person has'. *Jealousy* can also mean being angry because someone you love seems far too interested in somebody else!

> **Answers**
> 2 happiness   3 sadness   4 anger   5 fear

❷ Tell the class to complete the answers to the quiz on their own, before checking with the key. They give themselves a mark for each answer, then look at what their total says about them.

> **Answers**
> 2 anger   3 fear   4 happiness   5 jealousy

❸ Allow time for individuals to read the key and think about what it says about them.

> **Answer key to quiz**
> 1 a 2, b 0, c 1   2 a 1, b 0, c 2   3 a 1, b 2, c 0
> 4 a 2, b 1, c 0   5 a 0, b 1, c 2

Extension idea With some classes, you may feel it is appropriate for pairs to discuss the answers and/or get them to report back to the class.

Listening Part 4

❶ Point out that they will hear the rest of this dialogue in the exam task to follow. Ask them to look quickly through this first part of the conversation and sum up the situation: two friends separated by one of them going to live somewhere else. They keep in touch, but one of them isn't happy about not seeing the other. Elicit the language they use to express opinions, possibly getting students to underline the actual words used. Then elicit more expressions.

> **Answers**
> 1 I don't think, I'm a bit surprised, it seems to me, for me   2 (Suggested answers) in my opinion, I think, I believe, I'm sure (that), I feel (that), as I see it, if you ask me, I'd say, I'm afraid, my view is that; the use of *might/could/may* for possibility.

❷ Play it twice without pausing, then check.

> **Answers**
> 1 A   2 B   3 A   4 B   5 A   6 B

Extension idea Give pairs or groups a copy of the transcript on page 142, and get them to underline all the expressions used for expressing opinions, e.g. *I don't think*.

Recording script   CD1 Track 22

Erica:	So, Ben, how often do you and Liam actually get together these days?
Ben:	Whenever I can, Erica. Usually about once every two months.
Erica:	I don't think that's enough, really, to keep a friendship going. Couldn't you visit him each month, or ask him to come here?
Ben:	Well, it's a long way to go. More than 400 kilometres, I think.
Erica:	How long does it take?
Ben:	Over six hours, each way. So you spend half the weekend on the coach, going up and down the motorway. It's so boring!
Erica:	How about taking the train? Wouldn't that be quicker?
Ben:	I don't think I could afford it. The fares are really high.

Erica:	Why don't you get a student travel card? Your tickets would be a lot cheaper.
Ben:	Hmm. That's an idea.
Erica:	And Liam could get one, too. Then he could sometimes come here on Saturdays and Sundays to see you.
Ben:	I don't think he's keen on doing that. He likes his new town a lot. He wants to stay there at weekends, he says.
Erica:	I see. So you go and see him, but he never comes here.
Ben:	I'm sure that's because there's so much to do there. It's an exciting town, and I know he's made new friends there. But we get on really well and we're not suddenly going to stop being friends.
Erica:	No, I'm not saying that at all. But maybe you need to remind him that you've been friends since you were little kids. And tell him how important a friend he is to you. He might not realise that, especially with all the changes in his life right now.

❸ Point out that the first two of these expressions are in the written part of the conversation in Exercise 1, possibly using *upset about* as an example. Adjectives followed by *about* will be covered in Vocabulary (adjectives + prepositions). This activity could be done in pairs. Check answers.

> **Answers**
> 2 e   3 f   4 a   5 b   6 d

Extension idea Elicit more examples with the expressions, then pairs ask questions, e.g. *When did you last feel upset about something?, When do you get together with your friends?*

❹ Students may have experienced, or know about, friendships that have had to adapt to someone moving to another town or country. If not, suggest they discuss what happens when a sibling or cousin moves away: how does it affect the relationship?

Grammar
Can, could, might and *may* (ability and possibility)

❶ Pairs study the three extracts. Elicit the answers, including the contracted forms of *cannot* and *could not*.

> **Answers**
> *can, could, might (not); might not is negative; not goes after the modal verb (might); mightn't; can't and couldn't*

❷ ⊙ Pairs or small groups note down the kind of error made in each case. Go through the corrections. If your students tend to make any other errors, e.g. adding third person *s* to modals (e.g. *he mights*), highlight these, too. Focus on Question 4, eliciting the question form *could we*, and further examples such as *Where can we go?* and *May we leave?*. You may also want to mention the negative question forms *can't we* and *couldn't we*, as in *Why can't we stay longer?*

> **Answers**
> 2 ~~may seems~~ → may seem – the main verb following a modal is an infinitive without *to* so it does not add 's' in the 3rd person (*he/she/it*)
>
> 3 ~~I'm not can~~ → I can't – forms of *be* are not used before modals; most modals form the negative by adding *not* or a short form of it at the end
>
> 4 ~~we could~~ → could we – the question form of modals normally needs a change in word order of modal and subject and doesn't use the auxiliary verb *do*
>
> 5 ~~can doing~~ → can do – modals are not followed by the -*ing* form of the verb
>
> 6 ~~you will might see~~ → you might see – the future form of most modals is the same as the present form
>
> 7 ~~It's could be~~ → It could be – forms of *be* are not used before modals
>
> 8 ~~could met~~ → could meet – modals are followed by the infinitive without *to*, not a past form of the verb

❸ Elicit the rules. Point out that we sometimes use *could* for past (general) ability, e.g. *I could swim when I was six*, with the senses, e.g. *I could hear them talking*, and in conditional forms: *I could finish this job if I had more time.*

> **Answers**
> 1 can/could   2 may/might/could

❹ Get the class to read quickly through the text and say who wrote it and why (it is a response by Kylie, the person receiving the email in Exercise 3, suggesting they leave seeing each for now, but talk on the phone soon). Pairs then choose the correct alternatives.

> **Answers**
> 2 might   3 couldn't   4 can't   5 can't   6 can
> 7 Could   8 can't

❺ Encourage them to say what they *could, couldn't, may* or *mightn't* do. Remind them not to use auxiliary *do* with these.

Alternative treatment Pairs discuss the emails in Exercises 3 and 4, asking and answering questions, e.g. *How might Kylie feel about the fact she can't see her* *best friend? What could she do on Thursday instead? Can talking on the phone to a friend be as good as seeing them?*

> **Suggested answers**
> I can't see my school friends, I can't stay out very late; I can go out with friends, I can stay in bed late, I can play computer games all morning, I might go to the cinema, play tennis, go dancing

Should, shouldn't, ought to, must, mustn't, have to, and *don't have to* (obligation and prohibition)

❶ Elicit the meaning of *ought to* (*should*), and explain that although *oughtn't* is possible, we more often use *shouldn't* as the negative of both.

> **Answers**
> 1 B   2 A

❷ Point out that any of these modals can be used for either picture.

> **Suggested answers**
> **A** you ought to / should get a haircut, have a wash, mend your trousers, get some new shoes; you shouldn't go out like that, wear those clothes, have your hair like that
>
> **B** You shouldn't go to school tomorrow, do any work, get too close to people; you ought to / should see the doctor, go to bed, lie down, have hot drinks, take an aspirin

Extension idea Think of other situations in which people need advice, e.g. someone riding a motorbike without a helmet, not revising, spending too much time on the PlayStation®, and elicit sentences using *should / shouldn't / ought to.*

❸ Pairs discuss the pictures and sentences. Check their answers, then focus attention on the modal in each sentence. Point out that whereas the meanings of *must* and *have to* are similar (though not identical: *must* involves obligation imposed by the speaker, *have to* an 'external' obligation), *mustn't* and *don't have to* are quite different from each other: *mustn't* involves prohibition and *don't have to* a lack of obligation. If necessary, elicit or give more examples. Finally, point out that *needn't* has the same meaning as *don't have to.*

> **Answers**
> 2 D   3 C   4 E
>
> *Must*: it's necessary to do it (because the speaker says so); *Mustn't*: you're not allowed to do it; *Have to*: it's necessary to do it (because it's a rule or law); *Don't have to*: it's not necessary to do it.

❹ Check everyone has the correct answers.

> **Answers**
> **b** 3   **c** 2   **d** 1

❺ Remind the class to refer back to the meanings of these modals. They will need to use one of them twice. Go through the answers, asking which of the sentences could also be completed with *needn't* (1 and 4).

> **Answers**
> 2 must   3 mustn't   4 don't have to   5 have to
> 6 must

❻ Set a two-minute limit for students working alone to do this, then elicit the answer. Remind them that understanding the purpose of a text is a reading sub-skill that is tested in Reading Part 4, Question 1. Check comprehension of language in the text, particularly IT expressions such as *site, online* and *page.*

> **Answer**
> B

❼ 🎧 Play the recording once or twice, pausing if required. If time allows, ask why each answer is correct, and the alternative wrong.

> **Answers**
> 2 don't have to   3 have to   4 doesn't have to
> 5 must   6 shouldn't   7 mustn't

Recording script   CD1 Track 23

Presenter: Internet sites like *MySpace, Bebo* and *Facebook* are a great way for young people to keep in touch with friends, but there are things you <u>should</u> do to stay safe. On some sites you <u>don't have to</u> use your real name if you don't want to, so invent a name for yourself. On most sites it's a rule that you <u>have to</u> give an email address, but this <u>doesn't have to</u> be your normal one – you can use any address. You can write lots of interesting things on your online page, but something you <u>must</u> never do is put your house address or phone number. In fact, you <u>shouldn't</u> give any information that could let strangers know your identity, because on the Internet you never know who is looking. Remember, too, that you <u>mustn't</u> put your friends' personal details on your page, or you could put them in danger. So the message is: have fun, but take care.

❽ Allow time for pairs to discuss these. Possibly elicit any amusing ideas, e.g. things they ought to do but never find the time for.

> **Suggested answers**
> **2** I mustn't eat at my desk.   **3** I don't have to go out early.   **4** I must work harder.   **5** I shouldn't eat cream cakes but I sometimes do!   **6** I ought to tidy my room but I probably won't.

Vocabulary
Adjectives and prepositions

❶ Elicit the answers. Point out that here the prepositions all come immediately after the adjectives, but that this is not always the case.

> **Answers**
> **1** with   **2** of   **3** about

❷

> **Answers**
> **1** of   **2** with   **3** about

❸ Encourage groups to think of real sentences they have heard, particularly those using the most common of these adjectives.

> **Suggested answers**
> **of**: confident (also *confident about*), envious, frightened, etc.; **with**: pleased, cross, fed up, etc.; **about**: relaxed, excited, mad, etc.

> ***Extension idea*** Highlight some other adjective + preposition combinations. They have already seen *keen on*, but a common error is to say 'keen of'. Others might include *interested in*, *sorry for*, *similar to*, etc.

❹ Tell the class that once they have written in the correct prepositions this is a light-hearted activity. They don't have to think too deeply about their answers; in fact, they don't actually need to be true!

> **Answers**
> **2** with   **3** of   **4** with   **5** of/about   **6** of/about

Adjectives with *-ed* and *-ing*

❶ Allow two minutes for this, explaining that they don't need to fill in any of the gaps at this stage.

> **Answers**
> He wanted to contact her (and needed her details / phone number from them); They met again and got married.

❷ Explain that verbs ending in *e* drop this to form the adjective. Focus attention on the rewritten sentence and elicit the *-ed* adjective. Point out this kind of change in structure may be tested in Writing Part 1. Then ask for answers to the two final questions, reinforcing the point that *-ing* adjectives describe things (or events, people, e.g. *a boring speaker*, etc.), whereas *-ed* adjectives tell us how people feel about them. Finally, give and practise more examples using adjectives from the previous section: *frightened/frightening, tired/tiring*, etc.

> **Answer**
> boring, it drops the final *e* to add *-ing*

❸

> **Answer**
> bored

❹

> **Answers**
> boring, bored

❺ It may be necessary to pre-teach some of these adjectives, such as *embarrassing*. Give the class plenty of time to do this and go through the answers.

> **Answers**
> **2** relaxed   **3** surprising   **4** tired   **5** depressed   **6** embarrassing   **7** amused   **8** annoyed   **9** disappointed   **10** interested   **11** amazed   **12** excited

❻ Ensure that they write sentences using both forms, in each case.

> **Suggested answers**
> **1** I'm always excited when I meet new people. It's always exciting to meet new people.
> **2** Dancing for a long time is tiring. I get tired when I dance for a long time.
> **3** I was disappointed that he didn't phone. It was disappointing that he didn't phone.

❼ Explain that they are going to hear four short monologues about emotional experiences, and they must identify those emotions. They will have to do this by noticing the speaker's tone. When they have listened to the recording, possibly twice, check their answers. These monologues also provide models for students to follow in Exercise 8.

> **Answers**
> **1** c   **2** d   **3** a   **4** b

Speaker 1:   My brother took some CDs out of my room without asking. I wasn't happy about it because I wanted to play one of them.

Speaker 2:   Usually my family all meet at our house on December 31st, but this year my cousins can't come. It's a shame.

Speaker 3:   (bored tone) I don't want to go to that youth club again. There's never anything to do there and there's nobody to talk to.

Speaker 4:   And then Jessica walked in. I couldn't believe it, because I thought I'd never see her again.

8 If the students' culture makes it difficult for them to talk about being personally embarrassed, for instance, suggest they describe a scene in a film or play in which somebody suffers embarrassment.

Extension idea Ask for two or three volunteers to tell their short story to the rest of the class. As in Exercise 7, they have to listen and identify the emotion.

Reading   Part 5

1 Give the class a minute to read and absorb the text, then ask for answers. Keep the discussion fairly brief, but try to reach a consensus.

2 Get pairs to talk about the pictures and then broaden out the discussion. The final question focuses on the theme of the Reading text to follow, so fairly short answers are fine here.

3 Give students no more than two minutes to read the text, and then ask for answers to the three gist questions.

> **Suggested answers**
> **1** when something bad happens to us   **2** all the time / every day   **3** our lives will get much better / we'll become much happier

4 This exercise practises the technique suggested in the Exam advice box. Allow time for them to look through all the items (but not the text) and note down their answers. Check their answers.

> **Answers**
> **a** 2, 5, 6   **b** 4, 8, 10   **c** 1, 7, 9   **d** 3

Extension idea If time allows, first practise the technique used in the exam task at sentence level:
1 Look at questions 1–4 below. Which tests: **a** modal verbs? **b** adjectives + preposition? **c** words with similar meanings? **d** adjectives ending with -ed or -ing?
2 For each question, choose the correct answer, A, B, C or D.
1 Megan is proud … what she did yesterday.

A for   B with   C about   D of
2 I was feeling very … so I went to sleep.
A relaxed   B excited   C tiring   D boring
3 On an aeroplane, people … not smoke.
A need   B must   C might   D ought
4 Thank you, I'm very … for your help.
A helpful   B careful   C grateful   D successful

> **Answers**
> **a** 3   **b** 1   **c** 4   **d** 2   **1** D   **2** A   **3** B   **4** C

5 Students do the exam task on their own. Go through the text and items when everyone has finished.

> **Answers**
> **1** B   **2** A   **3** C   **4** A   **5** B   **6** C   **7** B   **8** B
> **9** A   **10** D

6 This could begin with a class discussion, to generate ideas. Students then write down those they feel are most important to them. Refer back to the content of the text, encouraging them to try the technique suggested in the final two paragraphs.

Vocabulary
Adjectives and their opposites

1 Students can refer back to the Reading text to study *miserable* and *negative* in context.

> **Answers**
> **2** d   **3** a   **4** c   **5** b

2 Check their answers and elicit example sentences using some or all of the adjectives and their opposites.

> **Answers**
> **2** relaxed   **3** positive   **4** depressed   **5** mean

3 Do this quickly, as a class. Check that everyone understands these, as they will be referred to in Exercises 4 and 5.

> **Answers**
> funny/serious, strange/ordinary

4 Encourage pairs or individuals to imagine each situation as they match it with an adjective.

> **Answers**
> **2** serious   **3** awful   **4** ordinary   **5** strange
> **6** fantastic

5 In Speaking Part 4 they will be talking about personal experiences. Encourage them to describe more than one situation using each adjective. If necessary, explain that *behind your back* means 'without you knowing'.

Extension idea Students work in pairs. One describes a situation they have experienced and the other has to guess which adjective best sums it up (e.g. their phone keeps on ringing but when they answer it there's never anyone there [annoying]).

Speaking Parts 3 and 4

❶ Encourage them to paraphrase if necessary. Suggest they think of more than one adjective to describe how they might have been feeling, and give reasons. Also introduce the question 'What do you think was his/her reaction?', as a form of this will appear in Exercise 3.

> **Suggested answers**
> **A:** I can see a girl. She looks like she's making a speech at her school or college. She seems nervous.
> **B:** I can see a boy. It looks like he's in a long queue for an event. He looks very bored.

❷ 🎧 Play the recording once, and again if necessary.

> **Answers**
> **A:** At the beginning, she felt nervous. After a few minutes she began to feel (more) relaxed. At the end, when everyone clapped, she was delighted.
> **B:** He was excited about going to the concert. After six hours in the queue he was very bored. In the end he was angry because some people bought tickets to make money.

❸ 🎧 Play the dialogues again, pausing if more time is needed to fill in the missing words.

> **Answers**
> **1** did, feel **2** happened, end **3** did, have
> **4** was, reaction

Extension idea The class practise these questions with the same intonation as the speakers on the recording. Play each of 1–4 again and chorus drill.

> **Recording script** CD1 Track 25
> Picture A.
> Girl: Well, once I had to make a speech to nearly the whole school, in front of hundreds of other students.
> Friend: How <u>did</u> you <u>feel</u>?
> Girl: At first I was really <u>nervous</u> and I couldn't remember what I had to say. I needed to keep looking at my notes. But after a few minutes I started to feel a bit <u>more relaxed</u>, and then I just talked and talked.
> Friend: What <u>happened</u> in the <u>end</u>?

> Girl: Everyone clapped. I was <u>delighted</u> when I heard that!
> Picture B.
> Boy: I was really <u>excited</u> about that concert, I just had to see it, but thousands of other people wanted tickets too. That's why the queue was so enormous.
> Friend: How long <u>did</u> you <u>have</u> to wait?
> Boy: Six hours. I was so <u>bored</u>! But just before I got to the ticket office, it closed! They'd sold all the tickets.
> Friend: What <u>was</u> your <u>reaction</u> to that?
> Boy: I was <u>angry</u>. A lot of people had bought ten or twenty tickets each, so they could sell them later and make money.

❹ Remind the class that Part 4 of the Speaking paper is always linked to the theme of Part 3. Monitor pairs as they talk, and give feedback when they have finished.

Writing Part 3

❶ Emphasise the importance of relevance when replying to a letter. Then ask for the answers – and for reasons why the others are irrelevant.

> **Answers**
> 1, 4, 5; include reasons why you like to relax in that way.

❷ Give the class time to read through the letter. Ask what style it is written in (informal), but leave specific examples for Exercise 3.

> **Answers**
> **1** (Where) her own room **4** (When) weekends
> **5** (How) read an interesting book
> **Reasons** (why): warm and cosy, she can listen to her favourite music, nobody comes in, no phone calls

❸ Explain any expressions they may be unsure of.

> **Answers**
> Lots of love (E), All the best (E), Don't forget to write soon (E), Dear George (B), Well, that's all for now (E), Thanks for your letter (B), This is just a quick letter to say (B), It was great to hear from you (B), Hi Lisa (B), Give my love to everyone (E), Sorry I've taken so long to write back (B)

❹

> **Answers**
> Used in letter: Hi Nathan, Thanks for your letter, it was great to hear from you, Write soon and let me know, All the best

❺ Allow a minute for them to scan the letter for this.

> **Answer**
> so (nobody comes in)

❻ Point out that the word order in these cause/result sentences sometimes has to change.

> **Answers**
> **2** I never get tired of going to the cinema because there are so many good films. **3** Since I don't have much homework to do, I often go out in the evenings. **4** I enjoy water skiing a lot because it's really exciting. **5** I've got some really good games, so I'm on my PlayStation® every day.

❼

> **Sample answer**
> Dear Libby,
>
> It's nice to hear from you. You ask about something exciting I do and the answer is easy: horse riding in the mountains!
>
> It's great because on a horse you can get to beautiful places that are impossible to reach by car, or even by bike. Sometimes we're so high up that in winter and spring everything is covered in snow and the views are fantastic!
>
> The paths along the mountainsides are very narrow, so it can be a bit frightening if you look down, but you're completely safe because the horses know the way – they've been there hundreds of times!
>
> In your next letter tell me about the exciting things you do!
>
> Bye for now,
>
> Keira

Unit 5 photocopiable activity: What are you talking about?

Time: 20 mins +

> **Objectives**
> - To review and practise adjectives and their dependent prepositions from Unit 5
> - To let students act out mini role plays in a semi-controlled task
> - To practise paraphrasing

Before class

Make one copy of the activity, and cut into ten cards.

In class

❶ Divide your class into pairs. There should be no more than ten pairs in the class, so if you have more than 20 students (or an uneven number), some will need to work in groups of three.

❷ Give each pair one of the conversation prompt cards. They should not show these to the other students in the class. If you have fewer than ten pairs, you will not need to use all of the cards.

❸ They imagine they are having a conversation with each other, and that one of them has just said the sentence at the end of their card. They are going to continue the conversation, but they are not allowed to use any of the words in **bold**.

They have five minutes to plan what they are going to say. They can make notes, or write a short script for their conversation.

Copy the following onto the board:

> *Adjectives*: crazy depressed disappointed fond impatient jealous nervous proud satisfied tired
>
> *Prepositions*: about of with
>
> *Phrases*: … sports like motor racing. … going to my new school. … people who are rich.
> … learning English. … moving to a new city.
> … my exam results. … my parents.
> … our team's football score. … people who are always late. … pizzas and burgers.

❹ After five minutes, ask them to stop. Tell them that they are now going to act out their conversation, *without using the words in bold on their card*. The other pairs should listen to the conversation and decide what the 'opening' sentence was. They then reconstruct this, using the words and phrases on the board.

Each sentence should begin with *I'm*, followed by an adjective, a preposition and a phrase, in that order.

❺ The pair with the Conversation 1 card begins speaking. They have a maximum of one minute. After they have acted out their conversation, the other pairs have about 30 seconds to construct the opening sentence, which they write on a separate sheet of paper.

❻ Repeat Step 5 with the other pairs / conversation cards until they have all finished. Review their answers. The pairs win one point for each correctly constructed sentence. You can also award a point to the 'speaking' pair each time their unspoken 'opening' sentence is identified.

> **Answers**
> See the photocopiable cards on the next page.

What are you talking about?

Conversation prompts

✂ Cut along the dotted lines to divide these into cards.

Conversation 1

Here is the first sentence of your conversation. Do not read this sentence out, and do not use the words in **bold** at any time in your conversation. You have a maximum of one minute. 'I'm **satisfied** with our **team's football score**.'

Conversation 2

Here is the first sentence of your conversation. Do not read this sentence out, and do not use the words in **bold** at any time in your conversation. You have a maximum of one minute. 'I'm **proud** of my **parents**.'

Conversation 3

Here is the first sentence of your conversation. Do not read this sentence out, and do not use the words in **bold** at any time in your conversation. You have a maximum of one minute. 'I'm **crazy** about **sports** like **motor racing**.'

Conversation 4

Here is the first sentence of your conversation. Do not read this sentence out, and do not use the words in **bold** at any time in your conversation. You have a maximum of one minute. 'I'm **nervous** about **going** to my **new school**.'

Conversation 5

Here is the first sentence of your conversation. Do not read this sentence out, and do not use the words in **bold** at any time in your conversation. You have a maximum of one minute. 'I'm **fond** of **pizzas** and **burgers**.'

Conversation 6

Here is the first sentence of your conversation. Do not read this sentence out, and do not use the words in **bold** at any time in your conversation. You have a maximum of one minute. 'I'm **tired** of **learning English**.'

Conversation 7

Here is the first sentence of your conversation. Do not read this sentence out, and do not use the words in **bold** at any time in your conversation. You have a maximum of one minute. 'I'm **disappointed** with my **exam results**.'

Conversation 8

Here is the first sentence of your conversation. Do not read this sentence out, and do not use the words in **bold** at any time in your conversation. You have a maximum of one minute. 'I'm **impatient** with **people** who are **always late**.'

Conversation 9

Here is the first sentence of your conversation. Do not read this sentence out, and do not use the words in **bold** at any time in your conversation. You have a maximum of one minute. 'I'm **depressed** about **moving** to a **new city**.'

Conversation 10

Here is the first sentence of your conversation. Do not read this sentence out, and do not use the words in **bold** at any time in your conversation. You have a maximum of one minute. 'I'm **jealous** of **people** who are **rich**.'

Word list

Unit 5

Note: the numbers show which page the word or phrase first appears on in the unit.

amazed *adj* (48) extremely surprised

amusing *adj* (48) making you laugh or smile

anger *n* (44) a strong feeling against someone who has behaved badly, making you want to shout at them or hurt them

annoyed *adj* (48) slightly angry

ashamed *adj* (47) feeling guilty or embarrassed about something you have done

awful *adj* (49) very bad, of low quality, or unpleasant

bored *adj* (47) feeling tired and unhappy because something is not interesting or because you have nothing to do

cheerful *adj* (49) happy

crazy about *adj* (47) loving someone very much, or being very interested in something

delighted *adj* (49) very pleased

depressed *adj* (47) very unhappy, often for a long time

disappointed *adj* (47) unhappy because someone or something was not as good as you hoped or expected, or because something did not happen

embarrassing *adj* (48) making you feel embarrassed

emotional *adj* (44) showing strong feelings, or making people have strong feelings

exciting *adj* (48) making you feel very happy and enthusiastic

fantastic *adj* (49) very good

fear *n* (44) a strong, unpleasant feeling that you get when you think that something bad, dangerous, or frightening might happen

fond *adj* (47) expressing or causing happy feelings

frightening *adj* (48) making you feel afraid or nervous

generous *adj* (49) giving other people a lot of money, presents, or time in a kind way

get on well with someone *v* (45) to like and be friendly to someone

get together *v* (45) to meet in order to do something or spend time together

grateful *adj* (49) feeling or showing thanks

habit *n* (49) something that you do regularly, almost without thinking about it

jealousy *n* (44) jealous feelings

keen *adj* (45) wanting to do something very much

mean *adj* (49) A mean person does not like spending money, especially on other people.

miserable *adj* (49) unhappy

move away *v* (44) to go to a different place to live

negative *adj* (49) a negative effect is bad and causes damage to something; not having enthusiasm or positive opinions about something

ordinary *adj* (49) not special, different, or unusual in any way

positive *adj* (49) something that is positive makes you feel better about a situation; feeling happy about your life and your future

proud *adj* (47) feeling very pleased about something you have done, something you own, or someone you know

relaxed *adj* (48) feeling happy and comfortable because nothing is worrying you

remind *v* (45) to make someone remember something, or remember to do something

serious *adj* (49) A serious person is quiet and does not laugh often.

upset *adj* (44) unhappy or worried because something unpleasant has happened

Unit 6 Leisure and fashion

Unit objectives

- **Topics:** entertainment and media, clothes
- **Listening Part 1:** focusing on differences between three pictures
- **Reading Part 2:** introduction to task type, understanding descriptions of people, key words and distractors
- **Speaking Part 4:** expanding on a topic and eliciting views from your partner
- **Writing Part 2:** task completion, focusing on question and content points, writing a short message to say *thank you*
- **Grammar:** present perfect, *already, just, yet, for, since*, present perfect or past simple?
- **Vocabulary:** television programmes, going out, *been/gone, meet, get to know, know* and *find out*, describing clothes

Starting off

❶ Point out that *advert* is short for *advertisement*. We can also say *ad*.

> **Answers**
> 2 documentary   3 quiz show   4 the news
> 5 comedy series   6 chat show

Extension idea Draw a type of programme on the board for students to guess what it is, e.g. a laughing face = a comedy series.

❷

> **Answer**
> They talk about: documentary, comedy series, chat show, the news.

Extension idea Play the recording again but stop just after each expression **in bold** in the recording script. The students write down the expression they have just heard.

Recording script   CD1 Track 26

Lucy: Ben, you're watching TV again! What's on?
Ben: **It's a programme about** farmers in Kenya who are trying to save elephants. Did you know that the elephant population has fallen by 80% there?

Lucy: Yes, but how much TV do you watch a day?
Ben: **I'm not really sure. It depends on** whether I have a lot of homework or not. **I always watch** *Alphabet Road.*
Lucy: Oh? I haven't heard of *Alphabet Road.* **What's it about?**
Ben: Oh, it's the story of some neighbours on a crazy street. **It's on Thursdays and it always makes me laugh**. What's your favourite programme?
Lucy: **I don't watch much TV** but **I love** *The Luke Robinson Show.* He interviews all kinds of people, including famous people. Did you see his interview with Tom Cruise?
Ben: **You're joking! I can't stand** those kinds of programmes. **I prefer** play**ing** computer games **to** watch**ing** that.
Lucy: **Really?** Look, it's 9 pm. Why don't we switch over and watch the headlines? I like to know what's happening in the world.
Ben: **Good idea!** Here's the remote control.

❸ Encourage students to use some of the expressions from the recording in Exercise 2.

Reading Part 2

❶ ***Alternative treatment*** Choose eight students to represent the eight different events. They read the appropriate event description. Divide the rest into the five groups of people who should read their description. The groups of people visit the event representatives and decide which is the most suitable event for them.

> **Answers**
> 2 *Kids Rock*   3 *Found in Hong Kong*
> 4 *Best Friends*   5 *Prince of Mandavia*
> 6 *University Spotlight*   7 *Liala*   8 *Reggae Nights*

❷

> **Suggested answer**
> The important information has been underlined.

❸ Some students might be surprised that two girls are going to see *Fight Planet*. Remind them that all the answers come from the text and not what the students feel is correct.

> **Answers**
>
> G (*Fight Planet*) *suggested words to underline*: 'You haven't seen anything like this before' (as they *would like to see something completely different*)
>
> *Reasons why they do not choose the other options:*
>
> *University Spotlight* – it says book early; *Kids Rock, Prince of Mandavia, Liala, Found in Hong Kong* and *Reggae Nights* all contain music and Silvie and Kat *don't want to hear more music*
>
> *Best Friends* – there is *nothing different about this story*

❹

> **Suggested answers**
>
> **2** Teenagers visiting … with their parents, all love science fiction, Martha and Artie love live music, especially reggae, their parents want to see a musical
>
> **3** university students, want to have fun, can't afford … much money, like listening … music
>
> **4** Lily (19) … Ken (18) … five-year-old cousin, Mai … mad about animals …, wants to drive … doesn't want to pay for parking
>
> **5** Lara … mum prefer something funny to serious drama, go to bed early, buy some presents before they leave

❺ Encourage the students to cross off the options (e.g. *Fight Planet*) as they work.

> **Answers**
>
> **2** B **3** F **4** C **5** E
>
> *Suggested words to underline*: **2** Set in the year 2306, live musicians play, this show **3** play their records … disco, Admission free **4** monkey, elephant and bear, free parking for every two adult tickets
> **5** definitely good fun, not to be taken seriously, gift shop open during interval

❻

> **Suggested answer**
>
> Martha and Artie are teenagers and are going out with their parents. Their parents want to see a musical. *Reggae Nights* is a disco (not a musical) and is for over-18s only. It is likely that Martha and Artie are under 18. Also, there is no connection with science fiction, which they all like.

❼

> **Suggested answers**
>
> **1** Silvie and Kat are *best friends* (*Best Friends* is the title of H); they saw their *favourite band* last week (in C, 'Keith's Door' is everyone's *favourite band*) **3** Al and Ed are *university students* (A mentions students several times, e.g. *special discounts for students*) **4** Mai is *mad about animal*s (D mentions *no … animals here*; the musicians in E are dressed as *strange animals*)
> **5** Lara and her mum *prefer … funny to serious* (H mentions a *serious look*)

❽ Each group should appoint a spokesperson to explain their choice.

Vocabulary
Going out

❶ ❷ Encourage the students to cover the words in Exercise 1 as they do Exercise 2.

> **Answers**
> **2** admission **3** audience **4** live **5** review
> **6** subtitles **7** interval **8** venue

❸ *Fight Planet*

> **Recording script** CD1 Track 27
>
> Liam: Yes. It was brilliant! My uncle managed to get me a ticket for the <u>early performance</u>. When <u>Monkey</u> came on stage, the audience went wild. The only thing I didn't like was the venue. It was too crowded.

❹ Students might prefer to describe something else they have seen.

> ***Extension idea*** Students produce an entertainment guide for their area.

Grammar
Present perfect

❶ They decide to watch the film at home and have pizza there.

> **Recording script** CD1 Track 28
>
> Tom: Would you like to see a show tonight?
> Evan: Yeah! Why not? We haven't been out together for three months. What's on?
> Tom: Well, there's that musical, *Kids Rock*. Have you <u>seen it yet</u>?
> Evan: 'Fraid so. I saw it last week. I haven't <u>seen</u> the circus show, *Liala*, <u>yet</u>.
> Tom: I've <u>already seen</u> *Liala*. My cousin took me on Saturday.

Evan:	How about *Best Friends*?
Tom:	Fantastic idea. I've <u>just finished</u> reading the play.
Evan:	Oh no! It's not a play, is it? I don't fancy that!
Tom:	Let's stay in and watch a film on TV, then.
Evan:	We can't do that. My dad's just taken the TV to be repaired. <u>We couldn't go to your house and watch the film, could we</u>?
Tom:	<u>Of course</u>! Why don't we <u>get a pizza</u> on the way to my house and <u>we can watch the film and have pizza</u>?
Evan:	What a great idea!

② Check that the class know how to form the present perfect.

> **Answers**
> **1** seen it yet   **2** seen … yet   **3** already seen
> **4** just finished. The present perfect is used in all four extracts.

❸

> **Answers**
> **2** already   **3** yet   **4/5** (in any order) already, just
> **6** yet

❹ Students should read the complete skeleton letter first to understand the meaning.

> **Answers**
> **2** My dad hasn't found a new job yet.   **3** But he's/ has started a course in computing.   **4** My mum's/ has just won a prize in a photography competition.
> **5** Have you seen the new *Kung Fu* film yet?
> **6** I've/have already seen it three times. It's great!
> **7** What about you? Have you finished your exams yet?

Extension idea Students write a reply to Harry's email.

❺ ***Alternative treatment*** Write Evan's sentence from the recording: *We haven't been out together for three months* and ask the students to rephrase this with *since*. Elicit suggestions about the difference between *for* and *since*.

> **Suggested answers**
> **1** 1998, etc.   **2** three years, etc.   **3** last year, my birthday, etc.   **4** (Name of teacher) / four months, etc.   **5** (Name of sport / *the* + instrument) / 2005, last year, etc.

❻ Encourage the students to answer with full sentences, e.g. '*I've lived here for two years.*'

> **Suggested answers**
> **2** How long have you been at your school?
> **3** How long have you had your watch?
> **4** How long has (name) been your English teacher?
> **5** How long have you played (sport) /
> *the* (instrument)?

Present perfect or past simple?

❶ Encourage the students to look at the time adverbs in each sentence first and decide if the time is finished (past simple) or not finished (present perfect).

> **Answers**
> **2** Have … read   **3** saw   **4** haven't heard   **5** won
> **6** did … go   **7** have … taken

❷

> **Suggested answers**
> **1** Why did he decide to become a …?   **2** When did he begin his career?   **3** Where did he first work?
> **4** How did he feel when he first began working, do you think?   **5** How long has he been a …?
> **6** How many times has he won a competition?

❸ ❹ ***Extension idea*** Students find out about another interesting performer.

Vocabulary
been/gone, meet, get to know, know and *find out*

❶ Focus on the differences between the verbs.

❷

> **Answers**
> **1** been, been   **2** meet   **3** known   **4** gone
> **5** getting to know   **6** find out

❸ Fast finishers can use these verbs to write more questions.

Listening Part 1

❶ Make sure students find these items:
backpack, belt, blouse, boots, coat, dress, earring, glasses, glove, handbag, jeans, purse, pyjamas, sandals, shorts, skirt, socks, suit, sweater, sweatshirt, swimming costume, T-shirt, tie, tights, towel, tracksuit, trainers, trousers, umbrella, wallet

❷

> **Answers**
> **2** ~~beautifuls~~ → beautiful   **3** a long ~~and~~ white →
> a long white   **4** ~~fashion~~ → fashionable   **5** ~~T-shirt~~ →
> a T-shirt   **6** ~~a blue trouser~~ → blue trousers / a pair
> of blue trousers

❸

> **Suggested answers**
> *Underline*
> 1 Mark's sweater 2 Mary lost 3 John lost?
> 4 coat
> *Differences*
> 1 There are three cotton sweaters, A is plain with a V-neck, B is patterned with a V-neck and C is plain with a round neck
> 2 A is a towel, B a pair of earrings and C a purse
> 3 A are trainers, B socks and C sandals
> 4 There are three long coats, A has six buttons and two pockets, B two buttons and no pockets and C six buttons and no pockets

❹ 🎧 Students should listen to each recording twice. Remind them to take notes as they listen. Students can then compare their answers in pairs using any notes they have taken.

> **Answers**
> 1 C 2 B 3 A 4 C

Recording script   CD1 Track 29

	One. Which is Mark's sweater?
Mark:	Excuse me. I've lost my sweater. I left it by the pool. It's <u>a plain one – there's no pattern or anything on it.</u> Has anyone handed it in?
Girl:	Let me see … . We've only got three sweaters here, I think. Is it this one? It's got a V-neck.
Mark:	Sorry, no! <u>Mine's got a round neck.</u> Oh! There it is! It's that one there! The cotton one! It was very expensive.
Girl:	Well, be more careful with it next time! Here you are!

CD1 Track 30
Two. What has Mary lost?

Mary:	Hi! I was emptying my backpack in the sports centre café because I needed to pay for something and I couldn't find my purse.
Girl:	How much money was in it?
Mary:	Oh … it's OK, I found that, but <u>I had a pair of earrings inside my bag too</u> … in a little kind of pocket … and <u>I think they fell out</u> when I pulled my towel out. <u>Has anyone brought them here?</u>
Girl:	Sorry, no …

CD1 Track 31
Three. What has John lost?

| Dad: | We've come to pick up John and he's playing tennis in his sandals. |
| Girl: | Really? |

| Dad: | Yes! He's always losing things. We thought he'd lost his socks but we've found those. <u>Have you got his trainers?</u> |
| Girl: | What do they look like? |

CD1 Track 32
Four. Which coat is Barbara talking about?

Barbara:	I was wearing my sister's coat and now I can't find it. She's going to be so angry with me.
Girl:	We've got several coats. What does it look like?
Barbara:	<u>It's quite long with five or six buttons down the front.</u>
Girl:	Anything in the pockets?
Barbara:	<u>It hasn't got any pockets.</u>

❺ **Alternative treatment** Student A **telephones** Student B, the lost-property officer.

Speaking Part 4

As a warmer In pairs, students take turns to describe one of the photos.

❶ Remind the students that the Speaking Part 4 exam question generally has two parts, e.g. *things you like to do at home* **and** *things you like to do when you go out.*

❷❸ 🎧 Jon and Ivan do a model task, so these are also correct answers for them.

> **Answers**
> 2 ✔ 3 ✘ 4 ✔ 5 ✔ 6 ✘ 7 ✘

Note: **3:** Students should avoid changing the topic completely and talking about something they have already prepared, e.g. *where I live.* **5:** Candidates should look at their partner and not the examiner. **6:** Students should try to take turns to speak and not dominate the conversation.   **7:** Although students should always aim to speak for two to three minutes, if they run out of things to say, the examiner will ask a prompt question that is related to the topic, e.g. *talk about what you don't like.*

Recording script   CD1 Track 33

Examiner:	Your photographs showed people going out. Now I'd like you to talk together about what you like to do at home and what you like to do when you go out.
Jon:	So, Ivan, what do you like to do at home? Do you like watching TV?
Ivan:	Yes, I love watching TV. We normally switch on the TV after dinner and watch a film, a football match or a documentary. What about you? Do

Jon:	you like watching films?
Jon:	Yes, but I prefer watching sports to documentaries. I find documentaries a little bit boring. Did you see the basketball match last night?
Ivan:	No, I didn't. When I'm at home I also enjoy playing cards or other games with my two brothers. On Sunday afternoons, we often stay in and play together. Do you ever play cards at home?
Jon:	No, not really. When I go out with my friends we usually meet in the local shopping centre. It's not much fun. I love going to the cinema, but it's very expensive. Er, how often do you go to the cinema?
Ivan:	I agree with you. The cinema is very expensive but I go with my parents once a month and they pay. Have you seen the new *Batman* film yet?
Jon:	No, not yet. I like going to see shows with my family. I don't really like serious plays but I love musicals like *Cats, We Will Rock You!* and the *Lion King*. Do you like musicals?
Ivan:	Er … I like some musicals but I think I prefer the cinema. My sister really loves the ballet. I've been once but I thought it was too long and slow. I think it was *Swan Lake*. Do you like classical music?
Jon:	Oh no! My brother … er … plays the violin and we went to a classical music concert with him last year. It was awful! I wanted to wait outside but my mum said I had to sit there. It was two hours and there was no interval.
Ivan:	Two hours long? Poor you!

4 Point out that Ivan and Jon ask each other questions and both expand on the topic without changing the subject completely.

> **Answers**
> 1 True   2 False   3 False

5 6 These are Jon and Ivan's answers but any full answer which doesn't change the topic completely is fine.

> **Suggested answers**
> **2** No, I didn't. When I'm at home I also enjoy playing cards or other games with my two brothers. On Sunday afternoons, we often stay in and play together.
>
> **3** The cinema is very expensive but I go with my parents once a month and they pay.
>
> **4** No, not yet. I like going to see shows with my family. I don't really like serious plays but I love musicals like *Cats, We Will Rock You!* and the *Lion King*.
>
> **5** I like some musicals but I think I prefer the cinema. My sister really loves the ballet. I've been once but I thought it was too long and slow. I think it was *Swan Lake*.

Extension idea Photocopy the recording script on page 142. The students read and listen again and compare their suggestions in Exercise 5 with Jon's and Ivan's.

7

> **Answer**
> The clothes you wear during the week **and** the clothes you wear at weekends.

8 Remind students that they won't have any preparation time in the exam.

> **Suggested answers**
>
> | | |
> | --- | --- |
> | When we have sport. I wear a tracksuit. | What do you wear for sport? |
> | I often change my clothes when I get home from school. | Do you change your clothes? |
> | At weekends I like wearing fashionable clothes. | Why (not)? |
> | | What about you? |
> | On Sundays, I often have to wear smart clothes. | Do you like wearing smart clothes? |
> | I like choosing my own clothes. | Can you choose which clothes you buy? |
> | | If not, who chooses your clothes? |
> | I don't like wearing skirts very much. | What clothes do you <u>not</u> like wearing? |

9 *Alternative treatment* Record each pair doing the task. Play back each pair to the class, who listen and use the checklist in Exercise 2 to see how successful each pair is.

Writing Part 2

❶ Pre-teach *vase* and *naughty*.

> **Suggested answer**
> The cat broke the vase. It knocked the vase off the furniture. Water spilled on the floor.

❷ Point out that in the PET exam, the question is likely to be more mundane, e.g. like the question in Exercise 5, which is a more accurate reflection of a real exam task.

> **Suggested answers**
> aunt's cat, She … sent … money, an email to … Aunt Kath, thank, what … buy, describe … cat did, 35–45 words

❸ ❹ Point out that if a candidate does not include all three points, they cannot be awarded more than a 3.

> **Suggested answers**
> Although 1 (Bettina's answer) is very well written (with no spelling mistakes and a very good use of grammar), well organised and the message is clear, she has not included the three content points (she does not describe what the cat did). She can only be given a maximum of 3 marks.
>
> 2 (Katia's answer) is less accurate (see corrected version below) but it is well organised and the message is clear. She has included all three content points and so her teacher could give her 5 marks.

> **Suggested corrections**
> 1 Thank you very much for sending me some money. As you know, I love science fiction films and so I think I'm going to buy a new DVD. I haven't seen all the 'Star Wars' films yet. <u>Your cat broke my mum's flower vase but don't worry, she has another one.</u>
>
> 2 Money is <u>a great present</u> – thank you very much. I will buy a new game <u>for</u> my computer. The cat is <u>much worse</u> than my <u>little</u> brother. <u>I've had</u> a <u>bad</u> headache for a week!

❺

> **Sample answer**
> Dear Dorota,
>
> Thanks so much for the money you sent me for my birthday. You know how much I love new clothes. I'm going to buy those tight black jeans I saw last week. Why don't you come with me next week to buy them?
>
> Yours
>
> Magda

Vocabulary and grammar review Unit 5

Answers

Vocabulary

❶ 2 of 3 with 4 on 5 of 6 about 7 about 8 about 9 of 10 of

❷ amazing, interesting, embarrassed, frightened, amused

❸ **Across:** 3 mean 4 afraid 7 emotion 9 awful 11 ought 12 lucky 13 love
Down: 1 sad 2 habit 5 jealous 6 grateful 8 negative 10 proud

Grammar

❹ 2 can't 3 should 4 Could 5 don't have to 6 might 7 have to

Vocabulary and grammar review Unit 6

Answers

Vocabulary

❶ 2 Audiences 3 live 4 reviews 5 performances 6 admission 7 interval

❷ 2 C 3 A 4 A 5 B 6 B

Grammar

❸ 2 since three years ago → for three years / since 2007 3 he's gone → he went / he's gone to Dubai (with no time adverb) 4 gone → been 5 Already I've → I've already 6 I looked → I've looked 7 never → ever 8 has given → gave 9 just came → has just come 10 didn't decide → haven't decided 11 has opened → opened 12 what happened → what has happened

❹ 2 've/have never lived / 've/have not lived / haven't lived 3 since 4 've/have known 5 seen

Unit 6 photocopiable activity:
True or false? Time: 30mins +

Objectives

- To review the present perfect (comparison with the past simple)
- To practise asking questions to confirm whether something is true or false
- To reach decisions about whether they believe something to be true or false

Before class

Make one copy of the activity for each pair of students in your class. Cut into two sections along the dotted line and cut the bottom section into True/False cards.

In class

❶ Divide your class into pairs (if you have an uneven number of students, some will have to work in a group of three) and give each pair the main part of the activity. Do not give out the True/False cards yet.

❷ Explain that they are each going to write four sentences describing some of their experiences. The categories are on their activity sheet, and each student in the pair should choose four of these categories. In the space underneath, they should take it in turns to write complete sentences using either the past simple or the present perfect.

However, not all of their sentences need to be true: they can make them up. The only rule is that they need to be *believable* (for example, *'I've been to the moon'* would not be an acceptable sentence).

❸ Allow them about ten minutes for this, then ask them to stop writing. Give each pair a True and a False card.

❹ Ask one pair to come to the front of the class with their completed sentences. Ask *one* of them to read out *one* of their sentences to the rest of the class. The other students, in their pairs, should decide if the sentence is true or false for that student. They can do this by asking the student some questions, which should help them to establish whether he/she is telling the truth, or whether he/she is lying.

❺ After asking questions, the students then decide in their pairs whether the sentence is true or false. They vote by holding up one of their True/False cards. They then win points as follows:
- If the sentence is true and they vote 'True', they win one point.
- If the sentence is false and they vote 'False', they win one point.
- If the sentence is false and they vote 'True', the student pair who read out the sentence win one point. They also win one point if their sentence is true and the students vote 'False'.

❻ Steps 4 and 5 are repeated with the same student pair at the front of the class reading out *one* other sentence on their activity sheet.

❼ Steps 4 and 5 are then repeated with the other student pairs coming up and reading out their sentences. The winning pair is the pair at the end of the activity with the most points.

True or false?

Work with your partner. Take it in turns to write about things that you have done, or things that have happened to you, below. You should *each* choose four of the categories (in other words, you each write four sentences). You should not choose the same categories as each other. Your sentences can be true or false, but they must be *believable* (for example, you cannot say something like '*I've been to the moon*'). Write complete sentences, using either the **past simple** or the **present perfect** (for example, '*I went to Japan last year,*' '*I've been to Japan*'). If there are three students in your group, two of you should choose three categories, and one of you should choose two categories.

(Don't forget that if you use the past simple, you must say *when* it happened).

A film you have seen.

....

A country you have visited.

....

A famous person you have met.

....

An unusual food you have eaten.

....

A concert, show or other live event you have attended.

....

Something that you have *never* done before. *(You can only use the present perfect here.)*

....

Something funny that has happened to you.

....

A strange, unusual or exciting experience you have had.

....

✂ -

True | False

Word list

Unit 6

Note: the numbers show which page the word or phrase first appears on in the unit.

admission *n* (53) the money that you pay to enter a place

audience *n* (53) the people who sit and watch a performance at a theatre, cinema, etc.

button *n* (57) a small, round object that you push through a hole to fasten clothing

cartoon *n* (52) a film made using characters that are drawn and not real

chat show *n* (52) a television or radio programme where people are asked questions about themselves

comedy series *n* (52) a group of funny television or radio programmes that have the same main characters or deal with the same subject

cotton *n* (57) cloth or thread that is produced from the cotton plant

documentary *n* (52) a film or television programme that gives facts about a real situation or real people

earring *n* (57) a piece of jewellery that you wear on or through your ear

fashionable *adj* (57) popular at a particular time

find out *v* (56) to get information about something, or to learn a fact for the first time

get to know *v* (56) When you get to know someone, you learn more about them.

handbag *n* (57) a bag carried by a woman with her money, keys, etc. inside

interval *n* (53) a short period of time between the parts of a play, performance, etc.

know *v* (56) to be familiar with a person, place, or thing because you have met them, been there, used it, etc. before

live *adj* (55) A live performance or recording of a performance is done with an audience.

meet *v* (56) to see and speak to someone for the first time

the news *n* (52) the announcement of important events on television, radio, and in newspapers

old-fashioned *adj* (57) not modern

patterned *adj* (57) with a design of lines, shapes, colours, etc.

performance *n* (53) acting, singing, dancing, or playing music to entertain people

pocket *n* (57) a small bag that is sewn or fixed onto or into a piece of clothing, a bag, the back of a seat, etc.

purse *n* (57) a small container for money, usually used by a woman

quiz show *n* (52) a television or radio programme in which you answer questions

review *n* (53) a report in a newspaper, magazine, or programme that gives an opinion about a new book, film, etc.

round neck *n* (57) an opening for your neck on a piece of clothing which is in the shape of a circle

sleeve *n* (57) the part of a jacket, shirt, etc. that covers your arm

sleeveless *adj* (57) describes a piece of clothing with no sleeves

striped *adj* (57) with a pattern of stripes (a long, straight area of colour)

subtitles *n* (55) words shown at the bottom of a cinema or television screen to explain what is being said

sweater *n* (57) a warm piece of clothing which covers the top of your body and is pulled on over your head

tight *adj* (57) fitting your body very closely

venue *n* (53) a place where a sports game, musical performance, or special event happens

V-neck *n* (57) a V-shaped opening for your neck on a piece of clothing, or a sweater, dress, etc. with this opening

❶ **Complete the text with the correct comparative or superlative form of the word in** *italics*. **Remember that sometimes you will need to change the whole word and/or add other words.**

0   Lake Baikal is (*deep*) .... *deeper* .... than 1,700 metres in places. In fact, it's the (*deep*) ... *deepest* ... lake in the world.

   I love travelling and have spent much of my life on the road. I've had lots of good experiences, but some experiences have been (1) (*good*) .... than others. I loved Switzerland, for example, and last year I travelled around the country by bicycle. Switzerland has some of the (2) (*high*) .... mountains in western Europe, so in many ways it was (3) (*difficult*) .... than cycling in my own country. However, the countryside there is probably the (4) (*beautiful*) .... you will see anywhere in the world, and the (5) (*good*) .... way to see it is slowly, either on foot or by bike. The cities are probably the (6) (*safe*) .... in the world for cycling, because there are special roads for cyclists. The (7) (*bad*) .... experience I had there was when I lost my passport. Fortunately, someone found it and handed it in to the police. On another occasion I decided to cycle from Geneva to Basel without stopping. However, it was (8) (*far*) .... than I thought, and the road between the two cities was the (9) (*busy*) .... and (10) (*noisy*) .... in the whole country, so it wasn't a very pleasant experience!

❷ **Read the text below and choose the correct word for each space.**

The water is **0** .... B .... dirty, so don't swim in it.

0   A much   **(B)** extremely   **C** most   **D** absolutely

It's very cold today. In fact, it's (1) .... freezing. I hope it's better on Friday, because our history class is going on a school (2) .... to the countryside. I haven't been on one of these (3) .... , but everyone tells me they're great fun. We're going to look for old objects that are buried under the ground. This is (4) .... more exciting than it sounds, because some of these things can be quite valuable. For example, a boy I (5) .... at a party last year had found an ancient coin worth £1,000! I was (6) .... that something so small could be so valuable. Unfortunately, it's not always easy to find these things, because some of them can be (7) .... deep as two metres underground and we (8) .... use special equipment to find them. It would be great to find something very valuable, like a box of Roman gold, but we would probably be satisfied (9) .... an old plate or something like that. Of course, we (10) .... not find anything, but at least we get a day off school!

1	**A** too	**B** very	**C** so	**D** absolutely
2	**A** trip	**B** travel	**C** journey	**D** voyage
3	**A** just	**B** already	**C** yet	**D** now
4	**A** little	**B** lot	**C** much	**D** many
5	**A** found	**B** met	**C** discovered	**D** knew
6	**A** surprise	**B** surprised	**C** surprising	**D** surprises
7	**A** very	**B** almost	**C** so	**D** as
8	**A** must	**B** have	**C** should	**D** could
9	**A** of	**B** with	**C** for	**D** about
10	**A** should	**B** could	**C** can	**D** might

❸ Here are some sentences in which someone is talking about dolphins. For each question, complete the second sentence so that it means the same as the first, *using no more than three words.*

0 Dolphins can understand and follow simple instructions.

Dolphins are . *able to understand* . and follow simple instructions.

1 I was fascinated by dolphins when I was very young, and I still am.

I have been fascinated .... I was very young.

2 Did you know that dolphins are more intelligent than dogs?

Did you know that dogs are .... as dolphins?

3 Perhaps there are some people who don't realise how intelligent dolphins are.

Some people .... how intelligent dolphins are.

4 A few minutes ago I received an email inviting me to a lecture on dolphins.

I .... an email inviting me to a lecture on dolphins.

5 If you want to come too, it's not necessary to book tickets in advance.

If you want to come too, you .... to book tickets in advance.

❹ Read this conversation and use the words in italics to complete the sentences using the *past simple* or the *present perfect*. In some cases, you must change the form of the verb. When you use the present perfect, you should use short forms (*I have* = *I've*, *she has* = *she's*, etc.), because this is an informal conversation.

I can go out with you tonight because **0** (*I / already / do*) . *I've already done* .... my homework.

Angie:	Hi, Michael.
Michael:	Hello, Angie. How are things?
Angie:	Fine. My week (1) (*be / good*) .... so far, but it's only Wednesday. What about you?
Michael:	Great, thanks. (2) (*you / enjoy*) .... the party last Saturday?
Angie:	Party? Which party?
Michael:	Rosanna's.
Angie:	No, (3) (*I / not / go*) ....
Michael:	Really? Why not?
Angie:	(4) (*She / not / invite*) .... me.
Michael:	Oh, me neither. So, (5) (*what / you / do*) .... instead?
Angie:	Well, (6) (*I / go*) .... to a play at the theatre. A musical called *Rats*.
Michael:	Lucky you. (7) (*I / never / see*) .... a musical before.
Angie:	You're joking! (8) (*I / see*) .... lots. Next week I'm going to see *North Pacific*.
Michael:	Can I come with you?
Angie:	Well, I've got two tickets, but unfortunately (9) (*I / already / ask*) .... Jess to come with me.
Michael:	Oh well, never mind.
Angie:	Why don't you call the theatre for a ticket? Perhaps they (10) (*not / sell out / yet*) ....

❺ In these sentences, rearrange the letters in bold to make words.

0   When my mobile phone was stolen, I went to the **olicep ottisna**
.....*police station*..... to report the theft.

1   There's a **psnohigp neectr** .... near my house where you can buy inexpensive clothes and electrical items.

2   If you want to send an email and have a coffee at the same time, there's an **teintner éafc** .... in the town centre.

3   The **rat leglyar** .... on George Street has some really interesting exhibitions.

4   The **oyuht ucbl** .... , where I meet my friends on Saturday morning, is always very busy.

5   The **rtoitus feoicf** .... is a good place to go for information about the town and area.

❻ Correct the mistakes in these sentences.

0   I'm a bit depressed for my exam results because I only got an average score of 42%.
.... ~~depressed for~~ = depressed about.........

1   I love learning English at school and I never get boring with my lessons because our teacher is such fun.
....

2   Our football team won by 5 goals to 1, which was a really surprised result.
....

3   I'm quite a calm person, but I get really angry for people who drop litter in the street.
....

4   We were all looking forward to Peter's party, so we were all disappoint when he was ill and had to cancel it.
....

5   Carol is a good friend: she's a wonderful person and I've always been very fond about her.
....

❼ Complete these sentences with the correct form of these words or expressions. Use each word/expression once only.

be   find out   get to know   go   know   ~~meet~~

0   I .... *met* .... Joanne at a party and we got married two years later.
1   Tim has .... to the cinema, and I have no idea when he'll get back.
2   I .... a bit of Japanese when I was younger, but I've forgotten most of it now.
3   At first I didn't like Heidi, but when I .... her better, I thought she was great.
4   I was furious when I first .... that Jake had used my computer without asking me.
5   I've only .... to London once and I didn't like it very much.

Unit 7 Out and about

Unit objectives

- **Topics:** weather, transport
- **Listening Part 2:** focusing on instructions and questions, analysing options
- **Reading Part 1:** identifying text purpose
- **Speaking Part 2:** giving and asking for reasons and preferences, weak forms
- **Writing Part 1:** transformation dialogue, identifying parallel expressions
- **Grammar:** future: *will, going to,* present continuous and present simple
- **Vocabulary:** adverbs of degree, *too* and *enough,* prepositions of movement, *on foot, by car,* etc., compound words

Starting off

1 Students match the words with the correct pictures, then discuss the pictures briefly. Possibly revise vocabulary such as *impatient, bored, frightened, afraid, uncomfortable, sick.*

2 Pairs or groups fill in the words. Explain any new terms, or encourage them to use their dictionaries. Highlight weather collocations: high (not *hot*) temperature, wind blowing, strong (not *hard*) wind. Also mention 'raining heavily' (not *strongly, hardly,* etc.).

> **Answers**
> **2** temperature, hot, degrees, centigrade **3** showers, get wet **4** gale, blowing **5** thunderstorm, lightning **6** freezing, frost, snowfall

3 Check understanding of *extreme* and its opposite, *mild.* Opinions on the conditions may vary: –5°C in winter may seem quite mild to students from northern Russia; 40°C not at all extreme to those from parts of the Middle East! Encourage pairs to use more adjectives of emotion (Unit 5) such as *depressed, excited,* etc.

Extension idea Pairs ask questions about various places at the moment, e.g. 'What do you think the weather's like in London?', 'I think it's probably cold and raining.'

Listening Part 2

1 Explain that the purpose is to practise obtaining information from the instructions and items *before* they listen. This provides a context for the dialogue and should enable them to predict the gist of its content.

> **Answers**
> **1 a** Chloe **b** an interviewer **c** taking photos of extreme weather conditions **d** the weather in her country, when she began taking photos of bad weather, what she uses to photograph lightning, where she takes photos during thunderstorms, what she most likes photographing in winter, what she photographs when it's windy **e** the weather in the speaker's country, bad weather, lightning, thunderstorms, winter weather (ice/snow/frost), windy weather

2 Refer the class to the Exam advice box, then play the recording twice, in exam conditions. Then check their answers.

> **Answers**
> **1** B **2** B **3** C **4** C **5** A **6** B

Recording script CD1 Track 34

Interviewer: Tell me, Chloe, have you always been interested in the weather?

Chloe: Oh yes. It's really fascinating in this country because it can be quite different in the north, in the west and in the south, for instance, and it doesn't usually stay the same for long. It can be warm and sunny one moment; wet and cold the next. In fact, you can sometimes have all four seasons in one day!

Interviewer: So when did you first photograph storms and things like that? Was that while you were at university? Or in your first job?

Chloe: No no, I was much younger than that. I was just a kid, really. We were coming home from holiday and we got caught in a thunderstorm. I took some pictures and luckily they came out really well. Since then I've done lots of other kinds of photography, especially when I was a student, but I still love photographing lightning.

Interviewer: That must be quite difficult. How do you get good pictures?

Chloe: Well, the first thing is the right camera. It doesn't have to be expensive, or particularly modern – <u>I've had mine for many years</u> – and I avoid using digital ones. But the main thing is where you go to take your pictures.

Interviewer: Which are the best places?

Chloe: Well, some people take photos from their bedroom windows, but I live in a flat where there's no real view of the night sky and so I have to go out. Standing in fields and on hills during a thunderstorm is rather dangerous, so I <u>drive into the countryside, park, open the window and start taking pictures</u>. You're much safer with all that metal around you, like on a plane.

Interviewer: So what about photography during the day?

Chloe: I really enjoy taking winter photos, when it's really freezing.

Interviewer: Which are your favourite? Snowy scenes?

Chloe: I used to like doing those, just after snowstorms, and sometimes those beautiful shapes like flowers that you see on glass when it's frosty. But nowadays I prefer mountain scenes with lots of ice. Especially when you have <u>water flowing down valleys and over waterfalls, and it gets so cold that it freezes solid</u>.

Interviewer: Mm. And during the rest of the year?

Chloe: Um … storms, I think. You can get some great pictures when the wind is really blowing, particularly on the coast. <u>Whenever there's a gale, I go down to the beach and take loads of photos of the waves</u>. They can be amazing. And I'd like to take pictures of clouds, though it's often too dark to photograph them when it's stormy. Also forests, with everything bending in the wind. I've always wanted to try that, too.

❸ Allow time for them to study the extract and discuss the questions. Point out that each question is 'cued' like this one, so that they know when to expect the answer.

> **Answers**
> The extract answers Question 3; the expressions 'photographing lightning' and 'How do you get good pictures?' show the information that you need to complete 'To photograph lightning, she uses …' will soon follow; **A:** <u>I avoid using digital ones</u>, **B:** <u>It doesn't have to be expensive</u>, **C:** <u>I've had mine for many years</u>; Yes, these are all close together; No, the order Chloe talks about them is not the same order as the options A, B and C.

Alternative treatment Give pairs copies of the entire script on page 143. They should notice that all the options for each item are dealt with in a fairly short section of text. Point out that there is some untested speech after each item. Go through all the options for each item, eliciting the paraphrase used for the options and any other reasons why they are right or wrong.

> **Answers**
> **1 A** it can be quite different in the north
> **B** <u>it doesn't usually stay the same for long</u>. It can be warm and sunny one moment; wet and cold the next **C** It can be warm and sunny one moment; wet and cold the next … you can sometimes have all four seasons in one day
>
> **2 A** Or in your first job? … No no, I was much younger than that **B** <u>I was just a kid</u> **C** Was that while you were at university? … No no, I was much younger than that
>
> **3 A** I avoid using digital ones **B** It doesn't have to be expensive **C** <u>I've had mine for many years</u>
>
> **4 A** Standing in fields and on hills during a thunderstorm is rather dangerous **B** some people take photos from their bedroom windows, but I live in a flat where there's no real view of the night sky **C** <u>I drive into the countryside, park, open the window and start taking pictures</u>
>
> **5 A** <u>water running flowing down valleys and over waterfalls, and it gets so cold that it freezes solid</u> **B** Snowy scenes? … I used to like doing those, just after snowstorms **C** those beautiful shapes like flowers that you see on glass when it's frosty
>
> **6 A** Also forests … I've always wanted to try that, too. **B** <u>Whenever there's a gale, I go down to the beach and take loads of photos of the waves</u> **C** I'd like to take pictures of clouds

❹ Pairs discuss the attraction or otherwise of observing – not necessarily photographing – the kinds of weather mentioned in the recording and their effects, plus others such as hurricanes, typhoons, tornadoes, hail, heatwaves, etc.

Vocabulary

Extremely, fairly, quite, rather, really and *very*

❶ You may want to point out that 'quite' has the same meaning as 'fairly' and 'rather' when used with gradable adjectives, e.g. 'he was quite tired', but with non-gradable adjectives it means 'completely' or 'absolutely', e.g. 'he was quite exhausted'.

> **Answers**
> **1** really **2** rather **3** quite

Extension idea Point out that with comparative adjectives only 'rather' can be used, e.g. 'I found it rather easier this time', not 'quite easier'; 'It's rather warmer today', not 'fairly warmer'; 'This is rather more interesting', not 'quite more interesting'. Elicit more examples.

❷ Encourage pairs to use adjectives from this page and *Starting off*. Remind students of the difference between gradable and non-gradable adjectives (Unit 4) to avoid errors such as 'very freezing' or 'fairly boiling'.

Extension idea Pairs discuss 'the ideal climate', e.g. 'The sun shines most of the year. It gets quite warm in spring and the temperatures are fairly high in summer, but it never gets extremely hot. In winter it rains fairly often, making the countryside quite green. Sometimes it snows, so the mountains are really good for skiing'.

Too and *enough*

❶ Make sure they refer to the examples to answer all the questions. Elicit more examples, with and without a following verb.

> **Answers**
> **2** before, *to* infinitive   **3** uncountable, countable
> **4** as much as   **5** before, after, *to* infinitive

❷ ⊙ Remind the class to think about all the rules above, including those relating to the meaning (3 is a common confusion of 'too' and 'very'). Go through 1–8, asking why each is right or wrong.

> **Answers**
> **2** ~~money for to buy~~ → money to buy   **3** ~~too much~~ → very much   **4** ~~for get~~ → to get   **5** ~~too much expensive~~ → too expensive   **6** correct   **7** ~~for wearing~~ → to wear   **8** ~~enough warm~~ → warm enough

Extension idea Extend practice of both *too* and *enough* to their use with adverbs, beginning with simple forms such as 'you're working too slowly' and 'this computer doesn't run quickly enough'. Then introduce *to* infinitive structures, e.g. 'I was writing too slowly to finish my essay in time', 'she didn't sing well enough to win the competition'; and the *for* + object + *to*- infinitive structure, e.g. 'it's raining too heavily for us to go out', 'he didn't speak loudly enough for others to hear him'.

Grammar

The future: *Will, going to*; present continuous and present simple

❶ ∩ Allow time for the class to skim the text for the overall context, but discourage them from attempting to fill in any of the gaps at this stage. Play the recording once or twice, pausing if and

where necessary. Check that everyone has the correct answers.

> **Answers**
> **2** 's going to rain   **3** 'm meeting   **4** leaves
> **5** 'll take

❷ Check their answers, then elicit and/or give more examples, if necessary going into more detail by referring to the Grammar reference, page 125.

> **Answers**
> **b** 'll take   **c** it'll stop   **d** 'm meeting
> **e** 's going to rain

Extension idea Point out that in some cases more than one verb form is possible. For instance, there may be no difference in practice between a plan (*going to*) and an agreed arrangement (present continuous), e.g. 'We're going to have dinner together tonight' / 'We're having dinner together tonight'. In the case of *will* and *going to*, either may be used if it is not clear whether a prediction is based on fact (*going to*) or opinion (*will*): 'The bus will / is going to be late again', 'They'll/they're going to finish building the bridge soon'. Elicit and/or give more examples like these.

Recording script   CD1 Track 35

Mia: It's getting a bit late, Owen.

Owen: Yes, but look at the rain! I'm hoping <u>it'll stop</u> soon, though I don't think there's much chance of that.

Mia: No, the weather forecast said it's a big storm, so <u>it's going to rain</u> for hours. What time do you have to be at the station?

Owen: <u>I'm meeting</u> Jason and Mark there at 8.30, in the café near the main entrance. The train <u>leaves</u> at 8.45.

Mia: It's quite a long walk to the station, isn't it? And it's 8.15 already. Look, <u>I'll take</u> you in the car.

Owen: Thanks!

❸ Remind them to use contracted forms for the answers to most of these, as they are typical of informal dialogue. Check for accuracy in the question forms, and elicit some answers.

> **Suggested answers**
> **2** When are you seeing your friends next week? I'm seeing them on Friday.   **3** Where are you going to go this evening? I'm going to go to the cinema.   **4** What date do your holidays begin this summer? They begin on July 5th.   **5** When do you think you will get a job? I'll get a job in about eight years.   **6** Do scientists say the Earth is going to get hotter? Yes, they say it's going to get a lot hotter.   **7** When will you next send a text message? I'll send one right now!

4 Explain any differences in meaning resulting from a change of verb form, making them unlikely, e.g. 1 'I'll buy' would indicate a spontaneous decision, contradicting 'I've already decided'.

> **Suggested answers**
> **2** 'm going on Monday / 'm going to go on Monday.
> **3** 'll carry/take it for you.   **4** leaves   **5** 'll have a glass of orange juice.   **6** 'm meeting friends.
> **7** 's going to rain.

5 Pairs imagine they are with their partner in each situation, and tell them what they'd say using a future form. Once they have worked through 1–6, they could invent new situations for their partners to respond to, e.g. 'your sister has just written a letter and in a few minutes you will be walking past a letter box', 'you're in a car in the city and suddenly all the traffic lights stop working'.

> **Suggested answers**
> **2** I'll help you / fix it (if you like).   **3** It leaves / takes off at 9.30 in the evening.   **4** There's going to be a storm. / The waves are going to get a lot bigger.   **5** I'll call an ambulance.   **6** I'm going to study medicine. / I don't know what I'm going to study.

Reading Part 1

1 This follows up Reading Part 1 in Unit 2 (page 21). Elicit the answers quickly.

> **Answers**
> **2** email   **3** notice   **4** announcement/information
> **5** road sign

2 Explain that the second step in a Reading Part 1 task is to decide *why* the text was written. If necessary, focus on the first sign, asking the class what kind of idea 'no parking' expresses: a prohibition – in other words, something you must not do (d). This activity can be done in pairs.

> **Answers**
> **b 3** ('strong winds', 'take care')   **c 5** ('wait' imperative)   **d 1** ('no parking')   **e 4** ('closes 30 minutes before …')

Extension idea They quickly explain the meanings of texts 1–5 in their own words. The aim here is to show they understand the meanings of the texts, and practise putting them into their own words. Remind them to do this before they look at options A–C when they work on the exam task.

3 Focus on the first question and elicit the answers, plus reasons. Ask why option A is right and the others wrong.

> **Answers**
> **1 1** notice (near lift door, probably at an airport because of the reference to passport control)
> **2** Its purpose is to inform and advise (shown ⌐ ⌐ho common phrase 'out of order' and 'Please use')
>
> **2** message; to inform and suggest something
> **3** Internet item description; to advertise something for sale   **4** label; to give a warning   **5** notice; to say what is (and is not) allowed   **6** email; to inform and to suggest something

4 Allow plenty of time for students to answer these on their own. Then check their answers and deal with any queries.

> **Answers**
> **2** B   **3** B   **4** C   **5** A   **6** C

Extension idea Think of some common signs and change key words so that they are clearly wrong. Put them on the board or on a worksheet and get the class to spot the errors. Examples: 'Special offer – 2 for the price of 3', 'Dangerous items are allowed on this aeroplane', 'You must travel without a valid ticket', 'Low ceiling. Don't mind your head.', 'Shoplifters will not be prosecuted', etc. Then ask the class to think of more, possibly translating signs from their own country, then adding errors.

Vocabulary
Compound words

1 Point out that these are mostly nouns, although there are also some adjectives and verbs. Check they have formed all the compounds correctly before moving on to the definitions. Explain any new words such as *handle* or *tracks*. Once they have matched the ten compounds with the definitions, elicit the answers.

> **Answers**
> crossroads, guesthouse, guidebook, hitchhike, overnight, railroad, sightseeing, signpost, suitcase
>
> **1** guidebook   **2** suitcase   **3** crossroads
> **4** hitchhike   **5** railroad   **6** backpack   **7** signpost
> **8** overnight   **9** guesthouse   **10** sightseeing

❷ Set gist questions, e.g. 'Which three different ways will he/she travel?' (by air, rail and road), 'Where exactly does he/she want to go?' (Ayers Rock in central Australia), and allow two minutes for reading. Pairs fill in the answers using the ten compound words they formed in Exercise 1.

Background information Uluru (Ayer's Rock) is a huge sandstone rock formation in the centre of Australia. Standing 348 metres in height, and measuring nearly 10 kilometres in circumference, it is a sacred place to the local Aboriginal people. It appears to change colour during the day, glowing a beautiful shade of red at sunset. For more information, see http://www.environment.gov.au/parks/uluru/index.html.

> **Answers**
> **2** guidebook   **3** sightseeing   **4** railroad
> **5** guesthouse   **6** hitchhike   **7** backpack   **8** suitcase
> **9** crossroads   **10** signpost

Prepositions of movement

❶ 🎧 Students skim the text and say what it's about: Toby explaining to a friend, Leon, how to get to his new house. Then allow a couple of minutes to fill in the gaps before playing the recording once or twice.

> **Answers**
> **2** on   **3** on   **4** off   **5** on   **6** in   **7** out   **8** of

> **Recording script**   CD1 Track 36
>
> Toby: Hi Leon; Toby here. I'm really pleased you're coming to our new house next week.
> The quickest way here is <u>by</u> train to the city centre, which takes an hour and is usually <u>on</u> time. Then you can get <u>on</u> the number 64 bus to Edge Hill, getting <u>off</u> by the stadium. From there it's about fifteen minutes <u>on</u> foot.
> Or, if you don't feel like walking, you could jump <u>in</u> a taxi and ask the driver to take you to the new flats in Valley Road. When you get <u>out of</u> the taxi, you'll see the main entrance in front of you. See you soon!

❷ Elicit other means of transport and the prepositions that normally go with them, e.g. *on/off* a scooter, jetski and fairground ride; but *into / out of* a space rocket, carriage, cable car.

> **Answers**
> **1** on, off   **2** in, out of   **3** get, jump   **4** by, by, on
> **5** on

❸ 💿 Point out that these are very common errors. Give pairs a short amount of time to do these, then go through the answers.

> **Answers**
> **2** ~~into~~ → on/onto   **3** ~~at~~ → on   **4** ~~on~~ → in/into
> **5** ~~on~~ → by   **6** ✔   **7** ~~by~~ → on   **8** ~~into~~ → on/onto

Speaking Part 2

❶ 🎧 Check understanding of these means of transport, pointing out that the *metro* is also known as the *underground* or *tube* (especially in London) and the *subway* (in the USA). Play the recording once and get them to tick those they hear. At the end ask them which the speakers decide to use.

> **Answers**
> **1** Tick: bus, boat, metro, bike, tram   **2** They decide to use bike and boat.

> **Recording script**   CD1 Track 37
>
> Ingrid: So why are you <u>keen</u> on going by <u>tram</u>? It'll be very crowded in the rush hour.
> Mikel: Well, <u>because</u> it always keeps moving. Even when there's heavy traffic. So at least we'll get there quite quickly.
> Ingrid: I think I'd <u>rather</u> go on the <u>metro</u>, really.
> Mikel: I don't fancy that.
> Ingrid: Why <u>not</u>?
> Mikel: Well, for <u>one</u> thing, it's summer, so it's going to be really hot down there. And for <u>another</u>, it gets too crowded.
> Ingrid: So what <u>about</u> going on the <u>bus</u>, then? I know it's slow, but it's cheap.
> Mikel: Actually, what I'd most <u>like</u> to do is sail down the river.
> Ingrid: That's a good idea. We can ride to the harbour on our <u>bikes</u>, put them on the <u>boat</u> and be in the other end of town in half an hour.
> Mikel: Right, that's sorted, then!

❷ There should be enough clues here for students to complete these. If not, ask which of these words are followed by *on*, the infinitive with and without *to*, which verb can go with *most*, etc. They ignore the boxes for now.

> **Answers**
> **2** because   **3** rather   **4** not   **5** one   **6** another
> **7** about   **8** like

❸ 🎧 Play the recording and make sure everyone has completely correct answers. Then get pairs to put them into the functional categories by writing the correct letters in the boxes next to 1–8 in Exercise 2. Point out that this is useful language for Speaking Part 2.

> **Answers**
> **2** b **3** d **4** a **5** b **6** b **7** c **8** d

❹ 🎧 Play and pause where necessary, and get them to repeat several times. The aim is to highlight and practise the use of weak forms, i.e. the use of /ə/ when certain words are not stressed. Point out that this (together with the dropping of the final *g*) is why the *going to* future is sometimes written in very informal language, e.g. pop lyrics, young people's dialogue, as 'gonna', and *got to* as 'gotta'. It may be useful to write the phonemic script on the board: 1 /ə/, 2 /fə/, etc.

> **Answer**
> The underlined words are all weak forms.

Extension idea Replay the recording from an earlier part of this course that has a transcript in the Student's Book, such as the telephone message in Vocabulary on the previous page. Students identify the words that are pronounced with weak forms, and practise saying them. Point out that modal and auxiliary verbs are often unstressed, and may be missed if learners are not expecting the weak form, for example, /wəz/ for 'was', /wə/ for 'were' and /kəd/ for 'could'.

> **Recording script**   CD1 Track 38
> | | One. |
> | Ingrid: | why are you keen |
> | | Two. |
> | Mikel: | well, for one thing |
> | | Three. |
> | Mikel: | it's going to be really hot |
> | | Four. |
> | Mikel: | sail down the river |
> | | Five. |
> | Ingrid: | we can ride to the harbour |
> | | Six. |
> | Ingrid: | half an hour |

❺ This is practice for the exam task. If they don't live in a city, suggest they imagine they are going to cross the capital of their country, or somewhere like Buenos Aires, New York or Beijing. Encourage pairs to use the vocabulary and functional language on this page, and to pay attention to the pronunciation of the weak forms presented.

❻ Remind them that there is no right or wrong choice here, and a compromise involving more than one

means of transport might be the best solution. Monitor pairs, ensuring they are giving and asking for reasons and preferences. Give feedback.

Writing Part 1

❶ 🎧 The aims are to encourage the use of a wider range of structures and to raise awareness of the kinds of structures often tested in Writing Part 1. Pairs study the text and write their answers for 1–7. Tell them they don't need to write more than four words. Play the recording, pausing if necessary. There may be alternative answers.

> **Answers**
> **2** too awful   **3** quite close/near to   **4** so much
> **5** are going   **6** going everywhere on foot
> **7** I'd rather

Extension idea Go back through all the sentence transformations that students have done previously during the course. Get pairs to highlight the parallel expressions they find, and note them down for future reference. They could also write more examples of their own, using both structures. This activity could be set as homework.

> **Recording script**   CD1 Track 39
> | Pat: | Do you think people in 2020 will still go everywhere by car? |
> | Kelly: | No, I don't. For one thing, the traffic will be too awful for us to go anywhere. |
> | Pat: | Actually, we're quite close to that situation already. |
> | Kelly: | Yes, I agree. And cars cause so much pollution, especially in cities. I think a lot of countries are going to reduce the number of vehicles. |
> | Pat: | So do you think most of us will end up going everywhere on foot? |
> | Kelly: | Yes, I think we probably will, and I wouldn't mind that at all. In fact, I'd rather do that. |

❷ The answers should be checked after the exam items have been completed in Exercise 3. In order to practise the language presented in this unit, some of the structures tested are similar to those in Exercise 1.

> **Answers**
> **2** rise a lot   **3** sunny   **4** so … that   **5** be … wetter
> **6** the coldest

❸ Check the answers when individuals have finished.

> **Answers**
> **1** cool enough   **2** much higher   **3** will/'ll shine
> **4** too warm   **5** will/'ll rain   **6** colder

❹ This continues the theme of Exercise 3. Pairs compare their sentences.

> **Suggested answers**
> **1** The areas around the coast will be badly affected, because sea levels will rise and a lot of the land will be covered in water.
>
> **2** The dry part of the country in the south-east will have even less rain, which will turn the area almost into a desert.
>
> **3** In the parts of the country where there are high mountains, there will be less snow, even in winter, so it won't be possible to ski there any more.
>
> **4** In the green areas in the north and west of our country it will rain much less, so there will be fewer plants and trees, with a bigger danger of fires because everything will be much drier.

Unit 7 photocopiable activity:
Weak word crossword   Time: 20 mins

> **Objectives**
> - To identify words that have *weak* forms when spoken in sentences
> - To practise speaking weak forms

Before class

Make one copy of Part 1 on page 69 and one copy of Part 2 on page 70 for each pair of students in your class.

In class

❶ Divide your class into pairs, and give each pair Part 1 of the activity. Ask them to read the instructions, and allow them about five minutes to identify the weak forms and practise the dialogues.

❷ Tell them that you are now going to read the dialogues to them. They are going to listen to each dialogue twice and identify the weak forms, which they should underline on their activity sheet.

❸ Read each dialogue (see answers below), ensuring that you use the weak forms of the words in **bold**. Read each dialogue *twice*, pausing for a few moments between each one for the students to underline their answers.

❹ Give each student pair a copy of Part 2 of the activity. Explain that the weak words they heard can go into the crossword grid. There should be no gaps between the words. *3 across* has been done as an example.

❺ Stop the activity when one pair has successfully filled in the crossword grid, and review their answers.

❻ Allow the students to practise the dialogues again, paying particular attention to pronunciation of the

weak forms. You could perhaps begin this by choral drilling the dialogues before letting the students practise on their own.

You could also explain that some other words in their dialogues can also, at times, be weak forms, depending on the speaker. In the dialogue for *3 across*, for example, the letter *i* in the word *in* could be weak.

(The words in **bold** show the weak forms.)

Answers		
3 across	'It's so cold in here **that** I **can** see my own breath.'	'Well, put **a** coat on **and** turn up **the** heating.'
5 across	'What **a** nice day! What **shall** we do?'	'Well, we **could** go **for a** picnic on **the** beach.'
6 across	'Our train leaves **from** platform 5 **at** nine fifteen, which means we have half **an** hour **to** wait.'	'OK, let's go **to the** café **and** get **some** coffee.'
7 across	'How **are** we going **to** get **to** Paris?'	'Well, we **can** go by plane, **but** it's quite expensive.'
8 across	'Is it far **from** here **to your** house?'	'Not really. Half **an** hour if we take **the** bus.'
1 down	'How **do** you like **to** spend **your** free time?'	'Me? Playing football and swimming.'
2 down	'It **was** really windy on Monday, **and** it rained all day Tuesday.'	'I know! Sally **and** I went **to the** shops and **were** really wet when we got home.'
4 down	'Why **are** you keen on fishing?'	'Well, **for a** start, it's very relaxing.'

Weak word crossword

Part 1

Look at these 8 short conversations between 2 people. *Do not worry about the numbers and the words 'across' and 'down'.*

In your pairs, decide which words could have *weak* forms (= words that have a weak vowel sound when spoken in a sentence, as in the Speaking Part 2 section on page 68 of your coursebook). The words you are looking for only have 1 syllable. Practise speaking the dialogues together.

Answers		
3 across	'It's so cold in here that I can see my own breath.'	'Well, put a coat on and turn up the heating.'
5 across	'What a nice day! What shall we do?'	'Well, we could go for a picnic on the beach.'
6 across	'Our train leaves from platform 5 at nine fifteen, which means we have half an hour to wait.'	'OK, let's go to the café and get some coffee.'
7 across	'How are we going to get to Paris?'	'Well, we can go by plane, but it's quite expensive.'
8 across	'Is it far from here to your house?'	'Not really. Half an hour if we take the bus.'
1 down	'How do you like to spend your free time?'	'Me? Playing football and swimming.'
2 down	'It was really windy on Monday, and it rained all day Tuesday.'	'I know! Sally and I went to the shops and were really wet when we got home.'
4 down	'Why are you keen on fishing?'	'Well, for a start, it's very relaxing.'

Weak word crossword

Part 2

Complete this crossword with the *weak* words from the conversations. Do not leave any gaps between the words. *3 across* has been done for you (the *weak* words in the conversation are: *that, can, a, and, the*).

Word list

Unit 7

Note: the numbers show which page the word or phrase first appears on in the unit.

blow *v* (62) If the wind blows, it moves and makes currents of air.

board *v* (65) to get on a bus, boat, aircraft, etc.

check-in *n* (65) the place at an airport where you go to say that you have arrived for your flight

climate *n* (69) the weather conditions that an area usually has

crossroads *n* (67) a place where two roads cross each other

degree *n* (62) unit for measuring temperature

ferry *n* (65) a boat that regularly carries passengers and vehicles across an area of water

fog *n* (62) thick cloud just above the ground or sea that makes it difficult to see

forecast *n* (62) a report saying what is likely to happen in the future

frost *n* (62) a thin, white layer of ice that forms on surfaces, especially at night, when it is very cold

get wet *v* (62) to be no longer dry

guesthouse *n* (67) a small cheap hotel

guidebook *n* (67) a book that gives visitors information about a particular place

harbour *n* (68) an area of water near the coast where ships are kept and are safe from the sea

head back *v* (68) to begin to return to a place

helicopter *n* (68) an aircraft which flies using long, thin parts on top of it that turn round and round very fast

hitchhike *v* (67) to get free rides in people's vehicles by standing next to the road and waiting for someone to pick you up

icy *adj* (62) covered in ice

lightning *n* (62) a sudden flash of light in the sky during a storm

mild *adj* (62) When weather is mild, it is less cold than you would expect.

on time *prep* (67) not early or late

overnight *adv* (67) for or during the night

path *n* (66) a long, narrow area of ground for people to walk along

pedestrian *n* (66) a person who is walking and not travelling in a vehicle

railroad *n* (67) the metal tracks that trains travel on (US)

rider *n* (66) someone who rides a horse, bicycle or motorcycle

scooter *n* (68) a small motorcycle

season *n* (64) one of the four periods of the year; winter, spring, summer, or autumn

shower *n* (62) a short period of rain

signpost *n* (67) a sign by the side of the road that gives information about routes and distances

stormy *adj* (62) If it is stormy, the weather is bad with a lot of wind and rain.

suitcase *n* (65) a rectangular case with a handle that you use for carrying clothes when you are travelling

take off *v* (62) If an aircraft takes off, it begins to fly.

temperature *n* (62) how hot or cold something is

thunderstorm *n* (62) a storm that has thunder (= loud noise) and lightning

vehicle *n* (66) something such as a car or bus that takes people from one place to another, especially using roads

Unit 8 This is me!

Unit objectives

- **Topics:** people, personal identification
- **Listening Part 3:** spelling high-frequency words
- **Reading Part 3:** focusing on relevant sections, parallel expressions
- **Speaking Part 1:** focus on spelling, asking general questions
- **Writing Part 2:** punctuation, 'skilful linking' between content points, making a suggestion
- **Grammar:** zero, first and second conditionals, *when, if, unless* + present, future, *so do I* and *nor/neither do I*
- **Vocabulary:** describing people, phrasal verbs, prefixes and suffixes

Starting off

①/②

> **Answers**   1 A   2 A   3 C   4 A   5 B

> ***Extension idea***   Students produce their own 'All in the family!' quiz.

Reading   Part 3

② Encourage a discussion on what makes a good sports coach.

> **Answer**   Toni Nadal

③④

> **Suggested answer**
> A life coach helps people to think about what they want and how they are going to get it.

⑤

> **Suggested answers**
> **3** used to work … radio   **4** Jem … do a degree … before … Africa   **5** Jem's parents … like … his degree … another country   **6** singing … study … nearly perfect … science   **7** Irina … happy … any university   **8** Irina … always … keen on keeping fit   **9** Mo … worked … children younger than six   **10** Some … Regina's friends … new school play basketball

⑥

> **Answers**
> 2 B   3 C   4 C   5 C   6 D   7 D   8 D   9 E   10 E

⑦

> **Answers**
> **1** Correct – I get on very well with Irina
> **2** Incorrect – Until now, life coaches have helped adults … now it's the turn of our young people
> **3** Correct – a former radio producer
> **4** Incorrect – he has decided to take part in a volunteer project in central Africa first
> **5** Incorrect – This experience abroad will help him grow up before he goes to university here
> **6** Correct – Once she made up songs to learn by, she achieved 99 per cent in her tests
> **7** Incorrect – Now she hopes to get into a top university
> **8** Incorrect – She has even taken up exercise for the first time in years
> **9** Correct – Mo Ahmed has coached children as young as five years old
> **10** Correct – By joining the school basketball team Regina has made several new friends

⑧ Point out these expressions have a *similar* meaning rather than *mean exactly the same thing*. Point out words which have a different or opposite meaning (5, 7, 8).

> **Suggested answers**
> **3** *used to* → *former*   **4** *do a degree* → *got a place at university* (*before* and *first* have opposite meanings)   **5** *do his degree* → *study medicine / goes to university; in another country* → *abroad* (*here* has the opposite meaning)   **6** *used singing* → *made up songs; nearly perfect marks* → *99 per cent*   **7** *would be happy* → *hopes* (*top* has the opposite meaning of *any*)   **8** *keeping fit* → *exercise* (*for the first time in years* has the opposite meaning of *always*)
> **9** *younger than six* → *as young as five*
> **10** *some* → *several*

Vocabulary
Phrasal verbs

 ❶

> **Answers**
> bringing up, set up, sort out, grow up, found out, made up, has … taken up
>
> *Suggested answers for meanings*: bring up (a child) – to look after a child and teach them until they are old enough to look after themselves; find out (something) – to get information about something, or to learn a fact for the first time; get on with – if two or more people get on, they like each other and are friendly to each other; grow up – to become older or an adult; make up – to invent; set up (something) – to start a company or organisation; sort out (something) – to successfully deal with something, such as a problem or difficult situation; take up (something) – to start doing a particular job or activity

❷ Remind the students to be very careful with the position of the object, e.g. *my grandmother brought me up*. Refer students back to Unit 3, if necessary.

> **Answers**
> **2** brought me up   **3** sort out   **4** set up   **5** take up
> **6** get on (well) with   **7** make up   **8** found out

❸ ❹ Remind the students again to be careful with the verb and the object.

Grammar
Zero, first and second conditionals

❶ ❷ Limit the feedback on whether or not they think Kristian will become an actor to just one or two minutes.

> **Answers**
> **1** Kristian's dad says that Kristian isn't sure about his future.   **2** get training by going to acting classes after school; get experience by being a film extra

> **Recording script**   CD1 Track 40
>
> Mo: Hi, Kristian. How are you?
>
> Kristian: Er … OK. *[he doesn't sound very convinced]*
>
> Mo: <u>Your dad's got in contact with me because he says you're not very sure about your future</u>. Let's have a little chat about it. What are your favourite subjects?
>
> Kristian: No, that's not the problem … I'm very sure about my future. I'd really like to go to drama

> school. You see, everyone says I'm quite good at acting.
>
> Mo: How old are you, Kristian?
>
> Kristian: That's the problem. I'm only fifteen. I'll need my parents' permission if I <u>want</u> to go to drama school. They say I have to stay at school until I'm eighteen. But if I <u>stay</u> at school until I'm eighteen, <u>it'll be</u> too late.
>
> Mo: Too late for what?
>
> Kristian: If you <u>want</u> to be an actor, you <u>have</u> to start your training at an early age.
>
> Mo: Maybe we should look at other ways of getting training. <u>Have you thought about going to acting classes after school</u>?
>
> Kristian: Yes, but <u>I'd have</u> to give up football if I went to classes after school. That's why I think drama school would be a good solution. If I <u>studied</u> at drama school, <u>I'd have</u> enough time for everything.
>
> Mo: Have your parents seen you performing on stage?
>
> Kristian: No, not for a long time. I wasn't in this year's English play because none of my friends were in it.
>
> Mo: I see. <u>Let's think about ways you can get some more acting experience. Have you thought about being a film extra</u>?
>
> Kristian: What's that?

❸

> **Answers**
> **1** want   **2** stay, 'll be   **3** want, have   **4** 'd have, went   **5** studied, 'd have

❹

> **Answers**
> **1** No. Josh doesn't want Kristian to join the drama club because the football team will lose its best player.   **2** No   **3** (6) is a real possibility but (7) is not

❺

> **Answers**
> **b** Type 1: 2, 6   **c** Type 2: 4, 5, 7

❻

> **Answers**
> *Students should underline*: **b** snows, 'll make;
> **c** snowed, would go
>
> *Forms of the verb*: Type 0: *if* + present, present;
> Type 1: *if* + present, future; Type 2: *if* + past simple, *would* + infinitive without *to*

❼

> **Answer**
> We use a comma if the conditional sentence begins with the *if* clause. We don't use a comma if the sentence begins with the result.

❽

> **Answers**
> **1** The first conditional has been used because the weather forecast says it will rain, so this is a real possibility.
> **2** We would use the second conditional when rain is not likely (e.g. in the middle of a very dry summer – *If it rained, the plants would get some water.*).

❾ These answers will depend on individual circumstances, e.g. Question 1: some students never lose anything whereas others will quite likely lose their mobile phone.

> **Suggested answers**
> **2** If I saw a friend cheating in an exam, I wouldn't tell the teacher. / If I see a friend cheating in an exam, I'll tell the teacher.
> **3** If I get good marks at school, I'll be very happy.
> **4** If I found a lot of money in a rubbish bin, I'd take it to the police station.
> **5** If I got lost in a foreign country, I'd ask someone for directions. / If I get lost in a foreign country, I'll ask someone for directions.
> **6** If I get a lot of homework, I won't go out tonight with my friends.

❿

> **Suggested questions**
> **1** What would you do if you lost your mobile phone? / If you lost your mobile phone, what would you do? **2** What would you do if you saw a friend cheating in an exam? / If you saw …? **3** What will you do if you get good marks at school? / If you get good marks at school …? **4** What would you do if you found a lot of money in a rubbish bin? / If you found a lot of money …? **5** What would you do if you got lost in a foreign country? / What will you do if you get lost in a foreign country? / If you got lost …? **6** What will you do if you get a lot of homework from your teacher? / If you get …?

When, if, unless + present, future

❶

> **Answers**
> **A**: this teenager will definitely call her parents (**when** she gets there); **B**: this teenager may not call his parents (if he gets there too late); **C**: this teenager may not call her parents (only if she needs something)

❷

> **Answers**
> **1** when **2** if **3** unless

❸

> **Answers**
> **2** if **3** unless **4** unless **5** unless **6** unless

Listening Part 3

❶ Pre-teach *extra* in this context.

> **Answer**
> They are in the crowd scenes / background.

❷

> **Answers**
> **1** noun **2** noun **3** number **4** noun **5** day
> **6** name

❸

> **Answers**
> **1** (a) market(s) **2** website
> **3** 18/eighteen (years old) **4** face(s) **5** Sunday(s)*
> **6** Kavanagh* (* Spelling must be correct)

Recording script CD1 Track 41

Vanessa: What's an extra? An extra's an ordinary person – just like you or me – who's interested in TV or movies and would like to be on TV or in a movie. Extras aren't movie stars but they are people who appear in the background as members of a crowd, or <u>shoppers in a market</u> or fans in a sports stadium. Imagine the satisfaction of pointing to the screen and saying 'That's me!'.

Many people believe that films are only made in major cities like Los Angeles or New York. But that's where most people are wrong. Yes, movies *are* filmed in Los Angeles and New York City, but movie companies very often travel round the world to find suitable locations. <u>Check our website</u> regularly to see if something's being filmed near you soon.

Finding movie extra jobs is easy because it doesn't matter what you look like or how old you are, although your parents will need to give their written permission if you aren't yet eighteen years old. Directors are looking for all kinds of people. At the moment our directors are looking for young people who look about sixteen years old, who are no more than 1.7 metres tall and of course who have interesting faces.

Working as a movie extra isn't always exciting. Be ready to get up at 6 am or earlier and work very long days – anything up to sixteen hours – but very rarely seven days a week. Filming may begin on Monday, often with a break on Sunday. This will depend on the director. Remember to wear comfortable clothes and shoes as you may have to stand for long hours.

All movies need movie extras. All you have to do is let these directors know you are willing and available to work. Give our agency a ring and ask for Vanessa Kavanagh, that's K-A-V-A-N-A-G-H or visit our website: www.extrasextras.com.

Vocabulary

Describing people

❶ 🎧 Pre-teach *scar*. Encourage the students to talk about the differences between each picture before they listen.

> **Answer**
> B

Recording script CD1 Track 42

Marti: Harry, is that you?

Harry: Marti! How's things?

Marti: Great! Great! Look, Darrilus is looking for a teenager to play Dean Darrick's son in his latest movie. Have you got anyone?

Harry: Dean Darrick, eh? What should this teenager look like?

Marti: He should be medium height, look around sixteen with long, straight hair – although we could change that if we had to. He should probably be rather good-looking, too.

Harry: Um … we've got this new young actor, but he's got rather a large scar on his chin. Any good?

Marti: Mm. Not really. He needs to look young and fresh, preferably with no beard or moustache.

Harry: I've got this one here. He's got pale eyes; he's very attractive and everyone says he's honest and reliable.

Marti: Let's get in touch with him, then.

❷ Check the students pronounce these words correctly.

> **Suggested answers**
> *hair*: curly, straight, wavy, long, short, bald, grey, blond(e), red, dark, fair; *build*: slim, broad shoulders, medium height; *skin*: pale, dark; *other*: scar, beard, attractive, good-looking, moustache, beautiful, plain

❸ The opposite of *smart* could also be *casual* or *scruffy* but these describe appearance.

> **Suggested answers**
> **2** stupid **3** quiet **4** generous **5** polite/pleasant
> **6** nervous **7** shy, nervous **8** cold

❹

> **Answers**
> *im*patient *un*pleasant *dis*honest *un*reliable

❺ Check that students have spelt these new words correctly, e.g. *-ful* has one *l*.

> **Answers**
> wonder*ful* beaut*iful* hope*ful*/hope*less* cheer*ful* (also possible: cheer*less*)
>
> No – *hopeful* = feeling positive about a future event (e.g. *I'm hopeful about my future*) but *hopeless* = very bad (e.g. *I'm hopeless at sport*)

❻

> **Answers**
> Finn*ish* Turk*ish* Brit*ish* Swe*dish* Scott*ish*
> self*ish* child*ish* fool*ish* baby*ish*

Extension idea Remind students we can also add *-ish* to adjectives to say someone is *quite* tall, short, young, etc. *He's more tall than short. He's tall**ish**.*

❼ 👁

> **Answers**
> **b** ~~hair and eyes black~~ → black hair and eyes
> **c** ~~young handsome~~ → handsome young **d** ~~white beautiful~~ → beautiful white **e** ~~black short~~ → short black **f** ~~green big~~ → big green

Speaking Part 1

1 2 🎧

eɪ	iː	e	aɪ	əʊ	uː	ɑː
A, H, J, K	B, C, D, E, G, P, T, V	F, L, M, N, S, X, Z	I, Y	O	Q, U, W	R

Recording script CD1 Track 43

Man:	/eɪ/ – A, H, J, K
Woman:	/iː/ – B, C, D, E, G, P, T, V
Man:	/e/ – F, L, M, N, S, X, Z
Woman:	/aɪ/ – I, Y
Man:	/əʊ/ – O
Woman:	/uː/ – Q, U, W
Man:	/ɑː/ – R

3 4 🎧 **5** These are some of the most commonly misspelt words in the PET exam.

Answers
1 because   2 there   3 which   4 two   5 where
6 to   7 wear   8 their   9 too   10 different

Recording script CD1 Track 44

Write down the correct spelling of the words you hear.

	One.
Woman:	*because* – I'm going to bed <u>because</u> I'm tired.
	Two.
Man:	*there* – <u>There</u> isn't any milk in the fridge.
	Three.
Woman:	*which* – I did a maths test yesterday <u>which</u> was really easy.
	Four.
Man:	*two* – I've lived here for <u>two</u> years.
	Five.
Woman:	*where* – She can't open the door. She doesn't know <u>where</u> her keys are.
	Six.
Man:	*to* – Could you give this <u>to</u> your grandma, please?
	Seven.
Woman:	*wear* – Older people often <u>wear</u> hats at weddings in my country.
	Eight.
Man:	*their* – Rob and Simon didn't do <u>their</u> homework.
	Nine.
Woman:	*too* – I didn't get a part in the film. They said I was <u>too</u> young.

	Ten.
Man:	*different* – Do you think working in TV is <u>different</u> from working in radio?

Recording script CD1 Track 45

	One.
Woman:	*because* – B-E-C-A-U-S-E
	Two.
Man:	*there* – T-H-E-R-E
	Three.
Woman:	*which* – W-H-I-C-H
	Four.
Man:	*two* – T-W-O
	Five.
Woman:	*where* – W-H-E-R-E
	Six.
Man:	*to* – T-O
	Seven.
Woman:	*wear* – W-E-A-R
	Eight.
Man:	*their* – T-H-E-I-R
	Nine.
Woman:	*too* – T-O-O
	Ten.
Man:	*different* – D-I-F-F-E-R-E-N-T

5

Answers
Student A's words: 1 received   2 centre (US center)
3 and   4 beautiful   5 colour   6 comfortable
7 then

Student B's words: 1 interesting   2 together
3 restaurant   4 recommend   5 believe   6 favourite
7 thought

---

6 🎧

Answers
1 Brunner   2 Murakami   3 Switzerland
4 Japan   5 French   6 beautiful   7 future
8 yesterday evening   9 free time

Recording script CD1 Track 46

	One.
Examiner:	What's your name?
Angela:	My name's Angela.
Examiner:	Thank you. What's your surname?
Angela:	It's 'Tedesco'.
Examiner:	How do you spell it?
Angela:	T-E-D-E-S-C-O
Examiner:	Thank you. Where do you live?
Angela:	I live in Italy.

Examiner:	Do you study English?
Angela:	Yes, I do. I study it at school.
Examiner:	Do you like it?
Angela:	Yes, I love English because I like travelling and meeting people from other countries.
Examiner:	Thank you. Angela, do you think English will be useful for you in the future?
Angela:	I'm not sure, but when I'm older I'd like to be an architect and I think I'll need to read a lot of books in English.
	Two.
Examiner:	Now, what's your name?
Eduard:	My name's Eduard.
Examiner:	Thank you. What's your surname?
Eduard:	My surname's 'Brunner'.
Examiner:	How do you spell it?
Eduard:	B-R-U-N-N-E-R
Examiner:	Thank you. Where do you come from?
Eduard:	I come from Switzerland.
Examiner:	Do you study English?
Eduard:	Yes, I go to an English school twice a week.
Examiner:	Do you like it?
Eduard:	Yes, I like English, but I prefer French because it's easy for me.
Examiner:	Ah. Thank you. Eduard, what did you do yesterday evening?
Eduard:	Sorry, can you say that again?
Examiner:	Yes. Did you do anything yesterday evening?
Eduard:	Oh yes. I went to the cinema with my brother and cousins and we saw a film. It was very nice.
	Three.
Examiner:	What's your name?
Yuji:	Yuji.
Examiner:	Thank you. What's your surname?
Yuji:	Murakami.
Examiner:	How do you spell it?
Yuji:	M-U-R-A-K-A-M-I
Examiner:	Thank you. Where do you come from?
Yuji:	I'm from Japan.
Examiner:	Do you study English?
Yuji:	Yes, I have English lessons at school and I also do extra English at H & P English School.
Examiner:	Do you like it?
Yuji:	Yes.
Examiner:	Why?
Yuji:	I think English is useful for me and it's a beautiful language.

Examiner:	Thank you, Yuji. What do you enjoy doing in your free time?
Yuji:	Um … I really enjoy playing sports. Er, after school, I play ping pong with a team and I also like baseball. I also like reading books and watching TV.

❼ 🎧

> **Suggested answers**
> 1 Yes, they answer well because they use full answers with examples (Yuji: *After school, I play …*), reasons (Angela: *I'll need to read … in English*) and opinions (Eduard: *we saw a film. It was very nice*).
> 2 Sorry, can you say that again?
> 3 No, he answers with a (slightly) different question: *Did you do anything …?*

Grammar

So do I and *nor/neither do I*

❶ 🎧 After the students have chosen their reply, focus on the form of these replies.

Recording script	CD1 Track 47
Ken:	My name's Ken.
	I'm 15 years old.
	I've got two brothers.
	I live in Taipei.
	I don't like football.
	I went to the cinema yesterday.
	I haven't been to Paris.

❷ 🎧

Recording script	CD1 Track 48
Zosia:	My name's Zosia.
	I'm from Krakow. It's a very beautiful city in Poland.
	I've got one sister.
	I get on very well with my sister.
	I love going to the cinema with my friends.
	I went to the cinema yesterday with my best friend.
	I don't like staying at home.
	I haven't travelled very much …
	… but I've been to Warsaw, the capital city of Poland.

Writing Part 2

❶ For example: *Spanish uses a capital letter for countries but not for nationalities or languages.*

❷ ☉

> **Answers**
> **1** I am keen on **T**-shirts (also *t-shirt* or *tee shirts*), trousers and jackets.
> **2** I'll send a present to **M**arina. **I** hope she likes it.
> **3 S**ay 'Hi' to your sister. **S**ee you soon, Gari
> **4 I** can't come to your **E**nglish lesson on **M**onday.
> **5 M**y blanket is like a penguin's skin. **I**t's black and white.

❸

> **Suggested answers**
> meet your cousin Myra, station, never met … before, an email to Myra, describe yourself, ask Myra … describe herself, suggest … place to meet … station, 35–45 words

❹❺ Remind students that although the testing focus of Writing Part 2 is on task achievement, they could lose marks if their errors impede understanding.

❻

> **Answers**
> *Three points*: **1** Im tallish … cap   **2** what do you look like?   **3** Lets meet outside the resturant wich is in the station
>
> *Words to connect points (with correct spelling)*: because, with, and, which
>
> *Spelling mistakes*: **1** bec~~ou~~se → bec**au**se   **2** an → an**d**   **3** favor~~it~~ → fav**ourite** (UK) / fav**orite** (US)   **4** res~~tu~~rant → res**tau**rant   **5** ~~wich~~ → **which**
>
> *Punctuation mistakes*: **1** ~~Im~~ → I'm   **2** ~~i~~ → I   **3** ~~what~~ → What   **4** ~~Lets~~ → Let's   **5** ~~station~~ → station

> **Corrected letter**
> Hi Myra,
>
> I am very happy because you are coming.
> I'm tallish with short hair, blue eyes and I always wear my favourite (or favorite) blue cap. What do you look like? Let's meet outside the restaurant which is in the station.
>
> Pablo

Vocabulary and grammar review Unit 7

Answers

Grammar

❶ 2 big enough   **3** warm enough   **4** thick enough   **5** too sleepy   **6** old enough   **7** too cold   **8** too expensive

❷ 2 'm meeting   **3** 'll go   **4** leaves   **5** 'll   **6** are going

Vocabulary

❸ 2 f   **3** a   **4** b   **5** c   **6** e

❹ Across: 6 sail   **7** metro   **9** blow   **11** dry   **13** gale   **14** mild   **16** ferry
Down: 1 tram   **2** board   **3** wet   **4** cloudy   **5** cool   **8** flight   **9** bike   **10** warm   **12** ride   **15** icy

Vocabulary and grammar review Unit 8

Answers

Vocabulary

❶ 2 B   **3** A   **4** C   **5** D   **6** B   **7** A   **8** C   **9** D   **10** C

❷ 2 ~~becouse~~ → because   **3** ~~did'nt~~ → didn't   **4** ~~sisters~~ → sister's   **5** ~~italian~~ → Italian   **6** ~~wich~~ → which   **7** ~~were~~ → wear   **8** ~~belive~~ → believe

Grammar

❸

> **Suggested answers**
> **2** … someone broke my new skateboard.
> **3** … I can't wake up in the morning.
> **4** … I'd keep it.   **5** … I say something stupid.
> **6** … I'll have my party in the garden.   **7** … I pass all my exams.   **8** … my parents get angry.

❹ 2 has / has got / 's got   **3** so   **4** unless   **5** 'd/would travel

Unit 8 photocopiable activity: Friends and family   Time: 20-25 mins

Objectives
- To review adjectives used to describe physical appearance and personality
- To review prepositions of position
- To practise listening for specific information and making notes

Before class

Make one copy of the activity for each group of three or four students in your class. Cut into two sections and cut the first section into 12 cards. Shuffle the cards.

In class

1 Divide your class into groups of three or four, and give each group a set of picture cards. Ask them to spend a few minutes looking at the people on the cards and describing their physical appearance.

2 Ask them to turn their cards over. On the board, write the following names: *Alan, Andrew, Brian, Emma, Ernie, Samuel* and *Sue*. Then explain that you are going to read them a description of some of the people on their cards. The names of these people are on the board. While they are listening, they should make notes about what the people look like.

3 Read the following passage twice, at normal speed, pausing for a few seconds between each sentence. Your students should not write down everything you say: **they should focus only on the names and descriptions of the people and not where the people are standing yet**.

'Hi, I'm Samuel. I'm the good-looking one with wavy hair standing in the middle of the group. The tall man with the moustache to my right (that's your left), at the end of the group, is my father, Ernie. The woman next to him with the shoulder-length curly hair is my mother, Sue. The man standing between me and my mum is my Uncle Alan. He's quite short, like my mother, and has a beard. He's also got a scar, which he got when he was a boy. The beautiful, slim girl with long, straight hair directly to my left (your right) is my sister, Emma. The tall boy with the dark skin at the end of the group on my left is my best friend, Brian. The man with the bald head and broad shoulders standing between Emma and Brian is my neighbour, Andrew.'

4 Now ask your students to turn their cards back over, and match the names with the cards. There are five cards that they do not need and they should discard these.

5 Give your student groups the table from the second part of the activity. Tell them that you are going to read the passage from Step 3 again. This time, they should imagine that they are looking at a group photograph, and should put the pictures into the correct order in the table.

6 Read the passage again, once only. Allow them a few moments to put their cards into the table. They should write the name of each person in the space under each picture.

7 Review their answers. They should have the following:

Answers
From left to right: **H** (Ernie), **K** (Sue), **D** (Alan), **G** (Samuel), **L** (Emma), **B** (Andrew), **I** (Brian)

Unit 8 photocopiable activity
Friends and family

✂ Cut along the dotted lines to divide these into cards.

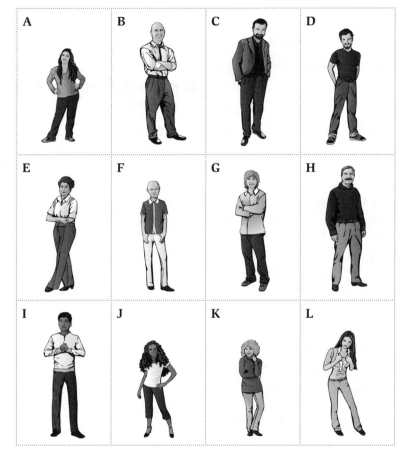

✂ -

Listen to the description and put the pictures in the correct boxes. Write the name of each person in the space below. There are five pictures that you do not need.

(The names you need are: Alan, Andrew, Brian, Emma, Ernie, Samuel and Sue.)

Word list

Unit 8

Note: the numbers show which page the word or phrase first appears on in the unit.

apostrophe *n* (77) a mark (') used to show that letters or numbers are absent

bald *adj* (74) with little or no hair

bring up *v* (71) to look after a child and teach them until they are old enough to look after themselves

broad shoulders *n* (74) wide shoulders

capital letter *n* (77) a large letter of the alphabet used at the beginning of sentences and names

childish *adj* (75) Childish behaviour is silly, like that of a small child.

coach *n* (70) someone whose job is to teach people to improve at a sport, skill, or school subject

comma *n* (73) a mark (,) used to separate parts of a sentence, or to separate the items in a list

confident *adj* (71) certain about your ability to do things well

dishonest *adj* (75) not honest and likely to lie or do something illegal

full stop *n* (77) a mark (.) used at the end of a sentence, or to show that the letters before it are an abbreviation

grandfather *n* (70) the father of your mother or father

grow up *v* (71) to become older or an adult

hard-working *adj* (75) doing a job seriously and with a lot of effort

honest *adj* (75) sincere and telling the truth

hyphen *n* (77) a mark (-) used to join two words together, or to show that a word has been divided and continues on the next line

lazy *adj* (75) Someone who is lazy does not like working or using any effort.

make up *v* (71) to say or write something that is not true

nephew *n* (70) the son of your brother or sister, or the son of your husband's or wife's brother or sister

plain *adj* (74) A plain person is not attractive to look at.

reliable *adj* (75) able to be trusted or believed

rude *adj* (75) behaving in a way which is not polite and upsets other people

scar *n* (74) a permanent mark left on the body from a cut or other injury

selfish *adj* (75) caring only about yourself and not other people

set up *v* (71) to start a company or organisation

shy *adj* (75) not confident, especially about meeting or talking to new people

smart *adj* (75) intelligent

sort out *v* (72) to successfully deal with something, such as a problem or difficult situation

stepmother *n* (70) the woman who has married your father but is not your mother

stepsister *n* (70) not your parent's daughter but the daughter of the person your parent has married

twin *n* (70) one of two children who are born to the same mother at the same time

uncle *n* (70) the brother of your mother or father, or the husband of your aunt

unreliable *adj* (75) not able to be trusted or depended on

Unit 9 Fit and healthy

Unit objectives

- **Topics:** health, medicine, exercise, sport
- **Listening Part 4:** identifying agreement, disagreement and decision making
- **Reading Part 5:** using the context to guess missing words
- **Speaking Part 2:** agreeing, disagreeing and deciding
- **Writing Part 3:** (*story*) text organisation, narrative verb tenses
- **Grammar:** defining and non-defining relative clauses, past perfect simple
- **Vocabulary:** illnesses and accidents; sports collocations
- **Pronunciation:** stressed words

Starting off

❶ Students answer individually, although they can discuss the language of the questions with their partners. Explain that *exhausted* means 'very tired'.

Alternative treatment Put students in pairs. Student A keeps their book closed while Student B asks each question and gives options A–C. Student A has to listen carefully before choosing the option that best describes him/herself.

❷ Allow time for everyone to read the interpretation of their scores at the back of the Student's Book. Then ask the class how they feel about what it says, and whether they think they should make any lifestyle changes to become 'fitter and more active'.

Extension idea As a non-classroom activity, students find out more about keeping active and getting fit – for example: how to live an active lifestyle, how to avoid sports injuries. Suggest they look at this website: http://www.nhs.uk/Livewell/fitness.

Listening Part 4

❶ 🎧 Give them a minute to read the transcript, then play the recording of this first part twice. Check answers for accuracy.

> **Answers**
> 1 I agree with you   2 I'm not sure about that

Recording script   CD1 Track 49

Kelly:	They keep saying on TV things like 'today's teenagers are unfit and unhealthy', and I just don't believe it.
Jason:	<u>I agree with you</u>. There's all this stuff about us not getting enough exercise because we're watching TV or playing computer games all the time, when in fact, nowadays everyone is mad about sports.
Kelly:	Well, <u>I'm not sure about that</u>, but certainly a lot of young people are doing active things. Perhaps more than older generations did.

❷ Keep this brief, as these expressions will be dealt with in the Speaking section. Elicit answers, together with their level of politeness. Point out that abruptly saying 'I don't agree at all', 'that's not true,' etc. may be considered rude, so encourage the use of the more polite expressions in an appropriate tone.
Give examples of 'I don't really agree', etc., using a polite tone, contrasting them with a ruder tone for 'that's not true', etc.

> **Suggested answers**
> <u>Agreeing</u>
> I totally agree; I agree completely; (you're) right; absolutely; that's true; yes, I think so (too) because …; yes, I do too; so do I; neither do I
>
> <u>Disagreeing politely</u>
> I don't really agree; I don't think so because …; you may be right, but …; I don't know; actually, I think …; I know, but …; I'm not (so) sure (about that)
>
> <u>Disagreeing (showing strong disagreement)</u>
> I don't agree with you (at all); I (completely) disagree; that's not true; I don't think so because …; that's not the way I see it

❸ 🎧 Let them study the questions, then play the recording twice. Students answer individually. Go through the answers.

> **Answers**
> 1 NO   2 YES   3 YES   4 NO   5 NO   6 NO

Extension idea 1 Give the class a copy of the transcript on page 144. Pairs study the six correct/incorrect statements and identify the expressions in the text with similar meanings, or that mean the opposite. Example: *people's diets now are less healthy than in the past: … that doesn't mean that what they eat is worse for them …*

Extension idea 2 The class identify the expressions used by Kelly and Jason to express agreement and disagreement. Play the recording again: whenever they hear such an expression, they call out or put their hands up. Stop the recording each time this happens, and give them time to note down the words used. Later, they can use some of these expressions in Exercise 4.

Recording script   CD1 Track 50

Jason:	It's true, isn't it, Kelly, that people eat more these days, so they're getting bigger and heavier?
Kelly:	Er, yes, I think so, Jason. But lots of people are vegetarian now, aren't they? And I think that kind of food is really good for you. So people might eat more nowadays but <u>that doesn't mean that what they eat is worse for them</u>.
Jason:	No, it's just different. But there's more to being healthy than just exercise and eating, isn't there? I mean, there's so much stress in everyday life. And there are a lot of people that don't get enough sleep.
Kelly:	I don't know whether people are any more stressed, but <u>you're right that everyone seems to go to bed late</u>, even when they've got school or work the next day. I suppose it's all the late films on TV, or staying on the Internet until two in the morning.
Jason:	Or on the PlayStation®. There are so many fun things to do. So even if people manage to get up on time the next morning, they're too tired to do anything.
Kelly:	Hmm, I'm not so sure. These days, <u>when they go to school, a lot more students are going by bike</u>. Especially now that in some cities you can hire one cheaply and then just leave it anywhere you like. And that's quite healthy, isn't it?
Jason:	Hmm, it might be. But the air's really bad nowadays, especially in the cities. There's all that pollution from cars and lorries.
Kelly:	Actually, <u>I think the situation has improved a bit</u> since they started making everyone pay to drive into the city centre. There's not so much traffic now.
Jason:	You may be right, but it still makes me cough in the morning. Which reminds me: don't you think people get sick more often nowadays? <u>I'm always fine, and I'm sure you are too</u>, but we know a lot of people whose health is terrible, don't we?

Kelly:	Hmm, I don't know about that. I think it's mostly coughs and colds and sore throats; perhaps a headache or a stomach ache which lasts a day or two. Usually nothing more serious than that. And teenagers have always had those kinds of illnesses. In most cases, I don't think their basic health is any different.
Jason:	Well, <u>that's not the way I see it</u>, but I *hope* you're right!
Kelly:	Me too!

Vocabulary
Illnesses and accidents

❶ 🎧 Play once or twice, highlighting the pronunciation of the underlined expressions. Get them to repeat these words: cough: /kɒf/; cold: /kəʊld/; sore: /sɔː/; throat: /θrəʊt/; headache: /hedeɪk/; stomach: /stʌmək/; ache: /eɪk/. Encourage them to explain each one (gesture or translation may be necessary): *cough*: make air come out of your throat with a short sound; *cold*: common illness that makes you sneeze and makes your nose produce liquid; *sore throat*: pain inside the throat; *headache*: pain inside your head; *stomach ache*: pain in your stomach.

Recording script   CD1 Track 51

Kelly:	coughs and colds and sore throats; perhaps a headache or a stomach ache

❷ Help with any new expressions and their pronunciation, and distinctions such as *injury* /ɪndʒəri/ and *wound* /wuːnd/ (a wound is often caused by a weapon).
Possibly explain that an X-ray is a photo taken of the inside of the body, often to diagnose fractures. Ensure that everyone completes the table.

> **Answers**
> *accidents*: injury, cut, bruise, wound, sprain, fracture
> *illnesses*: flu, disease, high temperature, earache
> *treatments*: medicine, plaster, pill, tablet, bandage, aspirin, X-ray, operation, injection, plaster cast

❸ Some languages use the definite article with parts of the body ('The foot hurts!'), so stress that we normally use the possessive in English. Point out that we use *some* with the uncountable *medicine*, but *a* with countables such as *tablet*, *disease*, or *bandage*. We talk about having or catching *a cold*, but we *have flu* – though sometimes we may talk about having *the flu*. An article is also possible with expressions such as 'to have *(an) earache*', and must be used in 'to have *a headache*'.

Suggested answers
1 My brother fractured his leg.   2 I think I've sprained my ankle.   3 You've cut your finger.
4 She's bruised her leg.   5 I've got a bad earache.
6 The patient has a serious wound.   7 A nurse put a plaster cast on his broken arm.   8 You should have an X-ray.   9 I don't like taking medicine.
10 You need to have an injection now.

❹ Encourage them to give a variety of symptoms.

Suggested answers
'I had a bad cough, a sore throat and a terrible headache', 'I had an X-ray, they put on a bandage and I took some tablets for the pain'.

Grammar
Which, that, who, whose, when and *where* clauses (defining and non-defining)

❶ Explain any difficult vocabulary, but don't check their answers yet.

❷ ♫ Play the recording once or twice, then go through the answers.

Answers
2 who   3 which   4 whose   5 that   6 when
7 where   8 that

Recording script   CD1 Track 52

Presenter: Most people <u>that</u> do regular sport are healthier, and often feel happier, than those <u>who</u> do little or no exercise. Care must be taken, though, to avoid the injuries <u>which</u> sport can sometimes cause. People <u>whose</u> favourite sports are running or jumping, for instance, may injure their ankles or knees. Training <u>that</u> involves doing the same exercise again and again can do serious damage, particularly to athletes in their early teens, <u>when</u> their bodies are still developing.
It is important not to do too much too soon. Everyone should 'warm up' before they begin – if possible in the place <u>where</u> they are going to exercise. It is essential, too, to follow any safety advice <u>that</u> they receive.

❸ They use their corrected answers from Exercise 1 as a model. Ensure that everyone has the rules filled in correctly, as they will be using them for reference.

Answers
2 who   3 that/which   4 which/that   5 when
6 where   7 whose

The other relative pronouns which are the object and could be left out are: 7 where and 8 that. Focus attention on (3) in the text above. Explain that *which* refers back to *the injuries*, so it is the object of the verb *cause* (the subject is *sport*) – in other words, 'Sport (subject) can sometimes cause injuries (object)'. Then get the class to find a similar structure: in 8, *that* (referring to *safety advice*) is the object of the verb *receive*.

❹ Allow a minute or two for this initial gist-reading activity, then elicit answers.

Answers
1 stress caused by busy living   2 find something they enjoy doing every day

❺ Give pairs a couple of minutes to fill in the gaps (reminding them that for people and things there are alternative answers). Don't give the answers yet.

❻ ♫ Play the recording – twice, if necessary. Go through the answers.

Answers
(Possible variations in brackets) 2 whose   3 which (that)   4 that (which)   5 when   6 which (that)   7 where

Recording script   CD1 Track 53

Presenter: People <u>who</u> work very hard, and individuals <u>whose</u> lives are busy in other ways, may suffer from a kind of stress <u>which</u> can actually damage their health. One way <u>that</u> they can reduce stress levels is to find a time, every day, <u>when</u> they can relax. They should find something <u>that</u> they enjoy doing, such as reading, in a place <u>where</u> they feel comfortable and unlikely to be disturbed.

❼

Answers
We could leave out: 4 which   5 when   6 that
7 where

8 Learners have to decide which relative pronoun (if one is needed) to use, and where in the sentence it goes. Check their answers, possibly also eliciting the reason for omission/non-omission in each case.

> **Answers**
> **2** who/that swim   **3** where accidents
> **4** not necessary / illness that   **5** whose tooth
> **6** not necessary / time when

Extension idea Take a section of intermediate-level text, possibly from a reading passage the class have already studied, and delete some or all of the relative pronouns, using correction fluid. Make photocopies and get pairs to replace them, indicating where the omission of the relative pronoun makes no difference to the meaning.

9 Encourage pairs to make a number of complete sentences using each prompt.

> **Suggested answers**
> **2** I do my homework / I listen to music   **3** I hate / I really like   **4** I stay in bed late / I go swimming   **5** always helps you / listens to you   **6** ticket wins a prize / health is really good

10 Check answers and elicit or give more examples of non-defining relative clauses, using a range of relative pronouns including one with the relative clause at the end of the sentence. Examples: *Mr Lomas, who is Canadian, studied at McGill University in Montreal. This coffee, which is made in Columbia, is my favourite. I lost some money on the way home, which was very annoying.*

> **Answers**
> **1** which   **2** which is very healthy   **3** separate it from the rest of the sentence   **4** yes   **5** no   **6** no

11 Explain they have to join the sentences using a non-defining relative clause, and they must make a small change to the second sentence.

> **Answers**
> **2** a doctor, works in the hospital.   **3** I went for a swim, was very cold.   **4** sister is a nurse, is my best friend.   **5** was 12, the sports centre opened.
> **6** really enjoy, is popular in my country.

12 ✪ Explain that these sentences contain a range of error types, including incorrect punctuation, missing relative pronoun, etc. Perhaps go through the sentences, asking what the mistake is in each case. Point out that 'which' is not possible in Question 7.

> **Answers**
> **2** I am visiting my mother, who is ill.   **3** He has a son, who is about my age.   **4** The last book (that) I read was *The Lord of the Rings*.   **5** I've met a guy whose name is Daniel.   **6** I'm in Brazil, which is a beautiful country.   **7** That is all (that) I can tell you.   **8** There are many places that/which are very beautiful.   **9** I'll tell everyone (who) I know.
> **10** I have to go to the airport, which is quite far from the city.

Vocabulary
Sports

1 Elicit the answers to the matching activity quickly, then ask for opinions on each of the sports.

> **Answers**
> **1** B   **2** C   **3** A

2 This can be done quickly, as preparation for the next exercise.

> **Answers**
> *do* gymnastics, *go* paragliding, *play* basketball

3 Pairs write the answers into their vocabulary notebooks, or on the page. Briefly explain – or translate – any unfamiliar sports.

> **Answers**
>
> | do | go | play |
> | --- | --- | --- |
> | gymnastics | paragliding | basketball |
> | boxing | cycling | ice hockey |
> | athletics | surfing | volleyball |
> | | running | football |
> | | swimming | squash |
> | | climbing | tennis |
> | | skiing | golf |
> | | jogging | baseball |

4 Patterns: *go* is usually used with outdoor sports over long distances; *play* often goes with sports that end -*ball* and ball sports generally. We often use *do* with sports that do not take *go* or *play*. (*Note*: in informal speech, *do* can be used with most activities [e.g. 'she *does* cycling in her free time'].)

Extension idea Ask the class to guess the verbs that go with some activities/sports that are popular in the students' country/countries. Then get pairs or groups to tell each other about other activities/sports, e.g. 'a lot of people go sailing / diving / mountain biking', 'people like to play rugby / handball / table tennis', 'doing aerobics / taekwondo / weightlifting' is very popular'.

5 ⊙ These focus mainly on sports that have not been introduced. If necessary, explain or translate them, and encourage students to work out which verbs collocate with them. For example, snowboarding is similar to skiing (*go*), table tennis is like tennis (*play*), aerobics has similarities with gymnastics (*do*), and windsurfing with surfing (*go*).

> **Answers**
> **2** ~~make~~ → do   **3** ~~make~~ → go   **4** ~~done~~ → played
> **5** ~~made~~ → did   **6** ~~played~~ → went

6 If necessary, prompt with descriptions, e.g. a *court* is usually rectangular with lines on the ground, but smaller than the area where football is played.

> **Suggested answers**
> court: tennis, squash, basketball, volleyball, etc.
> gym: gymnastics, aerobics, martial arts, etc.
> pitch: football, rugby, hockey, baseball, etc.
> ring: boxing, wrestling, kickboxing, etc.
> stadium: football, rugby, baseball, etc.
> track: athletics, running, cycling, etc.

Extension idea Give the names of other places where sports are played, e.g. *rink, course, piste, alley, circuit, table, green*. For homework, they use their dictionaries, or a search engine on their computer, to find out which sports are played there.

7 Also ask on which part of the body each item of clothing is worn, and how the equipment is used. Elicit other items associated with sports, e.g. *shorts, clubs* (golf).

> **Answers**
> clothes: boots (football, rugby, skiing, etc.); gloves (boxing, football goalkeeper, ice hockey, skiing, etc.); helmet (horse riding, motorcycling, baseball, etc.); trainers (running, jogging, tennis, etc.).
> Equipment: bat (baseball, cricket, table tennis, etc.); board (surfing, windsurfing, snowboarding, etc.); racket (table tennis, squash, badminton, etc.); net (tennis, table tennis, volleyball, etc.)

8 Elicit the irregular past forms of four of these verbs, particularly 'beat' in the past simple, and give examples: 'Australia *beat* Argentina 24–15, *winning* the Rugby World Cup again.' Pairs then complete the exercise.

> **Answers**
> **2** score   **3** draw, lose, win

Extension idea One student describes a sporting event he or she attended, saying where it was played, how people were dressed, what equipment was used and what happened – but without mentioning the name of the sport. Their partner listens to the complete description, then says what sport it is and how they know.

Reading Part 5

1 Elicit the sports shown (ice hockey, squash, aerobics, scuba diving) and check understanding of 'individual', 'team', etc. Pairs or groups do the task, using more than one adjective per sport where possible. They then think of more sports in each category.

> **Answers**
> **1** ice hockey: team, competitive   **2** squash: individual, competitive   **3** aerobics: individual, non-competitive   **4** scuba diving: individual, non-competitive

2 Allow a minute or two for this.

Alternative treatment If you feel some of the class are not interested in sports, divide them into sporting and non-sporting groups. Ask those who don't like sports to tell each other why, and what they do – or would like to do – instead. Then get the different groups to put forward their points of view to the class.

3 This could be done in pairs. Encourage them to refer back to earlier parts of this unit, particularly relative clauses and sports collocations. Don't go through the answers yet: the next stage is for them to compare with the options in the exam task.

4 Students do the exam task on their own. Go through the text and items when everyone has finished.

> **Answers**
> **1** A   **2** D   **3** B   **4** B   **5** A   **6** D   **7** D   **8** C
> **9** B   **10** C

Speaking Part 2

❶ 🎧 Play once or twice and check. Point out their usefulness in PET Speaking. Revise any similar expressions that came up at the beginning of this unit.

> **Answers**
> **2** sure **3** totally **4** so **5** way **6** all
> **7** true **8** too

> **Recording script** CD1 Track 54
>
> 1 You **may** be right, but isn't there another possibility? 2 I'm not **really** sure about that.
> 3 Yes, I **totally** agree with you. 4 I don't **think** so because that might not work very well.
> 5 That's not the **way** I see it. 6 I don't agree at all. 7 That's **true**. 8 I think so too.

❷ They could discuss these in pairs.

> **Answers**
> **a** agree: 3, 7, 8 **b** disagree strongly: 5, 6
> **c** disagree politely: 1, 2, 4

❸ 🎧 Play once or twice again. Point out that in some cases two consecutive words are stressed.

> **Answers**
> **2** really sure **3** totally agree **4** think **5** I
> **6** at all **7** true **8** I

❹ 🎧 Choral drill or tell them to practise in pairs.

❺ Pairs fill in the missing words.

❻ 🎧 Play the recording for them to check their answers.

> **Answers**
> **2** then **3** agreed **4** what **5** both **6** So **7** thing
> **8** glad

> **Recording script** CD1 Track 55
>
> Girl: Yes, that's a **good idea**. Let's do **that**, then.
> Boy: Right, we're **agreed**. **That's** what we'll do.
>
> Boy: OK, we **both** like the idea. So shall we do **that**?
> Girl: Yes, that's the **best thing** to do. I'm **glad** we agree!

❼ 🎧 Play again and elicit the stressed words. Get them to underline these or note them down.

> **Answers**
> Stressed words are: good idea, that, agreed, That's, both, that, best thing, glad

❽ Suggest they look again at the Reading text to consider which type of sport might suit them best, and that they use health and fitness vocabulary from this unit. Remind the class that all choices are equally valid. Monitor pairs, ensuring they are reacting politely to suggestions and that any decision is mutually agreed. Give feedback.

Writing Part 3

❶ Explain that these are similar to PET Part 3 instructions and remind the class that they will also have the option to write a letter. Elicit the answers, pointing out that the alternatives in Questions 2 and 3 are possibilities in the exam.

> **Answers**
> **1** story **2** title **3** first person
> **4** story, titles, frightening, experience, my (which answers Question 3)

❷ This activity focuses on text organisation. Point out that this is quite a common way of organising a short story, but it is not a model that they have to follow in every detail.

Alternative treatment This could be done in greater depth, with pairs studying the text to locate, for example, the part that describes each main event, words that set the scene, and identify exactly *who*, *what*, *where* and *when*.

> **Answers**
> **b** 1 **c** 3 **d** 3 **e** 3 **f** 1

Past perfect

❸ Focus on the whole sentence containing the extract, asking the class when the snowing started: before the writer reached the top. Point out that they will need to recognise the contracted form to find three of the uses in the text. When they have done so, elicit the form of the past perfect (*had* + past participle), the negative (*had not / hadn't* + past participle) and the interrogative (*had* + subject + past participle: *Had she gone over the edge?*). Remind them not to confuse the contracted form of *had* with that of *would* (also *'d*, but followed by an infinitive, e.g. *I said I'd tell her*).

❹ This practises narrative tense use, alternating with the past simple. Explain that the past continuous, for background actions and situations, is also often used with these tenses. Point out that the past perfect is often used with 'already', e.g. *The game had already begun when I switched on the TV.*

❺ Pairs apply the same questions from Exercise 1 to the exam task. They should notice an important difference: this time they must use a sentence to start their story. Point out that this must not be changed in any way.

❻ Students do this individually. Refer them back to the text in Exercise 2 for organisation and style. Explain that some of the features in a–f, such as *who, what, where*, etc., plus the main events and a clear ending, are essential.

Sample answer
I felt nervous when the game began. Fifty thousand people were watching me in the stadium, as well as a television audience of millions. I had always dreamt of playing for my favourite team, and at last I had my chance.

For the first hour everything went fine. We were playing well and I had started to feel less nervous. Then, suddenly, it all went horribly wrong: I made a terrible mistake and the other team scored. I felt awful.

Then I thought back to what the coach had said to me, about never giving up, and I knew that I simply had to win the match for my team. So, in the last few minutes, I scored the two most important goals of my life.

Unit 9 photocopiable activity: Relative clause sentence building

Time: 20 mins

Objectives
- To review and practise defining and non-defining relative clauses
- To look at the importance of commas in the construction of non-defining relative clauses

Before class
Make one copy of the activity for each pair in your class. You will also need dice (one for each pair).

In class

❶ Divide your class into pairs. Explain that they are going to play a game with their partner. They should decide who is Student 1 and who is Student 2.

❷ Give each pair a copy of the activity and a die. Tell them that the sheet contains eight sentences. Each sentence uses either a defining or a non-defining relative clause. However, the words are in the wrong order, and each word has been placed into its own box. They are going to rearrange the words to make sentences. There is an example at the top of the sheet. Allow them about five minutes to look at the words and use them to write sentences on a separate sheet of paper. They should make sure their partner does not see these.

❸ They then begin the activity, following the instructions in the box.

❹ Stop them after about 10–15 minutes, then ask them to stop. Review their answers. The student in each pair with the most correctly placed words is the winner.

Relative clause sentence building

Before you play the game, spend about five minutes looking at the words. On a separate sheet of paper, write the sentences that you think these words make. Pay particular attention to the *commas*: these will tell you if the relative clause in each sentence is *defining* or *non-defining*. Also pay attention to *capital letters* – remember that a sentence must always begin with one of these – and *full stops* – which must come at the end of the sentence). Do *not* let your partner see your answers!

Instructions:

1 Student 1 begins the game. You should roll the die once.

2 You should then rearrange the words to start making proper sentences and write these words in 'your' spaces [_____] below the original words. The number of words you can rearrange depends on the number on your die. So, for example, if you roll a four on your die, you can rearrange four words. YOU CAN DO ANY OF THE WORDS IN ANY OF THE SENTENCES, IN ANY ORDER.

3 When you have rearranged your words, it is Student 2's turn to roll the die. You can use a word Student 1 has already used if you think that they are wrong and you are right. Write the words in 'your' spaces [_____].

4 Repeat steps 1–3 until your teacher tells you to stop.

Example:

whose	English	is	friend	Peter,	teacher,	my	best	father	is	my
Peter,	whose	father	is	my	English	teacher,	is	my	best	friend.

1	is	I	day	out	Saturday	friends.	go	the	when	my	with

2	is	my	is	city.	which	favourite	France,	capital	Paris,	of	the

3	city	is	up.	I	grew	London	born	the	where	was	and

4	I	last	where	country.	holiday,	my	fascinating	is	Mexico,	spent	a

5	play	healthier	don't.	who	who	than	sport	those	are	People

6	really	something	games	enjoy.	that	Playing	I	computer	is

7	whose	are	busy	People	stress.	very	lives	from	suffer	can

8	when	was	Germany.	In	my	I	to	1996,	family	two,	moved

Word list

Unit 9

Note: the numbers show which page the word or phrase first appears on in the unit.

athletics *n* (84) the sports which include running, jumping, and throwing

bandage *n* (81) a long piece of soft cloth that you tie around an injured part of the body

bat *n* (84) a piece of wood used to hit the ball in some sports

beat *v* (84) to defeat someone in a competition

board *n* (84) a flat piece of wood, plastic, etc. used for a particular purpose

bruise *n* (81) a dark area on your skin where you have been hurt

challenge *n* (85) something that is difficult and that tests someone's ability or determination

cold *n* (81) a common illness which makes you sneeze and makes your nose produce liquid

competition *n* (85) when someone is trying to win something or be more successful than someone else

cough *n* (81) an illness that makes you cough (= action of making air come out of your throat with a short sound) a lot

court *n* (84) an area for playing particular sports

disease *n* (81) an illness caused by an infection or by a failure of health and not by an accident

earache *n* (81) pain in your ear

energy *n* (80) the power and ability to be very active without becoming tired

fit *adj* (80) healthy, especially because you exercise regularly

flu *n* (81) an illness like a very bad cold, that makes you feel hot and weak

glove *n* (84) a piece of clothing which covers your fingers and hand

gymnastics *n* (83) a sport in which you do physical exercises on the floor and on different pieces of equipment, often in competitions

headache *n* (81) pain inside your head

hurt *v* (82) If a part of your body hurts, it is painful.

ice hockey *n* (84) a game played on ice in which two teams try to hit a small hard object into a goal using long curved sticks

injure *v* (81) to hurt a person, animal, or part of your body

jogging *n* (84) running slowly for exercise

medicine *n* (81) a substance used to cure an illness or injury

net *n* (84) something made with a piece of net (= material made of crossed threads with holes between them), for example for sports

nurse *n* (81) someone whose job is to care for ill and injured people

operation *n* (81) when a doctor cuts someone's body to remove or repair part of it

pill *n* (81) a small, hard piece of medicine that you swallow

pitch *n* (84) an area of ground where a sport is played

racket *n* (84) a piece of equipment that you use to hit a ball in sports such as tennis

score *v* (84) to get points in a game or test

sore throat *n* (81) pain in the back part of your mouth and the passages inside your neck

stadium *n* (84) a large, open area with seats around it, used for playing and watching sports

stomach ache *n* (81) pain in the organ inside your body where food is digested

tablet *n* (81) a small, round object containing medicine that you swallow

track *n* (84) a path, often circular, used for races

wound *n* (81) an injury, especially one that is made by a knife or bullet

 Complete PET by Emma Heyderman and Peter May with Rawdon Wyatt © Cambridge University Press 2010 PHOTOCOPIABLE

❶ **Look at this text and put the verbs and any other words in bold into their correct future form (present continuous, present simple, *will* or *going to*). Sometimes more than one option is possible. Use short forms (*I will* = *I'll*, etc.).**

Are you hungry? I **0** (**make**) ...'*ll make*... you a sandwich.

So, you want to know my plans for the next few days? All right, I (1) (**tell**) ....
you. Tomorrow, I (2) (**meet**) .... Alan and Rosie for lunch at
that new Italian restaurant in the town centre. We originally wanted to go for a
picnic, but according to the weather forecast, it (3) (**rain**) ....
all day. After lunch, we (4) (**probably / have**) .... a drink at
their place because they (5) (**show**) .... me the video
they took on holiday. On Wednesday I (6) (**be**) .... busy
packing, because as you know, I (7) (**fly**) .... to New York on
Thursday. My flight (8) (**leave**) .... early in the morning,
so I think I (9) (**go**) .... to bed early on Wednesday and
(10) (**catch**) .... the first bus to the airport.

❷ **Read the text below and choose the correct word for each space.**

People (0) ...C... parents were very strict often treat their own children the same way.

0 A which   **B** their   Ⓒ whose   **D** have

I'm a very hard-working person, partly because I believe that (1) .... you work
hard, you will never succeed in life. My sister is the same. As a result, I rarely relax during
the week and (2) .... does she. I think we are like this because of our parents, who
have big plans for our future and make sure we work hard. They probably think this is the
only way to bring (3) .... children, but perhaps if they were less demanding,
we (4) .... have more time to relax and take things slowly.

The situation is made more difficult by our teachers. In my opinion, they always give us too
(5) .... homework, and we just don't get (6) .... free time to enjoy
ourselves. As a result, the weekends are the only time (7) .... we can do what we
like. Then we can watch television, (8) .... swimming and meet our friends.

I think that if I have children when I'm older, I (9) .... be a more relaxed parent,
because I think that children (10) .... are made to work too hard are often stressed
and grow up to be very unhappy.

1	**A** as	**B** because	**C** unless	**D** if
2	**A** so	**B** either	**C** also	**D** neither
3	**A** out	**B** off	**C** up	**D** on
4	**A** would	**B** will	**C** can	**D** had
5	**A** much	**B** many	**C** little	**D** few
6	**A** many	**B** enough	**C** some	**D** a
7	**A** which	**B** when	**C** where	**D** that
8	**A** do	**B** go	**C** make	**D** play
9	**A** would	**B** can	**C** can't	**D** will
10	**A** which	**B** what	**C** whose	**D** who

❸ **Here are some sentences in which someone is talking about keeping fit. For each question, complete the second sentence so that it means the same as the first, *using no more than three words*.**

0 Mark likes keeping fit and I do as well.

Mark likes keeping fit and .....*so do*...... I.

1 A good way to keep fit is by walking to school instead of taking the bus.

A good way to keep fit is by going to school .... instead of taking the bus.

2 My friend Mark runs to school every day and is very fit.

My friend Mark, ... school every day, is very fit.

3 He's a great tennis player and he always beats me when we play together.

He's a great tennis player and I always .... play together.

4 I like swimming in the sea, but the weather must be warm.

I only like swimming in the sea .... is warm.

5 It's not warm enough to go swimming today.

It's .... go swimming today.

❹ **In this text, replace the words in *italics* with one word only. The first letter of each word has been given to you.**

The trains to the city had been cancelled because of repairs to the (**0**) *tracks that trains travel on* (r *ailway*.........).

All of the trains had been cancelled, so I stood by the road and tried to (**1**) *get a free ride by standing next to the road* (h.................). It was a busy (**2**) *place where two roads meet and cross each other* (c.................), but nobody stopped for me. After two hours, I decided to find the (**3**) *small, cheap hotel* (g.................) in town that my (**4**) *book that gives information about places* (g.................) recommended and stay there (**5**) *during the night and until the morning* (o.................).

❺ **In this conversation, replace the words in *italics* with words that have an opposite meaning. In some cases, more than one answer is possible.**

My brother is very **0** *fat* . . . . . . *slim* . . . .

Livia and Valerie are looking at a photograph of Valerie's family.

Livia: Who's the boy with the (1) *long* . . . . , (2) *straight* . . . . hair?

Valerie: That's my brother William.

Livia: He's really (3) *plain* . . . .

Valerie: Yes, he looks just like my father. He takes after him in other ways too.

Livia: Such as?

Valerie: Well, they're both (4) *lazy* . . . . and (5) *mean* . . . .

Livia: Is that your father next to William? The one with the (6) *fair* . . . . skin and the (7) *narrow* . . . . shoulders?

Valerie: That's right.

Livia: He looks really nice. And that woman must be your mum. She looks just like you.

Valerie: Yes and like me she's (8) *reliable* . . . . and (9) *patient* . . . .

Livia: Oh come on, Valerie. That's just not true! The only negative thing I could possibly say about you is that you can be a bit (10) *confident* . . . . at times.

❻ **Fill in each gap with a preposition (*by, in, off, on, out* or *to*).**

I usually go to work **0** . . . . . . *on* . . . . foot.

I live (1) . . . . a town called Cassington, but work (2) . . . . another town called Yarnton. I go to work (3) . . . . train. It's usually (4) . . . . time, but occasionally it's late. As soon as the train gets (5) . . . . the station, I get (6) . . . . , find a seat and read the newspaper. There's a coffee machine (7) . . . . the train where you can get hot drinks, so I might have a coffee as well. The journey (8) . . . . Yarnton takes about 25 minutes. When the train arrives, I get (9) . . . . and take a taxi to my office. The ride takes about ten minutes. My working day really begins the moment I get (10) . . . . of the taxi.

Unit 10 A question of taste

Unit objectives

- **Topics:** food and drink, shopping and services
- **Listening Part 1:** analysing pictures, listening to the end of each recording
- **Reading Part 2:** predicting paraphrases
- **Speaking Part 3:** describing objects you don't know the name of (material, shape, etc.)
- **Writing Part 2:** writing a short message, ways to thank someone, explain, invite, apologise or suggest, checking work using a checklist
- **Grammar:** commands, *have something done*
- **Vocabulary:** food and drink, shops and services, *course, dish, food, meal* and *plate*
- **Exam round-up**

Starting off

As a warmer Revise the pronunciation of the alphabet letters (Unit 8). Students think of a type of food or drink which begins with each one (e.g. **a**pple, **b**anana, **c**arrot, etc.).

❶

> **Suggested answers**
> They have been organised according to colour.
> *white*: yoghurt, onion, cream; *red*: meat, pepper, steak; *yellow*: mustard, corn, oil, lemon; *orange*: peach, pumpkin, marmalade

❷ Encourage the students to give more than one word answers.

Reading Part 2

❶

> **Suggested answer**
> Students will probably have to match groups of people with suitable restaurants.

❷

> **Suggested answers**
> **1** teacher prefers … fish; interesting views; isn't too expensive
>
> **2** summer wedding anniversary; next Tuesday; hate being with other groups; normally orders steak; Jack … something different

3 try another character restaurant; this Thursday; aren't keen on fish; can't afford anywhere expensive

4 special views; on Sunday; Jon … prefer … meat rather than fish or vegetarian

5 on Sundays; love foreign food; eat alone; leaves Sweden

❸

> **Suggested answers**
> **1** cheap / inexpensive / reasonable / not expensive
> **2** They could hire the whole restaurant or book a private room. **3** Chef Mickey Mouse / Cowboy Café, etc. **4** No, restaurants in these places are unlikely to have windows with a view **5** Sweden (so they won't want to go to a Swedish restaurant)

❹ Point out to students that a useful way to check answers to a multiple-option question is to think about why the other options are incorrect (e.g. Sara and her friends don't choose the Ninja Castle. Although it is a character restaurant and it does have meat dishes, it is *not cheap*).

> **Answers**
> **1** B **2** F **3** A **4** H **5** C

Extension idea Students work in small groups and design their own unusual restaurant. Encourage the students to think about a theme for their restaurant first. Each group should then produce a poster including both text and pictures.

Grammar
Commands

❶ 🎧 Brainstorm two or three possible instructions for each restaurant, e.g. The Enormous Steak has a grill, so the waiter might say 'Don't touch the grill.'

> **Answers**
> **1** D **2** A **3** H

Recording script CD2 Track 2

One.
Waitress 1: Hi. How are you? Just before I take you to your table, <u>put on these gloves and snow boots</u>. Children, don't touch the walls, please! OK, follow me. Here's your table. I'll bring you <u>some hot soup</u> while you look at the menu.

Two.
Waiter: Here's the bill. I hope you enjoyed your meal, sir. And remember – bring your friends with you next time – but, <u>don't tell your enemies where we are – it's a secret</u>!

Three.
Waitress 2: Go over to the butcher's table. Choose <u>a steak</u>. The butcher will weigh it for you. <u>Take your steak to the barbecue</u> and tell the chef how you'd like your meat. <u>Don't touch the grill</u> or you'll burn yourself!

2 🎧 Remind students we add 'please' to make instructions sound less like orders.

Answers
2 don't touch **3** bring **4** don't tell **5** Take
6 Don't touch

Form of verb we use: **a** infinitive without *to*;
b *don't* + infinitive without *to*

Form of the verb does NOT change when we talk to more than one person

3

Suggested answers
1 Take off your coat and give it to me. **2** Mind your head. **3** Sit down here. **4** Here's your food. Don't touch the plate, it's hot. **5** Pick up your knife and fork. **6** Enjoy your meal.

4 If practical, set up the classroom like a restaurant and blindfold some 'guests'.

Vocabulary
Course, dish, food, meal and *plate*

1 2 ⊙ Pre-teach *cod*. Students should read the whole letter before filling in the gaps.

Answers
2 meals **3** plate **4** courses **5** dish

Extension idea Students write a reply to Alicia, talking about the food in their country using *course, dish, food, meal* and *plate*.

Listening Part 1

1

Answers
2 three **3** short **4** twice **5** try to tick (✔) the correct box

2 Remind students that it is also important to focus on the differences between pictures.

3

Answers
2 loaf of bread **3** packet of biscuits **4** tin of pineapple

4 🎧 The aim here is to show students that they need to listen to the whole recording. If they just listen to the first part, they will think that B is correct.

Recording script CD2 Track 3

One.
What did Jamie buy?
Jamie: I'm back, Mum! I got most of the shopping. <u>I got a tube of toothpaste and a loaf of bread</u>, but I <u>don't think they had any tins of pineapple left</u>. I couldn't see them anyway.

Answer
B

5 🎧 Point out the correct answer is now A.

Answer
A

Recording script CD2 Track 4

Mum: Don't worry. <u>What about the biscuits</u>?
Jamie: I couldn't find them at first because they've changed the packet. <u>Is one packet enough</u>?
Mum: Plenty. Thanks, Jamie. Keep the change!

6

Suggested answers
2 <u>What</u> will they <u>take</u> to the <u>party</u>? Listen to see if they take cake, ice-cream or soft drink and type (e.g. chocolate, cola, lemonade, etc.).

3 What <u>time</u> is the <u>boy's appointment</u>? Listen for the times: 4.10 pm, 4.45 pm and 6.30 pm, and decide which one is the correct time for the boy's appointment.

4 <u>What</u> did the <u>girl buy online</u>?

We know that the girl buys one or two objects. Listen to see if she buys a T-shirt and a pair of shoes, a T-shirt and a pair of pyjamas, or a pair of pyjamas only.

5 What is the free gift today? Listen to see if the free gift is a laptop, software or a mouse mat.

6 What is nearest to Rick's Diner?

You will need to listen to see which place, the bridge, station or roundabout, is the nearest to Rick's Diner.

7 Where has the mother been?

You will need to listen to see if she has been to the post office, fishmonger or hairdresser.

7 🎧 Students should listen to each recording twice.In the PET Listening Part 1 exam, students will listen to both informal dialogues and monologues.

```
Answers
2 B   3 A   4 C   5 C   6 A   7 B
```

Recording script   CD2 Track 5

Two. What will they take to the party?

Boy: Shall we take a chocolate cake to John's party?

Girl: Good idea, but I'm not going to make one and I'm sure they're expensive to buy. What about some cans of soft drink?

Boy: You're right about the cake. John said he was going to buy some lemonade and some orange juice. Have we got enough to buy some ice cream?

Girl: Not really, but my mum's got some in the freezer. Let's take that.

Now listen again.

CD2 Track 6

Three. What time is the boy's appointment?

Man: I'd like to make an appointment for my son to get his hair cut one afternoon this week. Could you manage that on Thursday? I can bring him here after school.

Woman: Um, Thursday's going to be busy … um … but we could do that if you come at say … half past six? Would that be okay? If not, I've got free appointments on Tuesday at ten past four or a quarter to five.

Man: Er, thanks. The earlier one that day would be best for us.

Woman: Fine!

Now listen again.

CD2 Track 7

Four. What did the girl buy online?

Girl: Shopping online? Everyone says shoes are my mum and they were fine. You'd also think it

would be safe to buy a T-shirt from the web but my mum bought one a month ago and it was just too tight.

CD2 Track 8

Five. What is the free gift today?

Announcer: Good afternoon, shoppers. To celebrate the fifth year of our very successful electronic department, we are offering great discounts off all software bought today. Computer expert, Gene Reedy, will also be in the store today to give you free advice on how to improve your laptop's performance. And for today only, you won't have to pay anything for one of our anniversary mouse mats – just pick one up from one of our shop assistants.

Now listen again.

CD2 Track 9

Six. What is nearest to Rick's Diner?

Message: This is Rick's Diner. We're open Monday to Saturday from 12.30 to late and you won't find better Moroccan food anywhere else outside Morocco! If you haven't visited us before, turn left at Links Roundabout into Trent Street and we're 100 metres on the right, just before West Bridge. And if you're coming by public transport, it's a five-minute walk from the station. See you soon!

Now listen again.

CD2 Track 10

Seven. Where has the mother been?

Boy: Hi, Mum, did you collect my parcel?

Mother: There was a terrible traffic jam and you know the post office closes at six. I had to get fish for dinner. Hope you don't mind. I wanted to buy some sausages, but by the time I managed to park the car, they were closed too! I'm having my hair cut tomorrow – I think I'll go by underground!

Boy: Could you get my parcel then?

Now listen again.

Vocabulary
Shops and services

As a warmer Play hangman as a class with the title 'Shops and services' and then brainstorm a list of shops and services onto the board.

❶

> **Answers**
> We use 's only with the place. (However, it is possible to describe the place with or without 's – hairdresser/hairdresser's.)

❷

> **Answers**
> **2** dentist   **3** dry cleaner   **4** library   **5** garage
> **6** butcher   **7** post office   **8** travel agent

❸

> **Answers**
> **1** (hairdresser's)   **2** (dentist's) (possible but not usual)   **3** (dry cleaner's)   **6** (butcher's)
> **8** (travel agent's) (possible but not usual)

❹ Tell students that 'book' an appointment is also possible.

> **Suggested answers**
> **1** dentist('s), garage, hairdresser('s)   **2** butcher('s), post office   **3** library   **4** travel agent('s)
> **5** dentist('s), dry cleaner('s), garage   **6** butcher('s), dry cleaner('s), garage, hairdresser('s), travel agent('s)

❺ 🎧 Encourage the students to give reasons for their answers.

> **Answers**
> **1** hairdresser('s)   **2** garage   **3** dry cleaner('s)

Recording script   CD2 Track 11

	One.
Madison:	What have you <u>done to your hair</u>, Layla?
Layla:	Oh, don't! I normally <u>have my hair cut at Gabrielle's</u> but I wanted something different, so I went to that new place on the High Street.
Madison:	Oh no! Was it very expensive?
	Two.
Andrew:	Are you coming to the party tonight, Lewis?
Lewis:	I can't. I'm not allowed to go out.
Andrew:	Why's that?
Lewis:	I had a little accident <u>on my scooter</u>. My dad says it was my fault.
Andrew:	What about your scooter? You only got it last week for your birthday.
Lewis:	That's why my dad is so angry. <u>We're having it repaired</u> and I'm going to have to look for a job to pay for it.
	Three.
Vicki:	Oh no! Callum! That's cola <u>you've spilt</u> down my dress.
Callum:	Sorry, Vicki. It was an accident.
Vicki:	My mum's going to go mad. <u>We had this dress cleaned last week</u> for this party and it wasn't cheap ...

❻ 🎧

> **Suggested answers**
> **1** Layla should complain and get her money back and then go to a better hairdresser.
> **2** Lewis should find a part-time job by looking in the newspaper, asking friends or family or asking in shops and cafés. (He should also take better care of his scooter!)   **3** Callum should offer to pay for the dry cleaning.

Grammar
Have something done

❶ Check the class has understood the meaning and highlight the form *have + something + done* in the present simple, present continuous and past simple.

❷

> **Answer**
> Vinnie

❸ Ask students to underline the verb form in the sentences in Exercise 2.

> **Answers**
> **1** has his meals cooked for him   **2** 's having her nails done today   **3** had his flat cleaned last year

❹ Encourage the students to focus on the time adverbs first.

> **Answers**
> **2** I had my bike repaired two weeks ago.
> **3** John is having his bedroom painted now.
> **4** We have our photo taken once a year.
> **5** Our grandma has her hair coloured every three weeks.
> **6** I can't send an email because we are having our computer mended at the moment.

❺ Allow students time to write down their questions first.

❻ Point out that students should underline examples of *have something done* and not phrases with *have*, e.g. *A boy of 11 has been told*.

> **Answers**
> he had his hair cut; have his head decorated; Jack has his head shaved; some of the teachers have their hair coloured regularly; footballers have their hair shaved

Speaking Part 3

❶ 🎧 Do not tell the students the names of the ten objects at this stage. Play the recording again and focus on the expressions each speaker uses to describe the object they do not know the name for.

> **Answers**
> They ask for: **B**, **I** and **G**.

> **Recording script** CD2 Track 12
>
>   One.
> Ekaterina: I'm sorry but <u>I've washed my hair</u> and I want a … um … <u>it's something for drying hair</u>.
> Girl: Oh. <u>You mean a *hairdryer*</u>. You can borrow mine.
>
>   Two.
> Mateos: I want to eat this orange. Can I have a … a … er … <u>it's made of metal</u> and <u>it's used for cutting</u>.
> Man: Do you mean <u>a *knife*</u>?
>
>   Three.
> Ruben: Hi. Have you got a … a … <u>it's something like stairs</u>.
> Woman: <u>A *ladder*</u>? What do you need one of those for?

❷ When the students have finished the activity, tell them the names of the objects.

> **Answers**
> **A** hammer **B** hairdryer **C** iron **D** plug (electrical) **E** fork **F** frying pan **G** ladder
> **H** tin-opener **I** knife **J** key

❸

> **Answers**
> **1** True **2** True **3** True **4** False (you don't have to talk about things 'outside' the photograph, e.g. feelings, previous activities, etc.) **5** False (you should use some of the expressions from the table in Exercise 2 in this section)

❹ 🎧 Point out that Natalie paraphrases *headscarf* and *tie*.

> **Answer**
> A

> **Recording script** CD2 Track 13
>
> Examiner: And now I'd like each of you to talk on your own about something. I'm going to give each of you a photograph of people shopping. So, Natalie, here is your photograph. Please show it to Lidia, but I'd like *you* to talk about it. Lidia, you just listen

and I'll give you your photograph in a moment. So, Natalie, please tell us what you can see in your photograph.

Natalie: Uh-huh. <u>In this picture I can see a lot of people in a shopping centre. The shopping centre is very big and quite crowded</u>. It looks very new, the floor is black and white. I can see <u>many shops</u> – for example: some clothes shops, a bag shop and a shoe shop. On the ground floor there are many people walking together and looking at the shops. I can see a woman <u>who is wearing a blue shirt</u>. She's also got a bag. On her head she's wearing um … er … I can't remember the word. It's something like a hat. There's a man behind her. <u>He's wearing</u> a white shirt, black trousers and um … a … it's made of cotton, I think. People often wear them for work. On the left I can see another man <u>who is carrying a bag</u>. He has got his mobile phone in his hand and <u>he is talking to someone</u>. On the second floor, I can see more people. <u>They are standing and looking at the people on the ground floor</u>.

❺

> **Answers**
> Students should tick (✔): 1, 3, 4 and 5

Writing Part 2

❶ ***Alternative treatment*** With books closed, read out the incomplete sentences from the exam round-up box and invite answers from the class.

> **Answers**
> **2** three **3** Connect **4** spelling **5** between
> **6** open and close **7** included

❷

> **Suggested answers**
> **1** have pizza with your class; celebrate … end … year; forgotten to ask Ryan; email to Ryan; apologise; invite; explain where … eat; 35–45 words
>
> **2** shopping centre; nearby city; school holidays; email to … Paula; invite; explain why you want to go; suggest … place … meet; 35–45 words
>
> **3** stayed at your cousin's; left something behind; email to Alex; thank him; describe what you left; suggest how … get … object back; 35–45 words

❸ Students then decide if they could use these sentences in any of the three exam questions in Exercise 2.

> **Answers**
> **2** because **3** to come **4** meet **5** inviting

❹

> **Suggested answers**
> *thank someone*: It was very kind of you to ...; Thank you very much for ...; *explain*: That's why ...; ... because ...; *invite*: How about ...; Would you like ...; *apologise*: I'm very sorry that ...; I'm so sorry for ...; *suggest*: Why don't we ...; Let's ...

❺ Remind students they are most likely to lose marks for not including all three points and writing outside the word limits.

❻

> **Model answers**
> **1** Hi Ryan,
>
> I'm very sorry that I forgot to invite you before. We're going out on Friday night. Would you like to come too? We'll have a great time. We've decided to go to the new pizza restaurant. Let me know if you can come.
>
> Yours,
>
> **2** Dear Paula,
>
> I'm going to the shopping centre tomorrow. Why don't you come too? I want to go there because I want to have my hair cut at Dani Bridell's new hairdresser's. Why don't we meet outside the station?
>
> See you soon,
>
> **3** Hi Alex,
>
> Thank you very much for inviting me to stay for the weekend. I had a lot of fun.
> I think I left my pencil case at your house. It's made of blue plastic. Can I come to your house tomorrow to get it?
>
> Lots of love,

Extension idea Display the final corrected versions on the classroom walls. Prepare a reading task by writing (or ask the student to write) a 'find someone who...' statement for each piece of writing, e.g. *Find someone who left their pyjamas at their cousin's house*, etc. Students walk around the classroom and find the answers to the reading task.

Vocabulary and grammar review Unit 9

Answers

Grammar

❶ 2 d that   3 f when   4 a who   5 b where   6 e whose

❷ 2 In summer, when the weather is good, we play tennis.

3 Stevie, whose team won, was the best player of all.

4 In the city centre, where we live, there is a lot of pollution.

5 My brother, who had an accident, is feeling better now.

6 Volleyball, which is a team sport, is played on a court. / Volleyball, which is played on a court, is a team sport.

❸ 2 had practised   3 felt   4 had/'d brought   5 had/'d put   6 was   7 had/'d rained   8 didn't seem   9 was   10 had left   11 started   12 realised   13 had/'d played   14 was   15 slipped   16 fell   17 knew   18 had/'d twisted   19 went   20 had not / hadn't broken   21 wore

Vocabulary

❹ 2 sore   3 beat   4 nurse   5 have   6 bat   7 athletics   8 pill   9 bruise   10 ring

Vocabulary and grammar review Unit 10

Answers

Vocabulary

❶

> **Suggested answers**
> 2 complain   3 book   4 borrow   5 repair

❷ *(Other answers are also possible)*
2 ~~interesting~~ *interested*   3 ~~resturants~~ *restaurants*   4 *Chinese food* ~~are~~ *is*   5 ~~kind~~ *nice*   6 *all* ~~kind~~ *kinds*   7 *chicken* ~~food~~ *dishes*   8 *I think chicken* ~~are~~ *is*   9 ~~my~~ *I think*   10 ~~enjoy with~~ *enjoy your meal*

Grammar

❸ 1 (Also possible: had <u>it</u> washed)   2 is having / has her hair / it cut   3 had it / one / a photo taken   4 have our windows / them cleaned   5 had the car / it repaired   6 had the walls / them painted

❹ 2 Put   3 didn't   4 had   5 I would/'d

Unit 10 photocopiable activity:
A perfect meal
Time: 20 mins +

> ## Objectives
> - To review food vocabulary from Unit 10
> - To practise explaining words and paraphrasing
> - To practise listening to other students for specific information

Before class

Make one copy of the activity for each student in your class. Cut each one along the dotted line to make two parts (Instructions / menu sheet and a name card). You will also need some paper clips (one for each student).

In class

❶ Before you begin the activity, you might want to explain that in many countries main meals are often divided into three parts, or courses: a *starter*, a *main course* and a *dessert*. The concept should be familiar in most cultures, but there are some where meals are 'structured' in a different way.

❷ Give each student a copy of the main part of the activity, a name card and a paper clip. Tell them to read the instructions and to write down their meals in the boxes. They will also need to copy this information onto a separate sheet of paper. While they are doing this, write the following sentence on the board:

'This is a small, soft, red summer fruit. I like to eat it with something soft, sweet and very cold that is made with milk or cream and which you keep in the freezer.'

❸ After about six to eight minutes, tell them to stop and to write their name on the name card. This should be attached to their completed menu sheet with the paper clip. When they have done this, they should pass the menu sheet back to you.

❹ Redistribute the menus around the class. The name cards are for your reference only, so that you do not return the menus to the students who wrote them (remove these as you redistribute the menus, *making sure that the students you give the menus to do not see them*). Ideally, you should try to distribute the menus to students who are not close to the students who wrote them and so are less likely to identify the handwriting.

❺ Explain that the students are now going to try to get 'their' menus back. They will do this as follows:

- Each student describes their meal to the rest of the class. They can refer to the duplicate information they wrote down, *but they are not allowed to use the words from this, or the words they wrote on their menu sheet.* Instead, they should try to paraphrase by describing colour, texture, taste, shape, size, whether it's eaten hot or cold, etc. The sentence you have written on the board is an example of this for strawberries and ice cream. If they cannot think of suitable words to describe, for example, taste and texture, help them by offering extra information (for example, if they are describing a soup, you could explain that it's a *liquid*).

- While they are doing this, the other students look at the menu sheet they have been given. If they think the description by the speaking student matches the information on their sheet, they write that student's name on that sheet.

The students then return the menus to the students who they thought wrote them.

A perfect meal

Instructions

Imagine that you are going to plan your favourite meal, deciding on a starter, a main course and a dessert.

Write down the name of each course (either in English or in your own language if it doesn't have an English-language equivalent) in the boxes below. If the main ingredients of the dish are not obvious from its name, write a short list of these. You have about six to eight minutes to do this. You should also copy the information onto a separate sheet of paper. It is important that no one else can see what you have written.

Your menu   DO NOT LET ANYONE ELSE SEE THIS CARD

<table>
<tr><td>Your favourite starter
What is it called and/or what are its main ingredients?</td></tr>
<tr><td>(Example: Chicken Caesar salad: lettuce, chicken, cheese, mayonnaise)</td></tr>
</table>

<table>
<tr><td>Your favourite main course
What is it called and/or what are its main ingredients?</td></tr>
<tr><td>(Example: Sukiyaki: beef, soy sauce, mushrooms, eggs)</td></tr>
</table>

<table>
<tr><td>Your favourite dessert
What is it called and/or what are its main ingredients?</td></tr>
<tr><td>(Example: Ice cream and strawberries)</td></tr>
</table>

 -

Name card

<table>
<tr><td>Write your name below and attach this to your completed menu sheet with the paper clip.</td></tr>
</table>

Word list

Unit 10

Note: the numbers show which page the word or phrase first appears on in the unit.

book *v* (88) to arrange to use or do something at a particular time in the future

borrow *v* (92) to use something that belongs to someone else and give it back later

butcher *n* (92) someone who prepares and sells meat

complain *v* (92) to say that something is wrong or that you are annoyed about something

course *n* (89) a part of a meal

dentist *n* (92) someone who examines and repairs teeth

dish *n* (89) food that is prepared in a particular way as part of a meal

dry cleaner *n* (92) a shop where clothes are cleaned with a special chemical and not water

food *n* (88) something that people and animals eat to keep them alive

fork *n* (92) a small object with three or four points and a handle, that you use to pick up food and eat with

garage *n* (92) a business that repairs or sells cars, and sometimes also sells fuel

glass *n* (94) a hard, transparent substance that objects such as windows and bottles are made of

hairdresser *n* (92)
1 someone whose job is to wash, cut, colour, etc. people's hair
2 the place where you go to have your hair washed, cut, coloured, etc.

hairdryer *n* (94) a piece of electrical equipment for drying your hair with hot air

hammer *n* (94) a tool with a heavy, metal part at the top that you use to hit nails into something

knife *n* (94) a sharp tool or weapon for cutting, usually with a metal blade and a handle

ladder *n* (94) a piece of equipment which is used to reach high places, consisting of short steps fixed between two long sides

library *n* (92) a room or building that contains a collection of books and other written material that you can read or borrow

loaf *n* (91) bread that has been baked in one large piece so that it can be cut into smaller pieces

make an appointment *v* (92) to arrange to do something at a particular time

meal *n* (88) when you eat, or the food that you eat at that time

metal *n* (94) a usually hard, shiny material such as iron, gold, or silver which heat and electricity can travel through

packet *n* (91) a small container that contains several of the same thing

plastic *n* (94) a light, artificial substance that can be made into different shapes when it is soft and is used in a lot of different ways

plate n (90) a flat, round object which is used for putting food on

post office *n* (92) a place where you can buy stamps and send letters and parcels

repair *v* (92) to fix something that is broken or damaged

taste *n* (88)
1 the flavour of a particular food in your mouth
2 the ability to judge what is attractive or suitable, especially in things related to art, style, beauty, etc.

travel agent *n* (92) someone whose job is making travel arrangements for people

tube *n* (91) a long, thin container for a soft substance, that you press to get the substance out

wood *n* (94) the hard material that trees are made of

Complete PET by Emma Heyderman and Peter May with Rawdon Wyatt © Cambridge University Press 2010 PHOTOCOPIABLE

Unit 11 Conserving nature

Unit objectives

- **Topics:** the natural world, the environment
- **Listening Part 2:** highlighting key words in stems and options
- **Reading Part 4:** matching options with relevant words in text
- **Speaking Part 4:** giving examples
- **Writing Part 3:** (*letter*) checking for mistakes
- **Grammar:** the passive (present and past simple), comparative and superlative adverbs
- **Vocabulary:** noun suffixes
- **Pronunciation:** word stress with suffixes, weak forms in passives
- **Exam round-up**

Starting off

❶ Ask what *conserving* in the title means, and elicit *conservation*. Explain or translate any new words, e.g. *left-handed, ostriches*. Allow time for discussion.

Answers
B 3   C 7   D 8   E 1   F 4   G 6   H 2

2 T   3 T   4 F Ostriches swallow small stones to help digest food, so they briefly have to put their heads into the ground to pick up stones. This is where the myth comes from. When frightened they run – at over 60 kph.   5 T   6 F In zoos, mice are often seen running close to their trunks but the elephants completely ignore them. Probably a myth from films like *Dumbo*.   7 F Bats have very small eyes but use them in daylight to navigate, particularly over long distances.   8 T

❷ Point out that this excludes zoos, etc. Allow time for discussion: some may (wrongly) think there are tigers in Africa, polar bears in the Antarctic, etc. Encourage the use of names of continents, countries and regions, correcting pronunciation where necessary.

Answers
1 tigers – Asia   2 polar bears – the Arctic
3 kangaroos – Australia   4 ostriches – Africa
5 lions – Africa/Asia   6 elephants – Asia/Africa
7 bats – all continents except Antarctica   8 bears – South America / North America / Europe / Asia

❸ These could be questions about any kind of animals, birds, fish, etc., including pets. Examples: *butterflies taste with their feet (true), penguins can jump nearly two metres in the air (true), all zebras have the same markings (false – they're all different).*

Alternative treatment Prior to the lesson, set this as a homework task for groups. They research the information and then quiz each other in the lesson.

Extension idea Broaden the questions so that they make statements such as *Africa is the driest continent.* (False – it's Antarctica), *There is more water in the Amazon than any other river.* (True – more than the next five biggest rivers in the world combined).

Listening Part 2

❶ Ask the class, prompting if necessary.

Alternative treatment Prior to the lesson, students research India using the Internet or encyclopedias. Make it a project to find the most interesting facts about the country, the people and its wildlife. Discuss these in class before doing the listening tasks.

Suggested answers
India: located in southern Asia – the world's biggest democracy and country with the second-largest population – independence in 1947 led by Gandhi and Nehru – religions include Hinduism, Buddhism and Sikhism – many languages are spoken but Hindi is the official language and English quite widely used – nowadays has a rapidly growing economy and is an emerging superpower

Biggest cities: Mumbai, Delhi (both over 10 million people)

Famous for: River Ganges, Taj Mahal; Bollywood films

Wildlife: tigers, elephants, monkeys, snakes and many other tropical rainforest plants and animals

❷ Allow time for discussion, referring back to earlier units if necessary. Then elicit the answers, ensuring everyone has the correct details.

Answers
2 one or two   3 twice   4 six   5 three   6 kind
7 key   8 similar   9 own   10 second

❸ Remind the class that they are unlikely to hear the same words as those used in the questions / unfinished statements and options, but they will hear expressions that have related meanings. These may mean the same, e.g. *wonderful view / the most amazing thing I've ever seen from the window of a hotel*, or the opposite: *relax on, big soft / uncomfortable* and *long way / actually inside*. Allow time for them to underline the words in 2–6, but point out that opinions may differ on what the key words are.

Suggested answers

2 guide, knew, tiger   A he, seen   B another, watching   C animals, noticed
3 got on, elephant   A ladder   B tree   C car
4 saw, tiger   A resting, meal   B sleeping
C looking, food
5 safe, believed A never attack, humans   B not attack, elephant   C too old
6 allowed   A get out   B feed   C photograph

---

❹ 🎧 Play the recording twice, in exam conditions.

Answers
1 B   **2** C   **3** C   **4** A   **5** B   **6** C

Recording script   CD2 Track 14

Interviewer: So tell us, Lucy, what happened when you got to the National Park?

Lucy: To be honest, I'd had a bad night travelling. The train wasn't very comfortable and I hadn't slept much. So I was happy to get to my hotel room and relax on the big soft bed there. Then I opened the curtains and there in the river, only 50 metres away, were several elephants having a bath! It was the most amazing thing I've ever seen from the window of a hotel. As the advertisement said, it was actually inside the park.
The next morning I set off by car with a guide and two other tourists, Jeff and Mel. Two hours later, our guide had a radio message to say there were reports of a tiger in the north, so we drove up that way. The guide that reported it said he had heard the monkeys warning each other of danger, and although he hadn't actually seen the tiger, their cries meant there was probably one nearby. We reached the area and there I saw our transport into the forest: an elephant! Ajay, the rider, told us to climb on, but it wasn't immediately clear how. There was no wooden ladder, and although there were plenty of trees

around, their branches were too high up. In the end we got up on the roof of the vehicle, then jumped on, and after some preparations, we set off.

It was great fun, and I found that an elephant can go just about anywhere. Suddenly Ajay pointed. 'There,' he said, and less than ten metres away was a magnificent 200-kilo male tiger. 'Quite small,' he said (though it looked huge to me). It was lying under the trees and at first I thought it was asleep. But then it raised its head slightly and looked, in a rather bored way, in our direction. It had obviously eaten recently. I was rather glad it wasn't feeling hungry, but Ajay told us that in India people are very rarely eaten by tigers. That was good to know! He also explained that tigers don't mind being approached by elephants, so we were in no danger. As we went slowly round the beautiful black, orange and white animal, I realised that was true. I'd read that most attacks on humans are by old or injured tigers, but this creature was young and fit. There were no rules against taking pictures of tigers, so I took lots with my new camera; but then, sadly, we had to leave. We passed some monkeys in the trees soon after and Mel wanted to throw them some food but Ajay stopped her, saying it wasn't good for them. Soon we reached the car and on our way back we drove around a lake. It was just wonderful there and I asked the guide if we could stop and go for a short walk. But he said we had to stay in the vehicle at all times. Except to climb onto an elephant, of course!

Vocabulary
Suffixes: *-ion, -ation, -ment*

❶ Focus on the suffixes in the heading, then pairs answer the three questions. Give more examples of verb-to-noun changes, e.g. *organise/organisation*. Point out the spelling change with *-ation* is usually from *-e* (the final *e* is dropped), but can also be from *-y* (*qualify/qualification* the *y* changes to an *i*).

There is no change if there is no final vowel: *relax/ relaxation*. Also explain that the final *e* is dropped before the suffix *-ion* if the verb ends in a vowel, e.g. *educate/education*. Other changes can occur, e.g. *introduce/introduction*, but leave those until Exercise 2.

Answers
1 advertise, prepare, direct   2 (suffixes are underlined) advertise*ment*, prepar*ations*, direc*tion*; *preparations* is the plural noun   3 *preparations* drops the final *e* from the verb form *prepare*; (because) the suffix begins with a vowel

❷ Stress that what matters here is the suffix added, not the noun ending, and that some need an extra spelling change (dropping the final *e* before *-ion* and *-ation*). Go through the answers, pointing out that verbs such as *apply*, *qualify* and *multiply* form nouns by dropping the final *y* and adding *-ication*, e.g. *application*.

Answers

-ment	-ation	-ion
announcement	admiration	attraction
development	confirmation	celebration
disappointment	examination	collection
enjoyment	information	completion
entertainment	invitation	connection
excitement	relaxation	creation
improvement	reservation	discussion
movement		education
replacement		invention
		pollution
		prevention
		protection
		translation

Extension idea Elicit more by prompting with the verb form, e.g. *communicate/communication, conserve/ conservation, argue/argument*, plus more irregular ones such as *describe/description, explain/explanation, register/registration, pronounce/pronunciation*. Ask them to spell both, and check for correct word stress in the nouns.

❸ Encourage pairs to say these out aloud, noticing that the stress normally falls on the syllable before the suffix, or on the *a* in the case of *-ation* suffixes. There are exceptions, e.g. *adver*tisement, *ar*gument, but penultimate syllable stress is usual.

Answers
att*ra*ction, celeb*ra*tion, col*le*ction, com*ple*tion, confir*ma*tion, con*ne*ction, cre*a*tion, de*ve*lopment, disap*poin*tment, dis*cu*ssion, edu*ca*tion, en*joy*ment, enter*tain*ment, exami*na*tion, ex*cite*ment, im*prove*ment, infor*ma*tion, in*ven*tion, invi*ta*tion, *move*ment, pollution, pre*ven*tion, pro*te*ction, rela*xa*tion, re*place*ment, reser*va*tion, trans*la*tion

❹ Begin with gist questions that require the students to read the whole text, e.g. *What do the scientists want people to do?* (Contact them if they find the ducks). *Why do they think this will happen?* (A reward is offered). Then they read more carefully and fill in the gaps with the noun forms, all of which they have seen in Exercise 2. Do not go through the answers yet.

❺ 🎧 Play the recording and get them to correct their own work.

Answers
2 invention   3 direction   4 movement
5 connection   6 translation   7 invitation
8 disappointment   9 attraction   10 celebration

Recording script   CD2 Track 15

Presenter: NASA scientists are aiming to get useful information about global warming from their latest invention: Arctic rubber ducks. They have put 90 of the toys into holes in a Greenland glacier, a huge mass of ice moving in the direction of the sea. They hope that icebergs and pieces of ice with the ducks inside will melt and then be found by local people. This will tell the scientists a lot about the movement of this glacier, why this is faster in summer, and its connection with global warming. Each duck has the words *science experiment* and *reward* on it, with a translation into two other languages. There is also an email address and an invitation to write to NASA. So far, to the disappointment of the scientists, nobody has emailed. But they believe the attraction of a big reward will bring results. So, if you find a NASA rubber duck on a beach near you, it could be a cause for celebration!

❻ 🎧 Play the recording of the ten answers from Exercises 4 and 5. Get them to repeat, ensuring correct word stress.

Answers
(*Underlinings show word stress*)   1 infor*ma*tion
2 in*ven*tion   3 di*re*ction   4 *move*ment
5 con*ne*ction   6 trans*la*tion   7 invi*ta*tion
8 disap*poin*tment   9 att*ra*ction   10 celeb*ra*tion

Recording script CD2 Track 16

Presenter:	One.
Man:	Inform<u>a</u>tion
Presenter:	Two.
Woman:	In<u>ve</u>ntion
Presenter:	Three.
Man:	Di<u>re</u>ction
Presenter:	Four.
Woman:	<u>Mo</u>vement
Presenter:	Five.
Man:	Con<u>ne</u>ction
Presenter:	Six.
Woman:	Transl<u>a</u>tion
Presenter:	Seven.
Man:	Invit<u>a</u>tion
Presenter:	Eight.
Woman:	Disap<u>po</u>intment
Presenter:	Nine.
Man:	Att<u>ra</u>ction
Presenter:	Ten.
Woman:	Celebr<u>a</u>tion

Grammar

The passive: present and past simple

❶ Allow time for pairs to discuss the sentences, then elicit the answers. These will be reinforced when they complete the usage rules in Exercise 2.

> **Answers**
> 1 A and C are active; B and D are passive 2 C and D describe an event in the past 3 B and D 4 A: subject – tigers; object – people. B: subject – people; agent – tigers (using *by*) 5 C: subject – guides; object – tourists. D: subject – tourists; no object 6 information not in sentence D: *who* allowed the tourists to take photos (the guides)

❷ Pairs study sentences A–D again and decide on their answers. Check answers and understanding of each point.

> **Answers**
> 2 A 3 P 4 A 5 P

❸ Check the answers.

> **Answers**
> 3 are seen 4 was chased 5 are the crocodiles fed
> 6 was not noticed

❹ 🎧 Play the recording more than once, pausing if necessary to repeat the unstressed auxiliary verbs. Model the /ə/ sound if students have difficulty with this phoneme: it may not exist in their first language.

Recording script CD2 Track 17

	One.
Man:	These are known as the 'Spring Gardens'.
	Two.
Woman:	The flowers were planted in March.
	Three.
Man:	The grass was cut in April and May.

❺ Students can do these individually or in pairs.

> **Answers**
> 2 Two giraffes were seen near the trees. 3 A poem was written about this waterfall. 4 Rice is grown in the east of the country. 5 The moon was hidden by one small cloud. 6 Cars aren't / are not allowed in the National Park. 7 The forest was partly destroyed by fire. 8 We weren't / were not told about the crocodiles in the river.

❻ 🎧 After they hear the answers, make sure everyone has the correct words, particularly the auxiliary verbs. Then they practise saying the passive sentences they have written. You may want to repeat the recording, or demonstrate the pronunciation of the negative auxiliaries *aren't* and *weren't*, which are not weak forms.

Recording script CD2 Track 18

	One.
Woman:	A lot of fish are caught here.
	Two.
Man:	Two giraffes were seen near the trees.
	Three.
Woman:	A poem was written about this waterfall.
	Four.
Man:	Rice is grown in the east of the country.
	Five.
Woman:	The moon was hidden by one small cloud.
	Six.
Man:	Cars aren't allowed in the National Park.
	Seven.
Woman:	The forest was partly destroyed by fire.
	Eight.
Man:	We weren't told about the crocodiles in the river.

Reading Part 4

❶ Answer questions on any expressions other than the eight in the task. Encourage the use of contextual clues to work out the meanings and match them with the phrases given. Remind the class that Reading Part 4 requires identification of words with similar meanings (parallel expressions).

> **Answers**
> **b 4** vehicles used by everyone – public transport,   **c 7** things that are thrown away – rubbish,   **d 3** using less electricity, gas, etc. – energy conservation,   **e 1** changes in the Earth's weather – climate change,   **f 6** big container for empty bottles – bottle bank,   **g 8** power from the sun – solar energy,   **h 5** using materials again - recycling

❷ Students work individually. Give them no more than a few minutes for this. The aim is to read quickly to establish the purpose of the text. Elicit the answer.

Background information The International Climate Champions project is run by the British Council: http://www.britishcouncil.org/climatechange-climatechampions.htm.

> **Answer**
> C

❸ Students try to answer Question 2 in their own words, then they focus on A–D. Point out that the distractors always come from within the text, so for this kind of item – unlike items 1 and 5 in Reading Part 4 – they can find evidence that each one is incorrect, or is not relevant. They can also find evidence for the correct answer. Elicit this and discuss the reasons why the distractors are wrong.

> **Answers**
> **1** D (correct answer)   **2** C (the word *import* tells us that the oil and gas come from abroad, not from under the sea)   **3** A (the text says the opposite: there is still *no pollution*)   **4** B (text says they are *in danger* – not that they have already disappeared)

❹ Students now apply the technique from Exercise 3 to the other two items that focus on specific parts of the text. To avoid underlining in the book, they could note down the expressions and mark each one A/B/C/D, or pencil in A/B/C/D next to the relevant parts. Check, and elicit the answers to exam questions 3 (C) and 4 (B).

> **Answers**
> **3** **A** 'the only way to prevent the situation getting even worse' (it is not certain it will get worse – there is one way to prevent it)
>
> **B** 'the air pollution that leads to global warming' ('leads to' means 'cause')
>
> **C** (correct answer) 'Chinese student Ding Yinghan'; 'it is unfair to say that just one country – his own – is causing climate change'; 'the air pollution that leads to global warming comes from many parts of the world'
>
> **D** 'the air pollution that leads to global warming comes from many parts of the world, including poorer countries' (poor countries also cause it)
>
> **4** **A** 'her articles have been published in her local newspaper' (passive – somebody else publishes them)
>
> **B** (correct answer) 'changes in the way teenagers behave are an important way of influencing choices that are made by parents'
>
> **C** 'For her, changes in the way teenagers behave are an important way' (she wants young people to do things differently rather than follow their parents' example)
>
> **D** 'She's against young people's general lack of interest in politics' (she thinks they should become interested in politics)

Extension idea For homework, students study any Reading Part 4 texts they have already done, either from this course or other PET material published by Cambridge University Press. They follow the same procedure as here, matching the relevant parts of the text with the options for questions that focus on detail, opinion or attitude.

❺ Remind the class that the information for Question 5 may be located in any part of the text. Allow several minutes for this, then check.

> **Answer**
> B

> **Suggested answers**
> **A:** 'I'm the only one from our country' (Every country has three champions: 'Each country involved selects three teenagers')
>
> **C:** 'already three of us from every country in the world' (Not 'every country in the world', only 13: 'At present, 13 countries are involved'; 'more countries are expected to join soon')
>
> **D:** 'Some of us are teenagers' (All of them are teenagers: 'young people of school age'; 'three teenagers')

> **Answers**
> 1 yes 2 opinion and attitude 3 general meaning
> 4 the text 5 yes 6 usually in one paragraph

❻ For the discussion of specific attitudes that could be changed, encourage the use of expressions such as *recycling, public transport* and *solar energy*. They can talk about changing the older generation's attitude to energy conservation, although there will be opportunities to discuss more ways of saving energy – and water – in the Speaking section.

Extension idea Groups discuss *how* young people might go about changing adults' opinions. If necessary, prompt them with ideas such as 'lead by example', 'embarrass them', 'show them the evidence', 'tell them they are harming their children's and grandchildren's future', or even 'point out the financial benefits'.
With some classes (and in certain cultures), you could extend this to influencing older people's attitudes in other areas, e.g. discrimination based on race, gender or disability.

Grammar
Comparative and superlative adverbs

❶ Two of the examples are from the Reading text. Allow a few minutes for pairs to do the task, then check. Point out that one-syllable adverbs, unlike adjectives, normally take *more/most* in the comparative and superlative, although adverbs which are the same as the adjectives (e.g. *fast, hard*) do not. Others, notably *badly* and *well* are completely irregular, while those ending in *y* usually change this to *i*, e.g. *more heavily, most noisily*, etc. The superlative sometimes takes *the*, as in *she worked the hardest*.

> **Answers**
> 1 Students should underline – comparative adverbs: more quickly, more efficiently, worse; superlative adverb: most brightly 2 by adding *more* in front of the adverb 3 worse 4 than 5 by adding *most* in front of the adverb

❷ Allow time to complete the table, then elicit the answers. You may want to get them to add other adverbs such as *strongly, frequently* or *quietly*.

> **Answers**
>
> | adverb | comparative | superlative |
> |---|---|---|
> | quietly | more quietly | (the) most quietly |
> | carefully | more carefully | (the) most carefully |
> | slowly | more slowly | (the) most slowly |
> | easily | more easily | (the) most easily |
> | fast | faster | (the) fastest |
> | badly | worse | (the) worst |
> | hard | harder | (the) hardest |
> | well | better | (the) best |

❸ Point out that most of the words in brackets are adjectives, and need to be changed to adverbs.

> **Answers**
> 2 hardest 3 more cheaply 4 worst 5 more cleanly 6 more heavily

❹ Pairs discuss the points raised in Exercise 3, possibly reporting back to the class.

Extension idea Using similar sentences, pairs continue the discussion on climate change. Feed in more adverbs such as *strongly, warmly, widely, violently* and *dangerously* for the weather, and *carefully, easily, sensibly, honestly* and *efficiently* for the suggested action. With a strong class, encourage the use of passive forms using modals, e.g. more *can be done*, money *should be spent*, fuel efficiency *needs to be improved*, ocean currents *could be used*, oil companies *mustn't be allowed* to.

Speaking Part 4

Extension idea If you want the class to practise Part 3 before they do Part 4, follow this procedure now. Put them in pairs and tell them they are going to talk on their own about a photograph of people doing jobs at home. Each says what they can see in their photograph (A or B above Exercise 1), for about a minute. Encourage them to paraphrase any objects they don't know the words for (refer the class back to Unit 10, page 94 if necessary). Limit the topic to what is shown in the picture and what people are doing: the environmental impact and how to avoid it will be discussed in Part 4.

❶ This section uses the pictures for two speaking tasks: practising giving examples in Exercises 2 and 3, and the Part 4 exam-type task in Exercise 4. The two topics of saving water and saving electricity should therefore be kept separate. If necessary, make the difference between 'use' and 'waste' (and possibly also 'lose') clear.

Suggested answers

A: They are wasting water by watering the lawn with a sprinkler instead of leaving the grass to go yellow / waiting for it to rain. They are watering the pots with a hose pipe / with an irrigation system instead of using a watering-can or using collected rainwater from the garden. They are consuming unnecessary water by having a water fountain and a swimming pool. They are using a lot of water to wash the car with a hose pipe and instead could wash the car by hand.

B: They are wasting water by using a washing machine and dishwasher instead of washing dishes and clothes by hand. They have left the tap running, instead of putting a glass of water in the fridge to cool down.

❷ 🎧 Play the recording once or twice and elicit the answers.

Answers
1 water plants later in the day   **2** use a bucket and a sponge to wash the car   **3** wash small quantities of plates or clothes by hand

Recording script   CD2 Track 19

Jake: Well, there's lots you can do to save water at home. In the garden, <u>for instance, it's best to water the plants later in the day</u>. Because if you water them at two o'clock, <u>say</u>, when it's hot, the sun just dries everything out again.

Lily: Right. And if you really must wash the car, <u>there are better ways of doing it than that. With a bucket of water and a sponge, for example</u>. You'd waste much less water, and get a bit of exercise, too.

Jake: It's the same in the kitchen, isn't it? All those things <u>like</u> dishwashers and washing machines that do everything for you. They use a huge amount of water.

Lily: I suppose they save people a lot of hard work when they're full. But if you don't have much to wash, <u>such as</u> a few plates or some socks, <u>you can do them much more quickly by hand. And avoid wasting all that water</u>.

❸ 🎧 Play it again, as many times as you feel it is necessary and pausing if required. Go through the answers, pointing out that *for instance, for example* and *say* often precede or follow a pause, whereas *such as* and *like* are more likely to follow one.

Answers
2 say   **3** for example   **4** like   **5** such as

❹ If necessary, prompt with suggestions, e.g. http://www.cambridgewater.co.uk/about_you/save_home.asp.

Possible answers
'If you want a cold drink, it's better to keep a jug of water in the fridge than run a tap until it gets cold'; 'Don't run the tap while you're brushing your teeth – use a glass of water'; 'Don't wash fruit, vegetables or salad under the tap – use a bowl'; 'Water used for cooking can be re-used, when it's cool, to water plants.'

Exam round-up Go through the answers with the class.

Answers
2 connected with   **3** keep to this topic   **4** a range of tenses   **5** take turns   **6** listening to   **7** asking for more details and their opinions   **8** give reasons and examples

❺ Before they begin the exam task, check understanding of the vocabulary in the 'Saving Energy' leaflet. Monitor pairs and give feedback when they have finished.

Writing Part 3

❶ The class read the instructions, then the model letter for gist, ignoring the errors for now. Check answers. Then they study the letter to find the three mistakes, all of which involve language presented in this unit.

Answers
1 paragraph A: the wildlife in your country; paragraph B: favourite animal; paragraph C: Are there many of them?

2 ~~seen~~ are seen (present simple passive), ~~better~~ best (superlative adverb), ~~easyly~~ easily (spelling of comparative adverb)

❷ ⊙ This revises language points and introduces a correction code. These should be done in pairs, then discussed as a class.

Answers
2 G, I really enjoy being here.   **3** G, ... a new film about animals which is called *The life of animals* ...
4 Sp, ... a film with plenty of excitement ...
5 WO, I don't know what the name of the mountain is.   **6** V, I hope I haven't made a lot of mistakes.

❸ *Exam round-up*

> **Answers**
> **2** True **3** False **4** True **5** False **6** True
> **7** False **8** True

❹ Students do this individually, referring back to Ana's letter for organisation. Don't collect in their completed work yet, as the final stage is peer correction in Exercise 5.

> **Sample answer**
> Hi Justin,
>
> It was great to hear from you. We love pets here and almost everyone has a dog, cat, bird, rabbit or other animal.
>
> People keep pets for different reasons. Many people, particularly those who live on their own, like to have a pet for company. Others need an animal at home – for instance, a huge dog to protect the house, or a cat to catch mice!
>
> Hamsters are my favourite pet. They're friendly, cute and – because they're so tiny – they don't take up much space! Sometimes our hamster Frankie is allowed out of his cage so that he can run round more freely. He really enjoys that!
>
> Well, that's all for now. I hope you can write again soon.
>
> Best wishes,
>
> Ana

❺ Students highlight errors in each other's work, but leave the actual correction to the writer. Give advice if it is not clear whether mistakes have actually been made, or what kind of errors they are. Give them plenty of time to talk through the corrections they have made. This activity provides useful practice with peer correction and could be done with all written work in future.

Unit 11 photocopiable activity: Passive connections Time: 15 mins +

Objectives

- To practise use of the passive (past and present)
- To review key vocabulary from Unit 11
- (In extension) To practise changing verbs to nouns using suffixes

Before class

Make one copy of the activity for each group of three or four students in your class. Cut each into 17 cards along the dotted lines (do not cut along the solid lines on the small cards). Shuffle each set of cards well.

In class

❶ Divide your class into groups of three or four, and give each a set of cards (including the large 'verb' card).

❷ Explain that there are 16 sentences on their cards. The first part of each sentence is on the right side of one card, and the second part is on the left side of another card. Their task is to match the right and left sides of the cards to make 16 complete sentences. The first card has 'Start' on it, and the last card has 'Finish'.

❸ However, to make this more challenging, the main verb in the second part of each sentence has been removed. They can find these verbs on their large card. They should put the verbs into their appropriate sentences, but they will need to change the form of each verb so that it is grammatically correct. All of the sentences use a passive construction (present or past simple).

❹ Stop the activity after ten minutes and review their answers. Award the groups one point for each sentence they correctly joined and one point for each verb correctly used in those sentences (the form must be correct). The winner is the group with the most points, or you could extend the activity as follows:

Extension idea The verbs they have used can also be made into nouns by adding a suffix (-*ion*, -*ation* or -*ment*) and, in some instances, by making other changes to the end of the verb. Most of these appeared in the vocabulary section of Unit 11. In their groups, they change these verbs into nouns (they could also use these nouns in sentences of their own). Stop them after another ten minutes. For each noun they correctly formed, groups get an extra point, which is added to their score from the original activity.

> **Answers**
> The cards are in their correct order on the activity sheet. The words needed to complete them are (in order): *treated, replaced, discussed, protected, entertained, invented, admired, permitted, celebrated, destroyed, reserved, invited, informed, completed, connected.*
>
> The noun forms are: *admiration, celebration, completion, connection, destruction, discussion, entertainment, information, invention, invitation, permission, protection, replacement, reservation, treatment.*

Passive connections

✂ Cut along the dotted lines to divide these into cards.

admire   celebrate   complete   connect   destroy   discuss   entertain   inform

invent   invite   permit   protect   replace   reserve   treat

START →	In the past, some animals in zoos were …	………… very badly.	The old heating system at our school was …
………… with one that was kinder to the environment.	At the meeting, many ideas were …	…………, but nobody could agree on anything.	Animals such as crocodiles and pandas are …
………… by international law.	I hate circuses because I think it's wrong when people are …	………… by animals.	Solar panels, which provide solar energy, were …
………… in 1954.	Sea creatures like dolphins and whales are …	………… by many people because they are beautiful and intelligent.	We could touch some of the animals at the zoo, but we weren't …
………… to feed them.	The 40th anniversary of *Friends of the Earth* was …	………… in 2009.	Somebody dropped a match and as a result half the forest was …
………… by fire.	Places on the nature trip around the bay were …	………… for us by our teacher.	I've always been interested in the environment and last year I was …
………… to a major conference on climate change.	We wanted to visit the nature park, but we were …	………… that it was closed to members of the public.	Work on the new Earth Environment Centre was …
………… at the end of 2008.	The trees in the forest are …	………… by bridges so people can see the wildlife in them more closely.	**FINISH**

Word list

Unit 11

Note: the numbers show which page the word or phrase first appears on in the unit.

advertisement *n* (99) a picture, short film, song, etc. which tries to persuade people to buy a product or service

announcement *n* (99) something that someone says officially, giving information about something

attraction *n* (99) something that makes people come to a place or want to do a particular thing

bat *n* (98) a small animal like a mouse with wings that flies at night

celebration *n* (99) when you celebrate a special day or event

climate change *n* (101) the way the Earth's weather is changing

collection *n* (99) a group of objects of the same type that have been collected by one person or in one place

confirmation *n* (99) an announcement or proof that something is true or certain

connection *n* (99) a relationship between people or things

creature *n* (98) anything that lives but is not a plant

crocodile *n* (100) a big reptile with a long mouth and sharp teeth, that lives in lakes and rivers

development *n* (99) when someone or something grows or changes and becomes more advanced

discussion *n* (99) when people talk about something and tell each other their ideas or opinions

duck *n* (100) a bird with short legs that lives in or near water

energy conservation *n* (101) when you are careful not to waste fuel, etc.

enjoyment *n* (99) when you enjoy something

entertainment *n* (99) shows, films, television, or other performances or activities that entertain people

giraffe *n* (101) a large African animal with a very long neck and long, thin legs

improvement *n* (99) when something gets better or when you make it better

invention *n* (99) something that has been designed or created for the first time

invitation *n* (99) when someone invites you to do something or go somewhere

pet *n* (105) an animal that someone keeps in their home

petrol *n* (101) a liquid fuel used in cars

pollution *n* (99) damage caused to water, air, etc. by harmful substances or waste

preparation *n* (99) the things that you do or the time that you spend preparing for something

protection *n* (99) keeping someone or something safe from harm

recycle *v* (101) to put used paper, glass, plastic, etc. through a process so that it can be used again

replacement *n* (99) the thing or person that replaces something or someone

reservation *n* (99) an arrangement that you make to have a seat on an aircraft, a room in a hotel, etc.

rubbish *n* (101) things that you throw away because you do not want them

save *v* (103) to keep something to use in the future, to stop something from being destroyed

snake *n* (98) a long, thin creature with no legs that slides along the ground

stand-by *n* (104) something that is ready to be used if needed

translation *n* (99) something which has been translated from one language to another, or the process of translating

waste *v* (104) to use too much of something or use something badly when there is a limited amount of it

wildlife *n* (98) animals, birds, and plants living in their natural environment

 Complete PET by Emma Heyderman and Peter May with Rawdon Wyatt © Cambridge University Press 2010

Unit 12 What did you say?

Unit objectives

- **Topics:** language and social interaction
- **Listening Part 3:** following the exam advice
- **Reading Part 3:** ignoring irrelevant difficult words
- **Speaking Part 3:** describing a photo
- **Writing Part 3:** (*story*) organisation and linking, typical mistakes with past tense and plural forms
- **Grammar:** reported speech (statements, commands, questions and other changes), indirect questions
- **Vocabulary:** slang words, *speak, talk, say, tell* and *ask for,* prepositions of place
- **Exam round-up**

Starting off

❶ Focus on the Martian picture to make sure students understand what a Martian is.

❷ Encourage the students to give full answers.

Reading Part 3

❶ *Geek* and *dork* have a negative connotation whereas *dude* is positive.

> **Answers**
> **1** geek **2** dude **3** dork

❷ In a monolingual class, students can compare to see if they use the same slang words. In a multilingual group, students should be encouraged to compare whether they have slang for the same words in their different languages.

❸

> **Suggested answer**
> The text is about *Martian*. This language has been created by Chinese teenagers to talk with their friends online.

❹

> **Suggested answers**
> **2** Young people … first … Martian … Taiwan;
> **3** film *Shaolin Soccer,* Zhao Wei comes … Mars;
> **4** Teenagers … use the Internet … called Martians;
> **5** Software companies … selling programs … help … write … Martian; **6** Ms Li … never … read messages … Mei's computer; **7** When Mei starts writing … Martian … uses other people's work;
> **8** Wang Haiyong allows … students … homework in Martian; **9** Bei Bei Song considers herself … up to date; **10** Bei Bei … approves of Martian

❺

> **Answer**
> Sentence 2; No, you don't need to understand *spread*.

❻

> **Answers**
> **1** Correct – 80% of teenagers aged between 15 and 19 in China use this language when they send messages or chat with each other online
>
> **2** Correct – It became popular in Taiwan in 2004 and three years later, it spread to mainland China
>
> **3** Incorrect – She isn't really a visitor from Mars
>
> **4** Incorrect – anyone who acts strangely there is known as a Martian … the language which teenagers in China enjoy creating is also known as Martian
>
> **5** Correct – people are buying special software to translate between Chinese and Martian
>
> **6** Incorrect – she could not understand the emails from Mei's friends
>
> **7** Correct – At first, I just copy words from texts which my friends have already written in Martian
>
> **8** Incorrect – I refuse to mark my students' work when they use this language
>
> **9** Correct – but she doesn't think she's old-fashioned
>
> **10** Incorrect – she thinks that this language is really silly

Extension idea Encourage the students to comment briefly on their reactions to the text.

❼

> **Suggested answers**
> 1 incorrect / false   2 words / information / details
> 3 text   4 word / phrase / sentence

Vocabulary
Speak, *talk*, *say*, *tell* and *ask for*

❶ *Alternative treatment* Write the example sentences from the *Cambridge Learner's Dictionary* on the board without the verbs. Invite the students to complete the sentences with a suitable verb, e.g. *She* . . . . *French*.

❷

> **Answers**
> 2 told   3 speak   4 say   5 told   6 ask for

❸ With a weaker class, write the suggested answers below on the board in a different order for the students to copy onto their mind map.

> **Answers**
> 1 talk   2 speak   3 say   4 tell   5 ask   6 ask for

> **Suggested answers**
> 1 (together) about a topic, online   2 to someone (about)   3 something to somebody, *cheese* (when you take someone's photo)   4 the time, the difference (between)   5 someone to do something, someone about something   6 more food, someone's opinion

❹ Give the class a couple of example questions first.

> **Suggested questions**
> 1 How many languages can you speak well?
> 2 Do you always say 'hello' to everyone when you walk into the classroom?
> 3 Are you good at telling jokes?
> 4 If you don't understand, do you ask questions?
> 5 Do you talk to your friends about your future plans?

Grammar
Reported speech and reported commands

❶ Ask students if they have raised money for a project (e.g. a trip) and how.

❷ 🎧 After listening, invite a discussion on which event the students would vote for.

> **Answers**
> **Scott**: disco; **William**: football match;
> **Gina**: non-uniform day

Recording script   CD2 Track 20

Ruby:	Shh! Be quiet! Close the door, Paul!
Paul:	OK!
Ruby:	Thanks. Er, Tania, can you take notes today?
Tania:	Oh, is it my turn to be secretary? OK.
Ruby:	Right. As you know, we have to decide what event we're going to organise for the *Schools for All project*. Er, any ideas? Yes, Scott?
Scott:	OK. Last year we organised a disco to collect money. We can organise a similar event again.
Ruby:	Hmm. I think Year 10 are going to organise a party this year. Has anyone else got any other ideas? William?
William:	Yeah, we've thought about organising a football match.
Ruby:	Another football match? There are matches here every Saturday.
William:	In my sister's school, the students are going to play against the teachers.
Ruby:	But the teachers here wouldn't want to play football.
William:	It doesn't have to be just teachers. Ellie's dad could play. He used to play football for United.
Ruby:	But how are we going to raise money?
William:	The adults will have to pay to play.
Ruby:	Sounds good. Hmm. Er, anyone else? Gina?
Gina:	Yes. Today we're all wearing school uniform and we all look the same. Who hates wearing school uniform?
All:	Well … I really don't like …
Gina:	So our idea is to have a day when we don't wear school uniform. We can wear what we want to school.
Ruby:	And the money?
Gina:	We'll pay to wear what we want.
Ruby:	Oh! Thanks. Right. Think about the suggestions. And don't forget the meeting tomorrow. We'll take a vote then.

❸ ❹ 🎧 The students will listen to a different recording to check their answers.

> **Answers**
> 1 had organised a disco to collect money 2 could organise a similar event again 3 'd/had thought about organising a football match 4 were going to play against the teachers 5 (that) it didn't have to be just teachers 6 were all wearing school uniform 7 would pay to wear

Recording script CD2 Track 21

Nina: Hi, Tania. Sorry I didn't get to the meeting yesterday. What did you decide?

Tania: Oh, hi, Nina. There's going to be another meeting today at 1 pm to take a vote. We have to think about the three suggestions.

Nina: What three suggestions? Did anyone take notes?

Tania: Yeah! I was the secretary. I've got them written here. Let me see. Oh yes, Scott said that they had organised a disco to collect money the year before and they could organise a similar event again.

Nina: But isn't Year 10 going to organise a party?

Tania: Er, yes, that's what Ruby said. Then William said they had thought about organising a football match.

Nina: Not another football match.

Tania: Well, not exactly … he said in his sister's school, the students were going to play against the teachers. He also said that it didn't have to be just teachers. It could be any adult – like Ellie's dad who used to be a football player. William said the adults would have to pay to play.

Nina: You said there were three suggestions, didn't you?

Tania: Yes, the third came from Gina. She reminded us that we were all wearing school uniform that day and that she hated wearing school uniform. She suggested a day when we wouldn't have to wear school uniform. She said we would pay to wear what we wanted.

Nina: Oh … good idea!

❺

> **Answers**
> 2 past continuous 3 past perfect 4 past perfect / past simple 5 *would* + infinitive 6 *was/were going to* 7 *could*

❻ For more information on other changes to adverbs, pronouns, etc. in reported speech, refer the students to the Grammar reference section.

> **Answers**
> 2 the year before 3 his/her 4 they/we

❼ Make sure that the students make the appropriate changes to the pronouns.

> **Answers**
> 2 (that) someone had left / left their/his/her MP3 player in the kitchen after the party 3 (that) he was having a great time there 4 (that) he wanted to sell his bike so he could buy a new one

❽ Encourage the students to write at least 50 words for each situation.

❾

> **Answers**
> 2 to close the door 3 to think about the suggestions 4 to forget the meeting

❿

> **Answers**
> 2 not to worry 3 not to touch anything 4 not to forget to phone

Listening Part 3

❶ If the answer is false, encourage the students to explain why.

> **Answers**
> 1 True 2 False (there is extra information which you don't need to understand to complete the notes) 3 True 4 True 5 False (use the second listening to check your answers) 6 False (make a guess – you will not lose marks for a wrong answer)

❷ Ask the students if they have ever entered a competition which tests a skill, e.g. a drawing or a short-story competition.

> **Suggested questions**
> 1 How old do I have to be to enter the competition? 2 Can I enter with a friend? 3 Can I choose the topic of my website? 4 What language should I write the website in? 5 When do I have to send you my website?

❸ Encourage the students to predict the missing information in the notes.

4 🎧 Encourage peer correction before open class feedback.

> **Answers**
> **1** coach   **2** 19   **3** (school) subject   **4** (online) library   **5** Australia   **6** November

Recording script   CD2 Track 22

Head: Quiet!! I'd like to introduce Gerry Tremain from *Web Challenge*. He's going to tell you about an exciting website competition.

Gerry: Thank you. Hi, everyone! I'm going to talk about the *Web Challenge*, which is an exciting competition for young people all over the world who are interested in designing websites. Although the website should be written in English, we do encourage you to provide links to translations into several other languages, including your own.

Firstly, you'll need to get your team together. All teams need a coach. The coach should be a teacher, librarian or assistant working in a school. In each team, there should be three to six members who are school students, in addition to the coach. The competition is open to students who are in full-time education who are no younger than nine and no older than 19. There are three age groups: 19 and Under, 15 and Under and 12 and Under.

Once you've got your team together, you'll have to choose a topic that interests you. Think about a favourite school subject, or things you like to do in your free time. You're now ready to build your website. Don't forget that your website will need to be uploaded to our server.

Prizes for competition winners include laptop computers, digital cameras and money for your school to spend on new technology. Every team that enters will have their site published on our online library. First-prize winners in each age group will win a seven-day trip to Australia where you'll take part in workshops, events and excursions.

And finally a word about dates. All interested teams need to register for the competition by the end of November. Your final website should be on our server by April 14th. Now winners will be announced on July 1st. You can get further information by contacting our hotline on 098764444 or by looking at our website: www.webchallenge.com.

Grammar
Reported questions

As a warmer Invite the students to recap on what they know about the Web Challenge competition.

1

> **Suggested questions**
> What software can we use to design the website?; Does the topic have to be very original?; How big should the website be?

2 3 🎧 Remind students that Gerry might not answer all the questions.

Alternative treatment Add a competitive element by awarding students a point if their follow-up question is answered.

> **Answers**
> **2** Jade   **3** Julian   **4** Hamad   **5** Haley

Extension idea Students think of sensible answers for any unanswered questions.

Recording script   CD2 Track 23

Head: Thank you, Gerry. I'm sure some of you have got questions. Yes, Nadia?

Nadia: Can I enter the competition on my own?

Gerry: Interesting question. No … the aim of the competition is to encourage young people to share ideas and work together.

Head: Who's next? Yes, Jade?

Jade: Does our coach have to work in our school?

Gerry: No, not in your school, but this person does need to be working in *a* school, for example it could be the French assistant in Woods High School

Head: Yes, Julian?

Julian: Sounds brilliant. How do we register for the competition?

Gerry: It's easy. Log on to our website and fill in the application form online.

Head: I think you're next, Hamad?

Hamad: What do we do if we have technical problems?

Gerry: Very good question. If you read the rules on our website, you'll see that if you are unable to upload your website because of problems with our server, we'll do everything we can to help you.

Head: Anyone else? Yes, Haley?

Haley: If we win, what will we see in Australia?

Gerry: Once again, full details of the prizes are on our website but I can tell you that it will be a trip you'll never forget!

4

> **Answers**
> 2 Does our coach have to work in our school?
> 3 How do we register for the competition?
> 4 What do we do if we have technical problems?
> 5 What will we see in Australia?

5

> **Answers**
> b usually changes like in reported speech
> c never   d isn't   e don't use

6

> **Answers**
> 2 she was   3 Do you want   4 they were going
> 5 if they had

Indirect questions

1

> **Suggested answer**
> Nadia says they took a boat trip around Sydney
> harbour and that their hotel had views over the
> harbour.

Recording script   CD2 Track 24

Journalist: Hello, Nadia. Congratulations on winning the prize! <u>I was wondering if I could ask you some questions about your trip.</u> It must have been amazing!

Nadia: Thanks. Yes, it was an amazing trip. We saw so many things.

Journalist: I'm sure. So, your flight landed in Sydney, didn't it? <u>Firstly I'd like to know what you thought of Sydney.</u>

Nadia: Well, before we won the prize, I thought Sydney was the capital of Australia, but it isn't. Canberra is the capital. Anyway, Sydney is enormous but the thing I noticed first was all the water. On the first day <u>we took a boat trip around Sydney harbour.</u>

Journalist: <u>I can't remember where you stayed in Sydney. Could you tell me where your hotel was?</u>

Nadia: Yes, we stayed in <u>a hotel with views over the harbour.</u>

Journalist: <u>Tell me what you visited in Australia, apart from Sydney.</u>

Nadia: Well, we went to …

2 Encourage students to try to complete the journalist's questions before they listen again.

> **Answers**
> 2 thought   3 you stayed   4 your hotel was
> 5 you visited

3

> **Answers**
> 2 you think of Sydney   3 you stay in Sydney
> 4 your hotel   5 you visit in Australia apart from
> Sydney

4 The students look at the examples in Exercise 2.

> **Answers**
> 2 stays the same   3 never   4 isn't   5 sometimes

5

> **Answer**
> In *reported* questions the *tense changes* and we
> *never* use a question mark. In *indirect* questions
> the *tense doesn't change* and we *sometimes* use a
> question mark.

Extension idea Invite the students to continue the journalist's interview with Nadia. Provide some information on Australia (e.g. www.australia.com). As a follow-up, students write an article for the school newspaper.

Vocabulary
Prepositions of place

As a warmer Describe the location of an object in your house, e.g. a picture, flower vase, etc. and the students should draw a diagram of its location.

1 2 Pause the recording between each question. Allow the students time to complete and compare their diagrams.

Recording script   CD2 Track 25

One. Where are Todd's keys?

Adam: Hi, Todd.

Todd: Hi, Adam. I was wondering if you could do me a favour?

Adam: Depends. What?

Todd: Look, I've left my keys at home. Can you bring them to school?

Adam: Sure. Where are they?

Todd: Right. <u>Go into my bedroom. On my desk, next to the lamp is a box. The keys should be inside the box.</u>

Adam: <u>OK. In a box on your desk.</u> I'll ring you back if I can't find them.

	Two. Where's the sports shop?
Karyn:	Dayton Sports. Karyn speaking.
Kylie:	Hi. I'd like to know if you've got any football gloves, size 8.
Karyn:	I'll just have a look for you … hmm … yes, we do.
Kylie:	Great. Could you tell me where your shop is?
Karyn:	Yes. Do you know where the central library is?
Kylie:	Er, yes.
Karyn:	Go past the library, **over** the bridge. We're **between** a bookshop and a hairdresser's, **opposite** the pet shop.
Kylie:	Ah! I think I know where you are.
	Three. Where's Elen, Imogen's cousin?
Nick:	I've never met your cousin Elen. What does she look like?
Imogen:	I think I've got a photo of her. Yes, here it is.
Nick:	Wow! Is that your family?
Imogen:	Yes. Can you see my aunt holding a baby? **In front of** her are my five little cousins.
Nick:	Ah! They look lovely. Has your aunt really got six children?
Imogen:	No! Three of them are my dad's brother's children.
Nick:	Oh! So where's Elen?
Imogen:	Well, **on the right** is my uncle. He's wearing sunglasses.
Nick:	Oh yes. Why didn't he take them off for the photo?
Imogen:	I don't know. My cousin Elen is standing **behind** my uncle. She's starting at our high school in September.
Nick:	She looks fun. I can't wait to meet her.

❸ Demonstrate this activity on the board first.

> **Suggested answers**
> **Picture 1**: label the box *on the desk*, the lamp *next to the box*, the keys *in/inside the box*
>
> **Picture 2**: write *over* above the bridge, label the sports shop *between bookshop and hairdresser*, also label sports shop *opposite pet shop*
>
> **Picture 3**: label five little cousins *in front of aunt*, uncle with sunglasses *on the right*, Elen *behind uncle*

❹ ❺ *Alternative treatment* Set a five-minute time limit to see which pair can complete their plans correctly within the time set. Those who don't do the task in English or look at their partner's plan have to stop speaking for five seconds.

(118) **Unit 12**

Speaking Part 3

 Ask the students to look at the two photos and predict the examiner's question.

> **Suggested answers**
> **1** on your own / one minute **2** describe what you can see **3** use one of the expressions from Unit 10 **4** use a suitable preposition

❸ *Alternative treatment* With a weaker class, model a good description first.

Writing Part 3

❶ *Alternative treatment* Divide the students into smaller groups of four or five. Student 1 begins the story, using one of the sentences as the first line. When you shout 'Stop!', Student 2 continues until you shout 'Stop!' again. Student 3 now continues and so on.

> **Answers**
> **1** A story **2** Your English teacher **3** About 100 words **4** One provides the *first sentence* of the story and two gives you the *title* **5** No, you can choose between a story and a letter

❸

> **Answers**
> **1** Question 1 **2** The ringing phone belonged to the teacher.

❹

> **Answer**
> All the sentences are correct, so the story is a good answer.

❺ According to the Cambridge ESOL examiners' reports, 'past tenses and plural forms, in particular, need to be checked by candidates, especially those with irregular forms.'

> **Answers**
> *Types of mistake*: past tenses and plural forms
> 1 ~~believed~~ → believe 2 ~~forgot~~ → forgotten
> 3 ~~student~~ → students 4 ~~left~~ → leave 5 ~~stoped~~ → stopped

❻

> **Model answers**
> **1 I realised that I hadn't locked the door.**
>
> I was at the bus stop. I telephoned my sister to ask her if she could go home but she didn't answer her phone. Then I decided to telephone my mum to tell her the truth. My mum told me to go home. As I got to my street I saw a fire engine outside my house. 'Oh no!' I thought. I saw a neighbour and asked him what had happened. He said that a cat was in a tree and couldn't get down. I was so happy. Finally I got to my house and locked the door.
>
> **2 The message began, 'Congratulations! You've won first prize!'**
>
> I couldn't believe it! I was the winner. Two months before, I had entered a drawing competition in a shop. I telephoned my best friend, who told me to phone the shop. She also asked me what the prize was but I said I didn't know. I decided to walk to the shop. I was so excited. I went into the shop and found a shop assistant. I told her my name and said that I had received a message. She said, 'Oh, you're the winner. Congratulations! You've won a weekend in Paris.' I was delighted.
>
> **4 As I got on the train, I saw an empty seat next to my favourite actor.**
>
> Davey Shaw was on the train. I couldn't believe it! I asked him if I could sit next to him. I told him that he was my favourite actor and I'd seen all his films. Davey asked me where I was going. I told him I was going to meet my friends to go to the cinema. The journey went really quickly and we were soon in the city centre. When I found my friends, I told them that I had sat next to Davey Shaw on the train but they thought I was telling lies again.

Vocabulary and grammar review
Unit 11

Answers

Grammar

❶ 2 was built 3 seems 4 rises 5 is washed 6 reaches 7 was completely flooded 8 disappeared 9 is done 10 know 11 were saved 12 was put up

❷ 2 more quickly 3 (the) best 4 more frequently 5 harder 6 (the) worst 7 more strongly 8 more carefully

Vocabulary

❸ *(More than one answer is sometimes possible)*
2 great/much excitement 3 a reservation 4 a quick examination 5 celebrations often 6 no information

❹ **Across:** 1 giraffe 5 snake 6 bat 8 ostrich 11 save 12 recycle
Down: 2 energy 3 rubbish 4 petrol 5 solar 7 duck 9 tiger 10 waste

Vocabulary and grammar review
Unit 12

Answers

Vocabulary

❶ 2 infront of → in front of 3 At the right → On the right 4 next → next to 5 in → on 6 behind of → behind 7 inside of → inside 8 on → over

❸ 2 told 3 said 4 ask for 5 asked 6 to tell / telling 7 tell

Grammar

❹ 2 what was the team called → what the team was called
3 why didn't I go → why I didn't go / why I hadn't gone
4 why was I crying → why I was crying
5 what was I going to do → what I was going to do
6 where should she go → where she should go
7 when am I going → when I am going

❺ 2 she was not / wasn't very keen 3 she loved comedies 4 she hadn't gone / didn't go 5 they had just finished 6 she would go to the cinema that day if she could

❻ **Suggested questions**
2 'Are you keen on thrillers?'
3 'Do you love comedies?'
4 'Did you go to the cinema last week?'
5 'Have you (just) finished your exams?'
6 'When will you go to the cinema?'

❼ **Suggested answers**
2 I asked you if you were keen on thrillers.
3 I asked you if you loved comedies.
4 I asked you if you went to the cinema last week.
5 I asked you if you had finished your exams.
6 I asked you when you would go to the cinema.

Unit 12 photocopiable activity: Reported speech dictation

Time: 25 mins +

Objectives
- To practise use of reported speech
- To listen for information and make notes
- (In extension) To make a piece of narrative text sound more natural

Before class

Make one copy of the activity for each group of four students in your class. Cut each one into six cards along the dotted lines.

In class

❶ Divide your class into groups of four students (if you have an uneven number of students, some will need to work in groups of five, but try not to have any groups of three). Ask them to divide into pairs: Students 1 and 2 and Students 3 and 4. Give Students 1 and 2 a copy
of the card marked *Dialogue 1* and give Students 3 and 4 a copy of the card marked *Dialogue 2*. They should make sure that the other pair does not see this. *Do not hand out the other cards yet.*

❷ Tell them that they are going to read the conversations on their cards to the other pair. They should tell the other pair their names (e.g. *John, Alice*) and then read the conversation at normal speed (not too slowly or too quickly). They should read it three times. The other pair should listen and make notes about what they hear on the second and third read-throughs. Their notes should be as detailed as possible. Allow them about seven to eight minutes for this.

❸ When they have finished, explain that they are going to use the information in their notes to complete a single piece of text using reported speech. Give Students 1 and 2 the card marked *Text 2*, and give Students 3 and 4 the card marked *Text 1*. Using the notes they made, they should try to fill in the gaps. Let them do this for about ten minutes, then ask them to stop and hand over their completed text to the other pair.

❹ Give Students 1 and 2 the card marked *Answers 1*, and give Students 3 and 4 the card marked *Answers 2*. They should compare the answers (the words highlighted in **bold**) with those that the other pair wrote. For each word in the gapped text that matches a word on their answer paper, they should award the other pair one point. The maximum they can score is 40 points. Some alternative answers are possible, so be prepared to offer your opinion if necessary.

❺ The winning pair is the pair in each group with the most points.

Extension idea The model texts they have been given are very basic, with limited cohesion (there are very few conjunctions, for example). In their pairs, they can rewrite the texts to make them sound more natural. For example, *Janice said that it was really hot, but Bill disagreed and said that he thought it was very pleasant because there was a cool wind blowing.*
They could also do the same with the conversations.
For example:
John: I'm bored. I'm going to the cinema.
Alice: What? But you went to the cinema yesterday.

Reported speech dictation

✂ Cut along the dotted lines to divide these into cards.

Dialogue 1 Students 1 and 2

John: I'm going to the cinema.
Alice: You went to the cinema yesterday.
John: I like films.
Alice: Can I come with you?
John: Of course you can.
Alice: Can you wait five minutes?
John: Why?
Alice: I want to put on some make-up.
John: We'll be sitting in a dark cinema. Nobody will see you.
Alice: I feel better when I look smart.
John: Hurry up, because I don't want to miss the beginning of the film.

Dialogue 2 Students 3 and 4

Janice: It's really hot.
Bill: I think it's very pleasant. There's a cool wind blowing.
Janice: I'm hot and I'm going to sit in the shade for a few minutes.
Bill: I've had enough of the sun. I'll join you.
Janice: I have an idea. We can get an ice cream.
Bill: I hate ice cream. It makes my teeth ache.
Janice: I'll have an ice cream and you can have a drink.
Bill: That sounds like a great idea.

Text 1 *For students 3 and 4 to complete.*

Yesterday evening, John and Alice were sitting together at home. John .... that he .... to the .... Alice .... him that he .... to the .... the day .... John .... that he .... films. Alice .... with him. John .... her that she .... Alice .... him .... five .... John .... her .... Alice .... that she .... to put on some make-up. John .... her that they .... in a dark cinema and nobody .... them. Alice .... she .... better when she .... smart. John .... her .... up because he .... to .... the .... of the film.

Text 2 *For Students 1 and 2 to complete.*

Last week, Janice and Bill were sitting on the beach. Janice .... that it .... really .... Bill .... her he .... it was very pleasant because there .... a cool .... blowing. Janice .... that she .... hot and she .... to sit in the .... for a few .... Bill .... that he .... enough of the .... and that he .... her. Then Janice .... she .... an ....: they .... an ice cream. Bill .... he .... ice cream because it .... his .... ache. Janice .... she .... an ice cream and he .... a .... Bill .... that that .... like a great ....

Answers 1 *For students 1 and 2 to mark Students 3 and 4's completed text.*

Yesterday evening, John and Alice were sitting together at home. John **said** that he **was going** to the **cinema**. Alice **told** him that he **had gone/been** to the **cinema** the day **before**. John **said** that he **liked** films. Alice **asked to go** with him. John **told** her that she **could**. Alice **asked** him **to wait** five **minutes**. John **asked** her **why**. Alice **said** that she **wanted** to put on some make-up. John **told** her that they **would be sitting** in a dark cinema and nobody **would see** them. Alice **said** she **felt** better when she **looked** smart. John **told** her **to hurry** up because he **didn't want** to **miss** the **beginning** of the film.

Answers 2 *For Students 3 and 4 to mark Students 1 and 2's completed text.*

Last week, Janice and Bill were sitting on the beach. Janice **said** that it **was** really **hot**. Bill **told** her he **thought** it was very pleasant because there **was** a cool **wind** blowing. Janice **told him / said** that she **was** hot and she **was going** to sit in the **shade** for a few **minutes**. Bill **said** that he **had had** enough of the **sun** and that he **would join** her. Then Janice **said** she **had** an **idea**: they **could get** an ice cream. Bill **said** he **hated** ice cream because it **made** his **teeth** ache. Janice **told him** she **would have** an ice cream and he **could have** a drink. Bill **told her** that that **sounded** like a great **idea**.

Word list

Unit 12

Note: the numbers show which page the word or phrase first appears on in the unit.

ask *v* (108) to say something to someone as a question which you want them to answer

ask for *v* (108) to say something to someone because you want them to give you something

behind *prep* (112) at or to the back of someone or something

between *prep* (112) in the space that separates two places, people, or things

communicate *v* (106) to share information with others by speaking, writing, moving your body, or using other signals

communication *n* (108) the act of communicating with other people

dork *n* (106) a stupid or silly person

dude *n* (106) a man

geek *n* (106) a man who is boring and not fashionable

graffiti *n* (106) writing or pictures painted on walls and public places, usually illegally

in front of *prep* (112) close to the front part of something

inside *prep* (112) in or into a room, building, container, etc.

joke *n* (108) something which someone says to make people laugh, usually a short story with a funny ending

lie *n* (108) something that you say or write which you know is not true

Martian *n* (106) in stories, someone from the planet Mars

next to *prep* (112) very close to something or someone, with nothing in between

on the right *prep* (112) on or towards the part of your body that is to the east when you are facing north

opposite *prep* (112) in a position facing something or someone but on the other side

over *prep* (112) above or higher than something

raise money *v* (108) to collect money from other people

say *v* (108) to speak words

slang *n* (106) informal language, often language that is only used by people who belong to a particular group

speak *v* (107) to say something using your voice

story *n* (108) a description of a series of real or imaginary events which is intended to entertain people

talk *v* (108) to say things to someone

tell *v* (108) to say something to someone, usually giving them information

truth *n* (108) the quality of being true

wonder *v* (111) to want to know something or to try to understand the reason for something

❶ **Look at this text and put the verbs in bold into their correct passive form (present or past simple). Don't forget to use the correct form of *be* in each case.**

This dress (**0**) (**clean**) ...... *was cleaned* ...... last week, but it's already dirty.

At school we have an hour for lunch and during that time we (**1**) (**allow**) .... to do whatever we want. I usually spend the time reading. I really like crime stories and last week I (**2**) (**send**) .... a book by a friend in California. It's a book of short stories about crimes that have gone wrong. All of the stories (**3**) (**take**) .... from newspapers and websites and my favourite is one about two unlucky criminals called Robert Harris and Jim White who lived in Detroit (a city that (**4**) (**know**) .... as the 'crime capital' of the USA). One morning, they parked their car outside a bank in the city, walked in, pointed guns at one of the assistants and demanded $10,000 in cash. They (**5**) (**give**) .... the money by the terrified assistant. However, while they were robbing the bank, their car (**6**) (**steal**) .... , which they discovered when they left the bank. While they were wondering how to get away, they (**7**) (**attack**) .... by an old lady who had been in the bank moments earlier. When she started hitting them with her umbrella, they tried to run away, but (**8**) (**chase**) .... by a large crowd of people who thought they were trying to rob the old lady. The two men were so frightened that they ran to the nearest police station for help, where they (**9**) (**protect**) .... from the angry crowd by several policemen. Later, they (**10**) (**tell**) .... by the policeman who arrested them that they were probably the unluckiest criminals in the country. I love that story!

❷ **Read the text below and choose the correct word for each space.**

After our starter we had two more (**0**) .... *C* .... , followed by coffee and chocolates.

| 0 | A plates | B foods | Ⓒ courses | D meals |

It was my birthday last week and because it was Saturday, I was able to relax. In the morning, I went to the hairdresser where I (**1**) .... my hair washed and cut. After that I went shopping for a new dress, but I couldn't find anything I liked, which was a bit of a (**2**) .... Then in the evening my friend took me to a restaurant, where we had a wonderful (**3**) .... For my (**4**) .... I had a seafood cocktail, and my friend had a large (**5**) .... of different Italian meats. Then we both had the (**6**) .... delicious steaks we had ever eaten. They had been cooked really (**7**) .... , not too much, not too little, and came with chips and a lovely pepper sauce. Neither of us likes (**8**) .... things like ice cream and chocolate, so we finished the meal with a selection of cheese (my friend (**9**) .... me that he thought it was French, but I think it was Italian). What I liked best about the restaurant was that we were sitting (**10**) .... the kitchen. It had a glass wall, so we could see the food being cooked.

1	A had	B made	C was	D did
2	A disappoint	B disappointed	C disappointment	D disappointing
3	A course	B plate	C meal	D food
4	A entrance	B dessert	C beginning	D starter
5	A plate	B cup	C place	D table
6	A best	B more	C most	D very
7	A well	B best	C good	D better
8	A salty	B sweet	C bitter	D sour
9	A said	B spoke	C talked	D told
10	A next	B opposite	C between	D over

❸ **For each question, complete the second sentence so that it means the same as the first,** *using no more than three words.*

0 My father said 'I'm going to cook dinner.'
My father said that .... *he was going* .... to cook dinner.

1 'Don't eat so much chocolate,' my mother said to me.
My mother .... to eat so much chocolate.

2 I prefer the taste of fresh fruit to chocolates and sweets.
I think fresh fruit tastes .... chocolates and sweets.

3 We can't cook dinner at home right now because someone is painting the kitchen.
We can't cook dinner at home right now because we .... kitchen painted.

4 In the restaurant, my brother sat on my left and my sister sat on my right.
In the restaurant, I .... brother and sister.

5 The waiter said 'Are you ready to order?'.
The waiter asked us .... ready to order.

❹ **Complete these short conversations with noun forms of the verbs in** *italics*. **In each case you should add a suffix (-*ion*, -*ation* or -*ment*). Sometimes you will also need to add or remove another letter.**

My town has several **0** (*attract*) ...*attractions*..., including an amusement park and theatre.

Claire:	Have you seen this (1) (*advertise*) .... in the paper?
Rick:	No, what's it about?
Claire:	Well, there's going to be a talk at the town hall about (2) (*pollute*) ....
Bob:	Anne and Rupert say they have an important (3) (*announce*) .... to make.
Roland:	Really? About what?
Bob:	I don't know. Perhaps they're going to get married.
Roland:	Well, that would certainly be cause for (4) (*celebrate*) .... !
Jane:	We can't go to your favourite restaurant tonight. I called to make a (5) (*reserve*) .... but they're fully booked.
Ryan:	Oh. I was really looking forward to it. What a (6) (*disappoint*) ....
Laurence:	I think that the best (7) (*invent*) .... of the last few years is a car that uses electricity instead of petrol.
Andy:	I agree. There have certainly been some amazing (8) (*develop*) .... in transport technology recently.
Teacher:	I'm afraid that your work has not shown much (9) (*improve*) .... recently.
Student:	I'm sorry, but I've had some problems at home.
Teacher:	All right, but your (10) (*examine*) .... is next week, and I don't think you'll pass.

❺ Correct the mistakes in these indirect questions. You will either need to remove a word, change a word or move a word to another part of the sentence.

0 Can you tell me how old are you? .... *Can you tell me how old you are?* ....

1 Could you tell me where do you live? ....

2 I can't remember what is your name. ....

3 I was wondering that I could ask you a few questions. ....

4 I will like to know what your plans are for the weekend. ....

5 Tell me about what you think about the new shopping centre. ....

❻ Look at this map and complete the sentences with the name of the shop or service and a preposition of location. You can use some prepositions more than once. You must complete both parts of each sentence correctly for one point.

0 If you feel unwell, you should go to the ....*doctor's*...., which is ....*next to*.... the dry cleaner.

1 You can have your teeth checked at the ...., which is .... the hairdresser.

2 Books can be borrowed from the ...., which is .... the right side of Bright Street.

3 You can get your hair cut at the ...., which is .... the garage and the butcher.

4 You can book a holiday at the ...., which you will find .... the shopping centre.

5 If you want to send a letter, go to the ...., which is .... Peach Road.

6 You can have your car repaired at the ...., which is .... the hairdresser.

7 If you have a jacket that needs cleaning, go to the ...., which you will find .... the corner of Bright Street and Peach Road.

8 The meat at the .... is much better than the meat from the supermarket. It's .... the library.

9 To get from one part of the shopping centre to the other, use the ...., which goes .... Main Street.

10 To relax after a busy morning in town, go to the .... This is .... the hairdresser and the garage.

Answer key

Progress tests

❶ 1 got 2 was going 3 are having / 're having
4 is shining / 's shining 5 am sitting / 'm sitting
6 want 7 don't have / haven't (got) 8 saw
9 was doing 10 went

❷ 1 B 2 A 3 D 4 D 5 C

❸ 1 used to play 2 (I) went 3 rarely / seldom play
4 have / have got / 've got 5 cost too much

❹ 1 What is your surname? 2 How do you spell that?
3 Where do you go to school? 4 What subjects do
you like to study at school? 5 What do you enjoy
doing with your friends?

❺ 1 unfit, unhealthy 2 untidy, impossible 3 impolite,
unpopular 4 impatient, incorrect 5 unkind, unfair

❻ 1 garage 2 garden 3 microwave 4 dishwasher
5 collecting 6 surfing 7 physics 8 chemistry
9 learning 10 studying

❼ 1 to try 2 to meet 3 going 4 giving up 5 to fly
6 tidying 7 breaking 8 to get 9 to phone
10 meeting

❶ 1 better 2 highest 3 more difficult 4 most
beautiful 5 best 6 safest 7 worst 8 further /
farther 9 busiest 10 noisiest

❷ 1 D 2 A 3 C 4 C 5 B 6 B 7 D 8 A 9 B 10 D

❸ 1 by dolphins since 2 not as intelligent 3 may/
might not realise 4 've/have just received 5 don't
need / don't have

❹ 1 's/has been good 2 Did you enjoy 3 I didn't go
4 She didn't invite 5 what did you do 6 I went
7 I've never seen 8 I've seen 9 I've already asked
10 haven't sold out yet

❺ 1 shopping centre (or center) 2 internet café
3 art gallery 4 youth club 5 tourist office

❻ 1 boring = bored 2 surprised = surprising
3 angry for = angry with or angry about
4 disappoint = disappointed 5 fond about = fond of

❼ 1 gone 2 knew 3 got to know 4 found out 5 been

❶ 1 'll tell 2 'm meeting / 'm going to meet 3 's going
to rain 4 'll probably have 5 're going to show
6 'll be / 'm going to be 7 'm flying / 'm going to
fly 8 leaves 9 'll go 10 catch (The auxiliary verb
will should not be repeated here because it is used
with *go* earlier in the sentence. Do not penalise your
students if they use *will*, but explain to them why it is
not needed.)

❷ 1 C 2 D 3 C 4 A 5 A 6 B 7 B 8 B 9 D 10 D

❸ 1 on foot 2 who runs to 3 lose when we 4 if/when
the weather / if/when it 5 too cold to

❹ 1 hitchhike 2 crossroads 3 guesthouse
4 guidebook 5 overnight

❺ 1 short 2 curly/wavy 3 handsome/good-looking
(you could also accept *attractive*, although this would
be less common) 4 hard-working 5 generous/kind
6 dark 7 broad 8 unreliable 9 impatient 10 shy

❻ 1 in 2 in 3 by 4 on 5 to 6 on 7 on 8 to
9 off 10 out

❶ 1 are allowed 2 was sent 3 are taken / were taken
4 is known 5 were given 6 was stolen (*had been
stolen* is also acceptable) 7 were attacked 8 were
chased 9 were protected 10 were told

❷ 1 A 2 C 3 C 4 D 5 A 6 C 7 A 8 B 9 D 10 B

❸ 1 told me not 2 better/nicer than 3 're/are having /
getting the 4 sat/was between my 5 if/whether we
were

❹ 1 advertisement 2 pollution 3 announcement
4 celebration 5 reservation 6 disappointment
7 invention 8 developments 9 improvement
10 examination

❺ 1 Could you tell me where you live? 2 I can't
remember what your name is. 3 I was wondering
if/whether I could ask you a few questions.
4 I would like to know what your plans are for the
weekend. 5 Tell me what you think about the new
shopping centre.

❻ 1 dentist('s), opposite 2 library, on
3 hairdresser('s), between 4 travel agent('s), in /
inside / in the middle of / within 5 post office, on
6 garage, next to / beside 7 dry cleaner('s), on/at
8 butcher('s), opposite 9 bridge, over 10 park,
behind/near/opposite

Writing reference

Part 1

Sentence transformations

Exercise 1
a spelling mistake (*first*)
b does not mean the same as the first sentence
c too many words
d grammatically wrong

Exercise 2
1 any flights   2 as cold as   3 us to
4 spent   5 the most

Exercise 3
1 *any* + change of verb *fly* to noun *flights*
2 comparative *-er* + *than* changes to negative *not as ... as*
3 direct to reported speech *asked us to*
4 *stayed ... for* changes to *spent* (no preposition)
5 *never ... such an* changes to superlative *the most ... ever*

Part 2

Messages

Exercise 1
1 Your friend Eva; you want to borrow her camera
2 Informal
3 An email
4 Explain why, suggest when you can collect it, say when you'll give it back

Exercise 2
Suggested answers (The useful expressions for explaining, thanking, inviting, suggesting, apologising and asking are underlined):
2 I'd like to borrow your camera <u>because</u> my camera (mine) is broken.
3 <u>Thank you ever so much for</u> the two weeks I spent in your house.
4 I know you've never visited my country. <u>Would you like</u> to come and stay in the summer?
5 <u>Why don't we</u> meet in front of the cinema?

6 <u>I'm so sorry for</u> forgetting your birthday. I feel terrible.
7 <u>Can you</u> tell me how to get to your house, please?

Exercise 3
1 *Dear ..., Best wishes, All the best, Yours*
2 *Hello, ..., Hi ..., Love, Lots of love, See you soon*

Exercise 4

	A	B	C
1	✗ (The candidate doesn't suggest when he can pick up the camera.)	✓	✗ (The candidate doesn't explain why they want to borrow the camera nor suggest when they can collect the camera so could only get a maximum of 2 marks.)
2	✓	✓	✓
3	✓ (*since* and *and*)	✓ (*but*)	✗
4	✓ (*Dear ... Love*)	✓ (*Dear ... Love*)	✓ (*Dear ... See you*)
5	✓ (41 words)	✗ (This answer is a little long at 50 words. The expressions *How are you?* and *I hope you're fine* are not necessary.)	✗ (This answer is short at 20 words and could only get a maximum of 2 marks.)

Exercise 5
Suggested answers:
A: The answer is well written and organised within the word limit but it could not get more than 3 marks because it does not include one of the content points.
B: The answer is a little long but it is a good answer which includes all three content points and it would probably be given 5 marks.
C: The message is easy to understand, but it does not include two of the content points and it is short. It could only get a maximum of 2 marks.

Exercise 6
Suggested words to underline:
1 You are going to miss (an English-speaking friend's birthday) party tomorrow   2 a note   3 (an English-speaking friend) Ian   4 apologise, explain why, suggest another day

Exercise 7

B: The candidate has included all three content points appropriately. The message is very clear.

Exercise 8

(suggested answers)

A (*six corrected mistakes are in* **bold**)

Hello, I am sorry but (~~tommorrow~~) **tomorrow** I can't go to your party (~~becouse~~) **because** I have my sister's wedding and she (~~live~~) **lives** in the USA. I must (~~bring~~) **take** the train from Lyon and afterwards the (~~plan~~) **plane** from Paris. Shall we meet next weekend? (~~Tanks~~) **Thanks**.

C (*changes in* **bold**)

Hi Ian, I'm sorry for not going to your party (~~yesterday~~) **tomorrow**. I (~~had~~) **have** a bad cold and my sister (~~had~~) **has had** an accident. I (~~went~~) **'ve been** to the hospital and the doctor (~~told~~) **has told** her that she (~~had~~) **has** a broken leg, so I (~~couldn't~~) **can't** be there. (~~I will see you tomorrow~~) **How about meeting next week?** Yours,

Part 3

Informal letter

Exercise 1

1 *letter, friend, answering … questions, about 100*
2 an English-speaking friend   3 They recently had their fourteenth birthday; they were with their family and enjoyed it a lot.   4 What happens when you have a birthday; What you do

Exercise 2

1 *What happens?* He gets excited before it; receives presents from parents, cards and a birthday cake. *What do you do?* Goes out with friends; can do what he likes
2 *Thanks, lots, cool, till, getting, nice, mum, dad, loads of, mates, Anyway, 've got to*
3 Exclamation marks, short forms, e.g. *isn't, there's, it'll*. Very short sentences: *There's a cake, too; Write soon*. Expressions: *take out* (phrasal verb), *the best thing, that's all, All the best*
4 Example: *like a concert*. Reasons: *because it's my birthday, because I've got to go out*; Linking words: *like; because*

Exercise 3

1 *letter, English-speaking friend, (about) 100 words*
2 Your English-speaking friend
3 He or she is going to visit your country next month.
4 More about your country, in particular where to go and what to do there.

Exercise 4

1 **1** ~~a good news~~ good news   **2** ~~for do~~ to do **3** ~~people which~~ people who   **4** ~~you to visit~~ you visit
2 No
3 Yes
4 Yes
5 Informal. Short sentences. Vocabulary such as *Hi, Thanks, I can't believe*. Short forms, e.g. *that's, it's*. Punctuation: dash (–), exclamation marks (!).
6 Yes. *Which are the best places to visit?* (second paragraph); *What can I do there?* (third paragraph)
7 *Hi …, Thanks for your letter, Please write again soon, Best wishes*
8 *because, as, because*

Story

Exercise 1

1 *teacher, story, title, lost wallet, 100 words*
2 title
3 about 100

Exercise 2

1 third person
2 *crowded, busy, upset, angry, nervous, anxiously*
3 a mystery
4 **a** *was standing* (past continuous), *was stolen* (past simple passive), *realised* (past simple), *had lost* (past perfect)
b *Upset and angry* (adjectives)
c *'I believe this is yours'* + reporting verb
d *looked anxiously inside* without saying yet what he saw
e *his card, but with someone else's photo*
f *they had wanted to steal his identity*

Exercise 3

1 *(English) teacher, story, begin, sentence, 100 words*
2 Your English teacher
3 *When the phone rang, I knew immediately who was calling*; at the beginning of the story
4 *phone, rang, I knew, who*
5 first person

Exercise 4

a 2   **b** 3   **c** 1

Exercise 5

1 Yes
2 Yes
3 ~~will~~ would (be announced), ~~beleive~~ believe, ~~of~~ in (the world)
4 *Suggested answers*: Past simple: *thought*; Past continuous: *was taking part*; Past perfect simple: *had completed*; Conditional: *would perform*; Conditional passive: *(would) be announced*; Present perfect: *You've won*

5 *immediately, Before, when, After, in two weeks, now*

6 Mainly formal. She uses the full form of verbs: *I had passed, I had completed.* The passive: *(would) be announced.* Complex sentences. No exclamation marks or dashes.

7 At the beginning, she makes the reader wait by saying *Before answering, I thought back* and then goes back in time, describing the events leading up to that in the second paragraph. She ends the second paragraph by saying *and now it was time*, and starts the final paragraph with *Nervously, I took the call.* Using the natural pause between paragraphs to create interest is similar to the way writers sometimes do this at the end of a chapter in an exciting novel.

8 She hears this over the phone: *'You've won the National Dance Competition.'*

9 *Nervously, amazed, couldn't bel(ie)ve it, a dream come true, the happiest person (in) the world*

Speaking reference

Part 1

Exercise 1

2 g **3** f **4** e **5** c **6** a **7** b

Exercise 2

~~five year~~ fifth year, at ~~the~~ school at school, ~~so many of the Internet~~ so much of the Internet, ~~as~~ Spain like / such as Spain, ~~We never did~~ We'd never done / We've never done

Exercise 3

2 True **3** False **4** True **5** False **6** True

Recording script CD2 Track 26

Examiner: Now, what's your name?

Emilio: My name's Emilio.

Examiner: Thank you. And what's your surname?

Emilio: Sánchez.

Examiner: How do you spell it?

Emilio: S-A-N-C-H-E-Z.

Examiner: Thank you. Now, where do you live?

Emilio: In Santiago. <u>In a district called</u> 'Independéncia', which is quite near **of** the city centre.

Examiner: And do you work or are you a student in Santiago?

Emilio: I'm a student. I'm in my **five** year at secondary school.

Examiner: And what subjects do you study?

Emilio: Er … <u>could you repeat the question, please</u>?

Examiner: What subjects do you study?

Emilio: Oh, um … maths, science, history, geography … things like that. <u>And English, of course</u>. I do that at **the** school, and I have lessons at home, too, with a teacher that comes to my house.

Examiner: Do you enjoy studying English, Emilio?

Emilio: Yes, I like learning it a lot <u>because</u> so **many** of the Internet is in English, and also because most of the music I enjoy is too.

Examiner: Do you think that English will be useful for you in the future?

Emilio: Yes, definitely. <u>For instance</u>, I'd really like to travel round Europe and North America, and for that <u>I'll need to know English</u>. Except in countries **as** Spain and Mexico, of course, where I'll be able to speak in Spanish.

Examiner: OK, Emilio. What did you do last weekend?

Emilio: Last weekend … Oh yes, <u>I was at the sports centre</u> on Saturday. We were playing basketball against one of the best teams in Santiago, and in the end we beat them. We never did that before!

Examiner: Thank you.

Exercise 4

Add more information: *as well as that, also, and sometimes*

Ask someone to repeat something: *could you say that again, please?, sorry, I didn't catch that, could you repeat that, please?*

Give examples: *for instance, like, for example, such as*

Exercise 5

Sorry, I didn't catch that, such as, also, like, for example, and sometimes

Recording script CD2 Track 27

Examiner: What do you enjoy doing in your free time?

Isabel: Er, <u>sorry, I didn't catch that</u>.

Examiner: What do you enjoy doing in your free time?

Isabel: My free time, right. Well, most of all I like doing sports – lots of different ones <u>such as</u> running and swimming. I love swimming, especially in the sea. <u>Also</u> sports that you play with a … er … racket, <u>like</u> tennis and badminton. There's a really big sports centre near my house, where you can do lots of different things. Gymnastics, <u>for example</u>. I really like that. <u>And sometimes</u> I play table tennis there, too.

Part 2

Exercise 1

1 That a classmate is leaving and the rest of you in the class want to get a present for him or her.
2 Discuss the possible presents shown in the picture; choose one of them
3 Six: (set of) books, (digital) camera, (set of) DVDs, mobile phone, (pair of) trainers, MP3 player

Exercise 2

2 Yes **3** Yes **4** Yes **5** Yes, the mobile phone
6 Stella. She deals with the task quite well, keeps the conversation going with her partner and talks quite fluently. Although she makes some mistakes, in general these don't prevent her communicating well and she uses a good range of grammar and vocabulary. Her pronunciation is influenced by her first language, but she can be understood without much difficulty. Lee is weaker on all these points, although he replies to most of what Stella says and knows how to take turns.

Exercise 3

Expressions used: *How about, I'm not really sure about that, You may be right, but, because, I'm not so keen on, Perhaps we should, Yes, that's true, That's a (very) good idea, So shall we … , then?*

Recording script CD2 Track 28

Examiner: In the next part, you're going to talk to each other. I'm going to describe a situation to you. A school friend of yours is going to live in another country. Talk together about the different things the class could buy him or her as a leaving present and decide which one would be best. Here is a picture with some ideas to help you. I'll say that again. A school friend of yours is going to live in another country. Talk together about the different things the class could buy him or her as a leaving present and decide which one would be best. All right? Talk together.

Stella: OK, er, if I start?

Lee: Yes, please.

Stella: How about buying her the books? I know she likes very much to read so maybe they will be nice for her to have.

Lee: I am no really sure. Very heavy for … er … carry on aeroplane. DVDs better.

Stella: You may be right, but is difficult to choose for somebody that you … er … not really know very well.

Lee: Uh-huh.

Stella: And if we ask what is her … er … favourite kind of film it's not a surprise when we'll give them to her. The same problem with music.

Lee: Maybe MP3 player, then?

Stella: Yes, then she can put any music she want. From the Internet. But I think that's not the better thing because she's got already an MP3 player. I'm sure I see her with one the other day, so not that.

Lee: Uh-huh. Shoes the same.

Stella: The trainers? Yes, probably she has some and I'm not so keen of them anyway.

Lee: So which of others we get?

Stella: Well, she's going to live in a new place, so perhaps we should get her the camera? Then she can make lots of photos.

Lee: Or mobile phone. She can also photo with mobile phone.

Stella: Yes, that's true. As well she could send the pictures to us here and we can see what is like her new life there.

Lee: Is very good idea, yes. Shall we do that then?

Stella: Yes, let's buy her a phone. She'll like that, I'm sure.

Examiner: Thank you.

Part 3

Exercise 1

(Accept other sensible suggestions)
Photo A: the place, weather, time of day, colours, clothes and activities
Photo B: the place, weather, time of day, colours, clothes and activities

Exercise 2

Sofia talks about the place, the weather, the colours, the clothes, the activities.
Tania talks about the place, the weather, the colours (dark), the clothes, the activities.

Exercise 3

Sofia 1 ✓ **2** ✗ There is some range: *a sunny day, trees, mountains* and *there are, I can see, I think* but this is all quite simple. **3** ✗ **4** ✗ (She says *the boy here* which suggests she is pointing at the picture.) **5** ✗ (She stops quickly by saying *That's all*.) **6** ✗ (Her answer is simple and rather short.)
Tania 1 ✓ **2** ✓ **3** ✓ **4** ✓ **5** ✓ **6** ✓ (Tania describes the photo well. She uses a wide range of vocabulary and structure to do this. She describes the location rather than points and speaks for about a minute.)

Recording script CD2 Track 29

Examiner: Now, I'd like each of you to talk on your own about something. I'm going to give each of you a photograph of people enjoying their free time. Sofia, here is your photograph. Please show it to Tania, but I'd like you to talk about it. Tania, you just listen. I'll give you your photograph in a moment. Sofia, please tell us what you can see in your photograph.

Sofia: Um … er … there are four people in the photograph. I can see a boy, no I think there are two boys and two girls. They all have a … um … a … this. I think they are on holiday. It's a sunny day and the weather it's warm. One of the girls wears short trousers and a red T-shirt. The boys wear … er … er … the boy here wears a shirt. The shirt is blue. They are looking at the trees, mountains and … that's all.

Examiner: Thank you. Can I have the booklet, please? Now, Tania, here is your photograph. It also shows people enjoying their free time. Please show it to Sofia and tell us what you can see in the photograph.

Tania: OK. In this picture, we can see three boys and a girl. I think they could be friends. On the right, we can see a boy wearing a shirt and dark trousers. Next to this boy, there is his friend. He appears to be happy because he's smiling. The other boy is carrying a … a … – it's made of wood and it's used for skating. Er … behind the girl and boys, we can see some buildings and the street so I think they're in a city, maybe New York or London. The weather looks nice and …

Examiner: Thank you.

Part 4

Exercise 1
Free-time activities you do **now** *and* free-time activities you'd like to try in the future

Exercise 2
Students' own answers

Exercise 3
Free-time activities

	now	in the future
Agnes	meet friends go to the cinema (very expensive) skiing (once) playing tennis, beach volleyball travelling listen to music dancing (used to do ballet)	go skiing again visit many places, e.g. China dancing lessons
Marcos	meet friends – have a walk, talk go to the cinema playing tennis (quite bad), skiing, snowboarding, snorkelling (last year) listen to music, especially rock dancing (quite bad)	skiing on the water (water-skiing) learn to play electric guitar

Exercise 4
1 ✓ 2 ✓ 3 ✓ 4 ✓ 5 ✓ 6 ✓ Agnes and Marcos are strong PET candidates. They do exactly what is required in this part of the test.

Recording script CD2 Track 30

Examiner: Your photos showed people enjoying their free time. Now, I'd like you to talk together about the things you enjoy doing in your free time and the things you would like to try in the future.

Agnes: OK. At the weekends, um, <u>I like meeting my friends</u>.

Marcos: Me too. <u>We meet on Saturday afternoon in the … the … town and have a walk or talk. Sometimes we go to the cinema.</u> What about you? Do you like going to the cinema?

Agnes: <u>Yes</u>, but it's very expensive. What about sport? Do you play any sports?

Marcos: Yeah, I agree the cinema is expensive. <u>I like playing tennis</u> but I'm quite bad. <u>In the winter we go skiing</u> to the mountains. I love it. <u>This year I've tried snowboarding.</u> It's fantastic. Have you ever tried it?

Agnes:	No, well, I mean ... <u>I once went skiing</u> with my uncle but that was two or three years ago. <u>I would like to go skiing again</u> but the mountains are very far. Like you, um, <u>I also like playing tennis</u>, especially in the summer. <u>We also play beach volleyball</u>. There is a place to play on the beach and we have a good time. What things would you like to try in the future?
Marcos:	We always go to the islands in the summer. <u>Last year I went snorkelling</u> with my cousins. It was so beautiful to see the fish under the water. You should try it. <u>I would like to try skiing on the water</u>. You know, you have skis and a boat takes you on the water. Yes, I want to do that.
Agnes:	Oh, you mean water-skiing. I've never done that. I'm a little scared of the water ... I prefer doing things on the land. <u>I really like travelling</u> and <u>when I'm older I would like to visit many places</u>. <u>My dream is to visit China</u>. We have studied so many things about China and I would like to see it. Would you like to travel when you're older?
Marcos:	Maybe. I haven't really thought about it. I don't really like cars and planes because I feel ... er ... I feel not good.
Agnes:	Yeah, it's true and sometimes the journey can be long and boring. Don't you think so?
Marcos:	Uh-huh. Something else. <u>I would like to learn to play the electric guitar</u>.
Agnes:	Really?
Marcos:	Yeah. My friend sings really well and there is another friend who can play the drums. We are thinking in making a group. You see, <u>we love all kinds of music but especially rock</u>. Do you listen to music?
Agnes:	<u>Sometimes.</u> Well, it depends. If I have to study then I can't listen to music or the TV or nothing but <u>when we have parties I like listening to music</u>. Do you like dancing?
Marcos:	<u>Yeah. I love it but I'm quite bad.</u> What about you?
Agnes:	When I was younger, <u>I used to go to ballet</u> but I didn't like it. <u>Now I like dancing and I would like to have lessons maybe</u>.
Examiner:	Thank you. That's the end of the test.
Both:	Thank you.

Authentic past PET paper from Cambridge ESOL

Paper 1 Reading and Writing

Reading Part 1
1 A **2** B **3** A **4** C **5** B

Reading Part 2
6 A **7** G **8** D **9** H **10** E

Reading Part 3
11 B **12** A **13** B **14** A **15** A **16** A **17** B **18** B
19 A **20** B

Reading Part 4
21 D **22** C **23** D **24** A **25** B

Reading Part 5
26 D **27** B **28** C **29** A **30** B **31** C **32** C **33** A
34 B **35** C

Writing Part 1
1 (see/watch) such an // (see/watch) a more
2 (about) having to
3 gave / showed
4 (much) better than
5 end of // referee ended/finished // final whistle of

Writing Part 2
There are 5 marks for Part 2. Candidates at this level are not expected to produce faultless English, but, to achieve 5 marks, a candidate should write a cohesive message clearly communicating all three content points.

Task-specific Mark Scheme for Writing Part 2

reason why candidate has moved
reference to what candidate likes about new home
invitation to English friend to visit candidate

These are two examples of real PET candidates' answers for Question 6 (Candidate A and Candidate B), followed by the examiner's comments and the marks awarded for each.

Question 6
Candidate A's answer

DeaR James
I have moved because my fatheR get anotheR job and
my parents hated ouR old flat. I like the football fields
and the fantastic tennis couRts. I'd like to invite you
to my new home to spend the day together
love

Examiner's comments for Candidate A and mark awarded

Candidate A
Points 1 & 3 are fine, point 2 is not clearly related to the home, so the communication is successful on the whole.
Mark 4

Question 6
Candidate B's answer

Thanks very much four your letter. It was lovely To hear
from you. I'm glad you're enjoying your new job. but
That you like Bristol, it's nice The people at work are so
friendly.

we're all missing you here in london! Bob and Hilary had
a party last weekend and everyone was asking how you
were it's was a good party! although I didn't get home
Till five in The morning so I spent most of sunday in
bed.

I hope you To visit us again here in londo To get much
fun TogeThe. The weather is very nice. well no more
news for The moment, I'll write again soon.

love

Examiner's comments for Candidate B and mark awarded

Candidate B
Despite the fluency, this is the wrong scenario and so content points 1 & 2 are missing. Point 3 refers to a repeat visit to the same place.
Mark 1

Writing Part 3

These are two examples of real PET candidates' answers for Question 7 (Candidate A and Candidate B), followed by the examiner's comments and the band awarded for each.

Question 7
Candidate A's answer

Dear John

How are you? I hope everything is O.K. with you and
your wife. I feel my town is going to be the same or may
be worse in 20 years. Young people leave the town and
they never come back. The problem is there is no future
for them here. The town is going to become really boring
and quiet and only elder people will live here. I think I'll
stay here because my entire live is here and my family as
well. That's my place and I want to spend rest of my life
here.

Take care

Examiner's comments for Candidate A and band awarded

QUESTION 7	Candidate A
ATTEMPT:	Very good
LANGUAGE/ AMBITION:	Ambitious use of language with a wide range of structures, e.g. 'I feel my town is going to be the same or may be worse in 20 years.', 'Young people leave the town and they never come back.'
RANGE:	
ORGANISATION & COHESION:	Well organised and coherent, with appropriate conclusion
ACCURACY:	A few minor errors, e.g. 'my entire live'
TARGET READER/ EFFORT:	No effort required
CONTENT:	On task
	BAND 5

Question 7
Candidate B's answer

Hi Gary

I don't think my town will be like in 20 years' time there are many changes just 20 years is too shot time for change evrything. The cost is to hight. One the other hand you never know what happen in future. All over the word is still developmpent. I don't think I'll alwas live there, but at the moment I have to because I living close to my children shool and work aswell near. I think maybe in future I'll live in country where is quiet live

Examiner's comments for Candidate B and band awarded

QUESTION 7	Candidate B
ATTEMPT:	Adequate
LANGUAGE/ AMBITION:	Ambitious but flawed, e.g. 'One the other hand you never know what happen … ', 'All over the word is still developmpent.'
RANGE:	Adequate range of vocabulary and structure, e.g. 'I don't think I'll alwas live there'
ORGANISATION & COHESION:	Evidence of organisation and some linking of sentences, e.g. 'but', 'because'
ACCURACY:	A number of errors, mostly non-impeding, e.g. 'is too shot time for change evrything'
TARGET READER/ EFFORT:	Requires some effort
CONTENT:	On task
	BAND 3

These are two examples of real PET candidates' answers for Question 8 (Candidate A and Candidate B), followed by the examiner's comments and the band awarded for each.

Question 8
Candidate A's answer

The best decision I'v ever made.

When I want to lering any languag I must my self don't have any thing. the teacher start the decision in the class nessary the student's who understand of me. There are some student's don't asked teacher him what he want. I draice any bady if will aske teacher him instudent is understand the teacher what did he seyed in the class I always ask my teacher about any thing I can't understand of me only because if I asked my teacher any quation about any thing and I don't knew it that is Problem well came. thank you. nice to read you.

Examiner's comments for Candidate A and band awarded

QUESTION 8	Candidate A
ATTEMPT:	Poor
LANGUAGE/ AMBITION:	Severely restricted command of language
RANGE:	
ORGANISATION & COHESION:	
ACCURACY:	Very poor control makes it difficult to understand
TARGET READER/ EFFORT:	Requires excessive effort
CONTENT:	
	BAND 1

Question 8
Candidate B's answer

The best decision I've ever made concerns my studies. When I was 18, I passed the baccalaureat I was studying in the city where I grew. I didn't know what to do, to continue or to begin to work. I was 18, I was very young. I decided to continue and leave in an other city. I chose three cities for the exam that I would like to do. Unfortunately all the answers were negatives. I was really disappointed. My mother told me to try another city but I was not sure because it was really far from my family. Finally, I decided to send my name to this school. When I received the answer I was happy because it was yes!

Today I'm really happy to have sent my name to this school because I passed my exam. I can begin to work and to do what I like in my job.

Examiner's comments for Candidate B and band awarded

QUESTION 8	Candidate B
ATTEMPT:	Very good attempt
LANGUAGE/ AMBITION:	Confident and ambitious use of language, e.g. 'I'm really happy to have sent my name to this school'
RANGE:	A wide range of structures, e.g. 'I didn't know what to do', 'My mother told me to try another city' and vocabulary, e.g. 'concerns my studies', 'really disappointed'
ORGANISATION & COHESION:	Well organised and coherent through use of linking devices, e.g. 'Unfortunately', 'When', 'but', 'Finally'
ACCURACY:	Errors are minor but are non-impeding, e.g. 'leave in an other city'
TARGET READER/ EFFORT:	Requires no effort by the reader
CONTENT:	On task
	BAND 5

Paper 2 Listening

Listening Part 1
1 A **2** C **3** A **4** C **5** A **6** B **7** A

Listening Part 2
8 C **9** B **10** C **11** A **12** C **13** A

Listening Part 3
14 R/roof(s)
15 (the) P/photo(-)graph(s)
16 P/piano(s)
17 (in/the) G/garden(s)
18 September
19 (£)13.50(p)

In Part 3 bracketed words do not have to appear in the answer.

Listening Part 4
20 B **21** A **22** A **23** B **24** A **25** B

Recording script CD2 Track 31

This is the Cambridge Preliminary English Test, Number 076.
There are four parts to the test. You will hear each part twice. For each part of the test there will be time for you to look through the questions and time for you to check your answers.
Write your answers on the question paper. You will have six minutes at the end of the test to copy your answers onto the answer sheet.
The recording will now be stopped.
Please ask any questions now, because you must not speak during the test.

PART 1

Now open your question paper and look at Part 1. There are seven questions in this part. For each question there are three pictures and a short recording. Choose the correct picture and put a tick in the box below it.

Before we start, here is an example. Where is the girl's hat?

Mum: Where's your new hat, Sally? I hope you haven't left it on the school bus.

Sally: Don't worry, Mum. I put it in my school bag because I was too hot.

Mum: Are you sure? I can't see it there. You probably dropped it in the road somewhere.

Sally: Oh, here it is – hanging in the hall. I forgot to take it this morning.

The first picture is correct, so there is a tick in box A.

Look at the three pictures for question 1 now.

Now we are ready to start. Listen carefully. You will hear each recording twice.

One.

Which band will the girl watch?

Girl: I'm going to hear my favourite band play tonight – you know – <u>The Arctic Blues</u>.

Boy: Oh, I know them. There are three of them, aren't there? I really like the drummer.

Girl: Oh, he left – they don't have a drummer any more. <u>But the singer and the guitarist are still the same.</u> And they've got a keyboard player now.

Boy: Oh, well, I might come along.

Now listen again.

Two.

Where does the boy feel pain now?

Doctor: Tell me what happened exactly.

Boy: Well, after I fell off the rock my back felt a bit sore for a time, then it seemed to be all right. But I woke up yesterday with <u>this bad pain in my left leg, and it still really hurts</u>.

Doctor: I see. Have you had any other pain, a headache for example?

Boy: Well, I did have a bit of a headache after I fell. I think I hit my head on the rock. But it's fine now.

Now listen again.

Three.

Where is the computer now?

Woman: I didn't really want a computer in the house, but my son does need one for his homework. Of course, he wanted it in his bedroom, but I said no – it's for all the family to use. <u>First we tried it in the sitting room</u>, but there's not much room in there, so then we put it in the room my husband uses as an office. But he wouldn't let anyone else use it, so <u>now it's back where it was before, and we've moved the sofa a bit</u>.

Now listen again.

Four.

How does the woman recommend travelling around the island?

Woman: Now the island is easy to get to by plane, and when you get there, you'll find there is a local bus system, so you don't have to hire a car, although they're available if you want. Some visitors in past years have hired bicycles, which they enjoyed very much. They're cheaper than a car and they do mean you can get to those parts of the island which are off the main bus routes. So, <u>as long as you can ride one safely, I'd say that's the best idea</u>.

Now listen again.

Five.

What do both girls decide to wear to the disco?

Karen: What are you going to wear to the disco tonight? I'm going in <u>my green T-shirt</u>, jeans and white jacket.

Lisa: Oh, <u>don't wear that T-shirt, it's the same as mine</u>. I'm going to wear that one, but with a skirt. I'm not taking a jacket, though, it'll be too warm.

Karen: <u>It doesn't matter if we go in the same clothes.</u> I haven't got anything else I want to wear anyway.

Lisa: Oh, all right. I suppose it's not important. See you later.

Now listen again.

Six.

Who gave the man the CD for his birthday?.

Brother: Thanks very much for the birthday present. I've always wanted to read that book.

Sister: That's OK. Hey – I went round to <u>Dad's</u> yesterday. <u>Did you like the CD that he bought for you</u>?

Brother: Yes! Great choice! How did he know I wanted that one?

Sister: I think he had some help from our little brother – they went shopping together last weekend.

Now listen again.

Seven.

What is the man going to order?

Man: Is that apple pie you've got? Mmm ... I think I'll have some of that. I'll get you another piece too, if you want.

Woman: I'd love another piece, it's delicious. Only I'm afraid this was the last one. They've got chocolate cake, though. Why don't you have that?

Man: Never mind. I just thought the apple pie looked good, that's all. I'll <u>get some coffee</u>, anyway. I need something before the film starts. <u>Should I get you one</u>?

Woman: Oh, <u>go on, then</u>. We've got time – the film doesn't start for another twenty minutes.

Now listen again.

That is the end of Part 1.

PART 2 CD2 Track 32

Now turn to Part 2, questions 8 to 13.

You will hear the pilot, Kate Gingford, talking about the last few days of her flight around the world in a small aeroplane.

For each question, put a tick in the correct box.

You now have 45 seconds to look at the questions for Part 2.

Now we are ready to start. Listen carefully. You will hear the recording twice.

Kate: So last week when I was talking about my flight around the world, I'd got as far as Norway. This week I'll tell you about the last part back to London.

When I landed in Norway, two friends were there to meet me. We stayed together in a hotel and talked a lot about my trip and the route I'd chosen. Next morning, we were given a wonderful cooked breakfast and then <u>my friends helped me get into the suit I have to wear when flying over water</u>. It's really tight.

I hadn't slept much, but I was excited and felt really wide awake on the flight to Denmark. <u>My son, who is also a pilot, called me on the radio.</u> He was flying a plane in Germany at the time and we chatted for a few minutes. I was flying across the sea in thick cloud, so I couldn't see much, but I arrived in Denmark safely on the Sunday evening.

On Monday I was worried about the plane. <u>There was a problem with one of the front wheels.</u> I knew I could still take off and fly, without any fear of an accident, but I knew that if I made a bad landing I could damage the plane and so not be able to continue. I called the airport in Holland, my next destination, to arrange some repairs, and fortunately I managed to land there without any problems.

That night I stayed with some friends on their farm in Holland. Next morning it was so foggy that I couldn't fly, but it <u>was</u> good to have a break. It was difficult to sleep so I walked around the farm instead. I hadn't spent any time in the countryside for months, and <u>I'd forgotten how much I missed the sound of birds</u>.

When the fog lifted in the afternoon, I was pleased to learn they had repaired my plane, and

I took off within minutes. My next destination was a flying club in the north of England and <u>I knew it would be impossible to land there once the sun had gone down</u>. But fortunately it was a lovely sunny evening, and I arrived in good time.

I left early again on Thursday for London. I felt nervous because it was my last day of flying. Then, when I finally landed, <u>I felt wonderful – the long, difficult journey had been worth it</u>. It was lovely seeing my family who were all there to meet me. I promised I wouldn't make another long trip like that again.

Now listen again.

That is the end of Part 2.

PART 3 CD2 Track 33

Now turn to Part 3, questions 14 to 19.

You will hear a recorded message about a tourist attraction called The Grand Palace.

For each question, fill in the missing information in the numbered space.

You now have 20 seconds to look at Part 3.

Now we are ready to start. Listen carefully. You will hear the recording twice.

Tour guide: This is the Grand Palace information service. We are pleased to announce that the Grand Palace is now open again. The emergency repair work on the roof is now complete, but work is still in progress to repair the outside walls of the building, which were damaged in storms last year. Visitors may like to look at an exhibition of <u>photographs</u> in the entrance hall, which show how this work is done. The exhibition is near the gift shop, where you can buy postcards of the Palace and slides of some of the paintings.

The Palace was built in the 18th century as a holiday home for the King and his family, and decorated in the classical style. You can admire the beautiful painted ceiling in the music room, which contains the Queen's <u>piano</u>. Upstairs are the royal bedrooms, containing 18th-century furniture. Visitors can also walk through the palace kitchens and into the dining room, where the table is laid for 40 guests, with silver dinner plates and beautiful glasses.

If you want refreshments, home-made cakes, sandwiches, tea and coffee are served in the Queen Anne tearoom. On fine days, refreshments are also served in the <u>garden</u>.

The tearoom is open every day from 3.00 to 5.00 pm, or 5.30 pm during July and August. The Palace itself is open every day, from 10.00 am to 6.00 pm in the summer season, that's June to September, and from 10.00 am to 5.00 pm from October to May.

There is an entrance charge of £5.50 for adults or £3.50 for students and children under 14. There is also a special family ticket available for £13.50. It's for 2 adults and 2 children, so you save £7.00.

If you would like further information, please call us on 01293 567488 during opening hours. Thank you.

Now listen again.

That is the end of Part 3.

PART 4 CD2 Track 34

Now turn to Part 4, questions 20 to 25.

Look at the six sentences for this part.

You will hear a conversation between a boy, Tom, and a girl, Jemma, who are studying in different parts of the country.

Decide if each sentence is correct or incorrect. If it is correct, put a tick in the box under A for YES. If it is not correct, put a tick in the box under B for NO.

You now have 20 seconds to look at the questions for Part 4.

Now we are ready to start. Listen carefully. You will hear the recording twice.

Jemma: Hi, Tom, I haven't seen you since we left school.

Tom: Jemma, what are you doing here? I thought you were at university.

Jemma: I'm back home with my parents for the holidays. I couldn't afford to stay in London.

Tom: Do you like city life? You must find it very noisy and busy after this village.

Jemma: Well, yes, but there's always something happening. Not like here.

Tom: There's the cinema in Kingsford.

Jemma: Yes, but it's 20 kilometres away. Where I live in London there are lots of cinemas with all the latest films, just round the corner.

Tom: Lucky you! By the time the films reach Kingsford cinema everybody else has forgotten about them.

Jemma: The trouble is, London's so expensive. At weekends I usually go to a club or a restaurant with my friends. That can cost more than £30.

Tom: Really! I can't believe that. An evening out round here never costs me more than £20. How do you afford it? Have you got a part-time job?

Jemma: Not yet. I've done a course at the local swimming pool to get a certificate in life-saving. I had to pay for the course, but it means I can be a pool lifeguard when I go back to London. I'm going to work early in the morning before my classes start.

Tom: It won't be very exciting, just sitting watching people swimming up and down.

Jemma: Maybe not, but the money's good. That's the main thing.

Tom: Actually, I've got a job in a children's holiday camp near here for the summer. I'm going to organise their sporting activities.

Jemma: Really? Can you give me the phone number? Perhaps I can get a job there too, while I'm at home!

Tom: You're probably too late. I applied five months ago, and I had to have an interview and a health check. But you can try.

Jemma: Well, there's nothing else for me to do here.

Tom: OK. I'll find the number.

Now listen again.

That is the end of Part 4.

You now have six minutes to check and copy your answers on to the answer sheet.

You have one more minute.

That is the end of the test.

Unit 1 photocopiable recording script

CD1 Track 3

Lucas:	When you're travelling abroad, Zoe, do you find that people do things at different times of the day?
Zoe:	Well, I guess the first thing you notice is how early people have dinner here in the UK, maybe at 6 o'clock. And often in the USA and Canada, too. But in Spain or South America, for instance, they don't usually have their main meal until late in the evening, and they often go out after that. By then, in a town like this, everything's closing, isn't it?
Lucas:	Well, I don't think that's *always* true. Some places stay open very late these days, particularly in the town centre.
Zoe:	But how do you get home here? The buses and trains all stop running around eleven- thirty.
Lucas:	There are usually taxis around after that. There always seem to be people getting into them, or waiting for them.
Zoe:	Well, even if you can get one, they cost far too much, in my opinion anyway.
Lucas:	You're right about that. That's why I never take them. But I suppose you could walk home.
Zoe:	All the way from the town centre? You must be joking! And that's another thing. At night in places like Italy or Greece or the Middle East, there are always lots of people around. Families, I mean. So you don't worry about anything bad happening there, but when I'm here in your town there are times when I feel, well, not as safe. I know it seems silly, but it's true.
Lucas:	You may be right that older people go to bed early most nights. But doesn't that make it more fun when you're out? Everyone you see is young!
Zoe:	That's true!
Lucas:	So do people in the south of Europe get up later the next morning?
Zoe:	Well, school starts just as early as in the north of Europe so I don't think they stay in bed any later. And the school day is normally about the same as here.
Lucas:	And when there's no school?
Zoe:	They have lunch later, perhaps at two or three. A proper meal, that is – not just a sandwich. After that people sometimes have a quick sleep.
Lucas:	I think that's sensible, if it's just for a few minutes. I'd like to do that, every day.
Zoe:	It's certainly a good idea when it's hot. Maybe the different routines in different parts of the world are because of the weather there?
Lucas:	That's possible, yes.

Unit 2 photocopiable recording script

CD1 Track 11

Linh: Do teenagers work in Colombia?

Marcelo: Yes, they do. Teenagers in my country work to earn extra spending money. What about in Vietnam?

Linh: Well, I don't work and actually very few teenagers in Vietnam work. In my country, most parents don't allow their children to have a part-time job. We have to go to school and study hard. In my opinion, it's not a good idea for teenagers to work and study at the same time. What do you think?

Marcelo: I'm not so sure. I agree that teenagers need enough time to study and do their homework. If they work too many hours, their marks will go down. However, working part-time can be a good experience ... don't you think so?

Linh: Maybe. For some teenagers, working could be a way to learn about money and society. However, we have to think about the future. I think that studying is the most important thing. Do you agree?

Marcelo: Yes and no. As I said before, I think having a part-time job can be a good experience. However, we need more rules. For example, teens shouldn't work more than 15 hours a week and only two or three days a week, like at the weekend. I think they can work more hours during the school holidays.

Linh: Have you got a part-time job?

Marcelo: Yeah. I sometimes work in my father's office. I have to deliver letters and documents around the building. I earn a little bit of extra money.

Linh: Really? That sounds interesting. What do your teachers say?

Marcelo: Teachers complain that students who work don't do their homework well and they often do badly in tests. I think that students can work

to earn some pocket money if they are good students.

Linh: Good point! I haven't got a job. I'm going to concentrate on my studies and look for a job when I'm older.

Unit 3 photocopiable recording script

CD1 Track 12

Spencer: Hi, I'm Spencer Watson and I'm here to tell you about four unusual ways to have a great day out. First, how about going back in time with a steam- train journey through the beautiful Scottish countryside? This is on the railway line made famous by the *Harry Potter* films. Starting at Fort William, near Britain's highest mountain, the train <u>departs each morning at twenty past ten</u>, getting into the lovely fishing village of Mallaig at 12.25. The return journey to Fort William starts at 14.10 and takes an hour and fifty minutes. The fares are good value for money and it's a great experience for steam-train fans of any age. It's very popular in summer, so it's best to book ahead.

For a really exciting day out, *Go Wild* adventure courses offer hours of fun in 17 different locations. For a fairly small admission fee, you can climb tall trees, go from tree-top to tree-top on a high wire, cross waterfalls far below, go through tunnels – and lots more. Before you start, though, they give you full safety advice. <u>To prevent accidents they put a belt round your waist and the tops of your legs</u>, and attach it to wires. And then you're off – completely on your own! To take part you have to be fit, over nine years old and at least 1 metre 40 tall. Opening hours are usually 9.30 to 3.30.

If the adventure course isn't really your thing, but you like seeing really big wildlife, you can't do much better than dolphin and whale watching in Wales. *Voyages of Discovery* organises regular trips out to sea, passing small islands with their enormous seabird populations and then on to even deeper waters. And there, very occasionally, you will see whales, while <u>on almost all the trips dolphins will appear</u>. You may also see huge sharks, although they are quite rare these days. The voyage isn't cheap, but most people who've done it agree that it's well worth the money.

If instead you'd like to be up in the sky, try a balloon flight, from any of the hundreds of sites across the country. It usually begins early in the morning when you meet the pilot, crew and other passengers, and the huge balloon slowly fills with hot air. It rises gently, and then you go whichever way the wind is blowing. The actual flying time is about an hour, and although <u>I think it could last a bit longer</u>, it's certainly a wonderful experience. It's also possible to book a flight just for two, for any time of the year.

Unit 4 photocopiable recording script

CD1 Track 21

Laura: In this photo <u>I can see a lot of boats on water</u>. It <u>looks like</u> a traffic jam. The water <u>looks</u> really dirty. I <u>think</u> it's a market in the morning – <u>it could be somewhere in Asia</u>. There <u>seems to be a lot of fruit and vegetables</u> on the boats. There <u>are some green vegetables</u> but I don't know what they are. On each boat, I <u>can see</u> a person … no … I can see men and women. Some people <u>are wearing hats</u>. I think <u>they're selling things</u> but there aren't any people buying …er… on one of the boats, there <u>appears to be</u> somebody wearing a colourful shirt. Next to this boat, there's another man but I can't see him very well. I think <u>it's the morning</u>. <u>The weather is hot and sunny</u>. I <u>don't think</u> it will rain. Er …

Unit 5 photocopiable recording script

CD1 Track 22

Erica:	So, Ben, how often do you and Liam actually get together these days?
Ben:	Whenever I can, Erica. Usually about once every two months.
Erica:	<u>I don't think that's enough, really, to keep a friendship going. Couldn't you visit him each month, or ask him to come here</u>?
Ben:	Well, it's a long way to go. More than 400 kilometres, I think.
Erica:	How long does it take?
Ben:	Over six hours, each way. So you spend half the weekend on the coach, going up and down the motorway. <u>It's so boring</u>!
Erica:	How about taking the train? Wouldn't that be quicker?
Ben:	<u>I don't think I could afford it. The fares are really</u> <u>high</u>.
Erica:	Why don't you get a student travel card? Your tickets would be a lot cheaper.
Ben:	Hmm. That's an idea.
Erica:	And Liam could get one, too. Then he could sometimes come here on Saturdays and Sundays to see you.
Ben:	<u>I don't think he's keen on doing that</u>. He likes his new town a lot. He wants to stay there at weekends, he says.
Erica:	I see. So you go and see him, but he never comes here.
Ben:	I'm sure that's because there's so much to do there. It's an exciting town, and I know he's made new friends there. <u>But we get on really well and we're not suddenly going to stop being friends</u>.
Erica:	No, I'm not saying that at all. But maybe you need to remind him that you've been friends since you were little kids. And tell him how important a friend he is to you. <u>He might not realise that</u>, especially with all the changes in his life right now.

Unit 6 photocopiable recording script

CD1 Track 33

Examiner:	Your photographs showed people going out. Now, I'd like you to talk together about what you like to do at home and what you like to do when you go out.
Jon:	So, Ivan, what do you like to do at home? Do you like watching TV?
Ivan:	Yes, I love watching TV. We normally switch on the TV after dinner and watch a film, a football match or a documentary. What about you? Do you like watching films?
Jon:	Yes, but I prefer watching sports to documentaries. I find documentaries a little bit boring. Did you see the basketball match last night?
Ivan:	No, I didn't. When I'm at home I also enjoy playing cards or other games with my two brothers. On Sunday afternoons, we often stay in and play together. Do you ever play cards at home?
Jon:	No, not really. When I go out with my friends we usually meet in the local shopping centre. It's not much fun. I love going to the cinema, but it's very expensive. Er, how often do you go to the cinema?
Ivan:	I agree with you. The cinema is very expensive but I go with my parents once a month and they pay. Have you seen the new *Batman* film yet?
Jon:	No, not yet. I like going to see shows with my family. I don't really like serious plays but I love musicals like *Cats*, *We Will Rock You!* and the *Lion King*. Do you like musicals?
Ivan:	Er … I like some musicals but I think I prefer the cinema. My sister really loves the ballet. I've been once but I thought it was too long and slow. I think it was *Swan Lake*. Do you like classical music?
Jon:	Oh no! My brother … er … plays the violin and we went to a classical music concert with him last year. It was awful! I wanted to wait outside but my mum said I had to sit there. It was two hours and there was no interval.
Ivan:	Two hours long? Poor you!

Unit 7 photocopiable recording script

CD1 Track 34

Interviewer: Tell me, Chloe, have you always been interested in the weather?

Chloe: Oh yes. It's really fascinating in this country because it can be quite different in the north, in the west and in the south, for instance, and it doesn't usually stay the same for long. It can be warm and sunny one moment; wet and cold the next. In fact, you can sometimes have all four seasons in one day!

Interviewer: So when did you first photograph storms and things like that? Was that while you were at university? Or in your first job?

Chloe: No no, I was much younger than that. I was just a kid, really. We were coming home from holiday and we got caught in a thunderstorm. I took some pictures and luckily they came out really well. Since then I've done lots of other kinds of photography, especially when I was a student, but I still love photographing lightning.

Interviewer: That must be quite difficult. How do you get good pictures?

Chloe: Well, the first thing is the right camera. It doesn't have to be expensive, or particularly modern – I've had mine for many years – and I avoid using digital ones. But the main thing is where you go to take your pictures.

Interviewer: Which are the best places?

Chloe: Well, some people take photos from their bedroom windows, but I live in a flat where there's no real view of the night sky and so I have to go out. Standing in fields and on hills during a thunderstorm is rather dangerous, so I drive into the countryside, park, open the window and start taking pictures. You're much safer with all that metal around you, like on a plane.

Interviewer: So what about photography during the day?

Chloe: I really enjoy taking winter photos, when it's really freezing.

Interviewer: Which are your favourite? Snowy scenes?

Chloe: I used to like doing those, just after snowstorms, and sometimes those beautiful shapes like flowers that you see on glass when it's frosty. But nowadays I prefer mountain scenes with lots of ice. Especially when you have water flowing down valleys and over waterfalls, and it gets so cold that it freezes solid.

Interviewer: Mm. And during the rest of the year?

Chloe: Um … storms, I think. You can get some great pictures when the wind is really blowing, particularly on the coast. Whenever there's a gale, I go down to the beach and take loads of photos of the waves. They can be amazing. And I'd like to take pictures of clouds, though it's often too dark to photograph them when it's stormy. Also forests, with everything bending in the wind. I've always wanted to try that, too.

Unit 9 photocopiable recording script

CD1 Track 50

Jason: It's true, isn't it, Kelly, that people eat more these days, so they're getting bigger and heavier?

Kelly: Er, yes, I think so, Jason. But lots of people are vegetarian now, aren't they? And I think that kind of food is really good for you. So people might eat more nowadays but <u>that doesn't mean that what they eat is worse for them</u>.

Jason: No, it's just different. But there's more to being healthy than just exercise and eating, isn't there? I mean, there's so much stress in everyday life. And there are a lot of people that don't get enough sleep.

Kelly: I don't know whether people are any more stressed, but <u>you're right that everyone seems to go to bed late</u>, even when they've got school or work the next day. I suppose it's all the late films on TV, or staying on the Internet until two in the morning.

Jason: Or on the PlayStation®. There are so many fun things to do. So even if people manage to get up on time the next morning, they're too tired to do anything.

Kelly: Hmm, I'm not so sure. These days, <u>when they go to school, a lot more students are going by bike</u>. Especially now that in some cities you can hire one cheaply and then just leave it anywhere you like. And that's quite healthy, isn't it?

Jason: Hmm, it might be. But the air's really bad nowadays, especially in the cities. There's all that pollution from cars and lorries.

Kelly: Actually, <u>I think the situation has improved a bit</u> since they started making everyone pay to drive into the city centre. There's not so much traffic now.

Jason: You may be right, but it still makes me cough in the morning. Which reminds me: don't you think people get sick more often nowadays? <u>I'm always fine, and I'm sure you are too</u>, but we know a lot of people whose health is terrible, don't we?

Kelly: Hmm, I don't know about that. I think it's mostly coughs and colds and sore throats; perhaps a headache or a stomach ache which lasts a day or two. Usually nothing more serious than that. And teenagers have always had those kinds of illnesses. In most cases, I don't think their basic health is any different.

Jason: Well, <u>that's not the way I see it</u>, but I <u>hope</u> you're right!

Kelly: Me too!